STEPS
TO A NEW
BEGINNING

STEPS TO A NEW BEGINNING

SAM SHOEMAKER
DR. FRANK MINIRTH
DR. RICHARD FOWLER
DR. BRIAN NEWMAN
DAVE CARDER

A JANET THOMA BOOK

THOMAS NELSON PUBLISHERS
Nashville

Some names, places, and events in this book have been altered in order to protect the privacy of the individuals involved. Any case examples presented are fictional composites based on the authors' clinical experience with thousands of clients through the year. Any resemblance between these fictional characters and actual persons is coincidental.

Published in Nashville, Tennessee, by Thomas Nelson, Inc., and distributed in Canada by Lawson Falle, Ltd., Cambridge, Ontario.

Scripture quotations are from the NEW KING JAMES VERSION of the Bible. Copyright © 1979, 1980, 1982, Thomas Nelson, Inc., Publishers.

Library of Congress Cataloging-in-Publication Data

Steps to a new beginning : leading others to Christ through the twelve-step process / by Frank Minirth . . . [et. al.].
    p.   cm.
  ISBN 0-8407-7697-7
  1. Evangelistic work. 2. Witness bearing (Christianity) 3. Twelve-step programs—Religious aspects—Christianity. I. Minirth, Frank B.
BV3793.S677 1992
269'.2—dc20   92-17110
                                   CIP

Printed in the United States of America
1 2 3 4 5 6 - 97 96 95 94 93

CONTENTS

Part Three: ESTABLISHING A SUPPORT GROUP OR RECOVERY GROUP IN YOUR CHURCH

THE TWELVE STEPS OF ALCOHOLICS ANONYMOUS

1. We admitted we were powerless over alcohol—that our lives had become unmanageable.

2. Came to believe that a Power greater than ourselves could restore us to sanity.

3. Made a decision to turn our will and our lives over to the care of God *as we understood Him.*

4. Made a searching and fearless moral inventory of ourselves.

5. Admitted to God, to ourselves, and to another human being the exact nature of our wrongs.

6. Were entirely ready to have God remove all these defects of character.

7. Humbly asked Him to remove our shortcomings.

8. Made a list of all persons we had harmed, and became willing to make amends to them all.

9. Made direct amends to such people wherever possible, except when to do so would injure them or others.

10. Continued to take personal inventory and when we were wrong promptly admitted it.

11. Sought through prayer and meditation to improve our conscious contact with God *as we understood Him*, praying only for knowledge of His will for us and the power to carry that out.

12. Having had a spiritual awakening as the result of these steps, we tried to carry this message to alcoholics, and to practice these principles in all our affairs.

ACKNOWLEDGMENTS

We are grateful to the many people who consented to be interviewed for this book. Some are trained experts in the recovery field, and some are experts by reason of experience. Graciously and vulnerably, these people have shared with us their insights, their stories, their experience, strength, and hope. Some, in the humble tradition of AA, chose to remain anonymous. Others, equally humble, did not object to the whole world knowing how they once lived and how God has worked a miracle of recovery in their lives.

Heartfelt thanks to those who have truly written this book with their observations and with their lives: Dan and Priscilla Reed, David Reed, Bob Bartosch, Bill Ritchey, Lyman Coleman, Richard Peace, Bob Osborne, "Stephen W.," Terry Davidson, Bob M., Mike M., Mona C., Jack B., Betty B., Sharron Galletano, Don Taylor, John Mendell, Jr., Florine Mendell, "Darcy Jennings," Susan Crawford, Linda Blaine, Jim Denney, Lenny W., Jane M., and Suzanne S. (Their kind assistance in this project, however, does not necessarily imply that each of these individuals agrees with or endorses all of the statements in this book.)

PART
1

STEPS
TO A NEW
BEGINNING

CHAPTER 1

I STAND BY THE DOOR

It was a place of warmth and safety under a dull, starless California sky.

In one corner of the otherwise empty parking lot, a few cars huddled together under the amber glow of the mercury vapor lamps. Little shadowy figures emerged from the cars and made their way through the gathering gloom toward the yellow glow of an open door. The sign by the door read "Fellowship Hall." Because it was Tuesday night, every other room in the church was dark and silent, but Fellowship Hall was alive with light and hope. On this night, perhaps more than any other night of the week, Fellowship Hall lived up to its name, for the ten people who gathered inside its walls, clustered in a circle by the fireplace, were about to become a *fellowship* in the deepest sense of the word.

"Let's begin by introducing ourselves," said Melissa, the group facilitator. "My name is Melissa, and I'm a compulsive overspender. I've been in Debtors Anonymous for three years, and I've really been hungering for a group where I can work the Twelve Steps alongside other Christians. When Pastor Thornton asked me to facilitate a Christian Twelve-Step group here in our church, I jumped at the chance! Seeing all of you here for our first meeting is a real answer to prayer." A broad, earnest smile shone from her face as she nodded to the woman on her left.

"Me? Oh, goodness!" the next woman laughed self-consciously. She was a strikingly attractive woman in her late thirties, with dark brown hair and delicate features, meticulously accented with just the right touch of eye shadow, blush, and lip gloss. "Well, most of you know me, but I don't think any of you know my story. My name is Laura, and I'm—"

Her voice faltered and choked. She paused, sighed deeply, and reached for the hand of the man next to her, gripping it like a lifeline. When she spoke again, her words quavered, and her meticulously applied mascara was seeping slowly down her cheeks. "My name is Laura," she said slowly, "and I'm an alcoholic. I haven't had a drink in ten years, but I'm an alcoholic nevertheless. I've never admitted that to anyone in this church before. But it feels good to let you know who I really am." She turned to the man next to her, giving his hand an affectionate squeeze.

"My name is Brad," the man said. He was fortyish, balding, and bearded. He glanced lovingly at Laura. "I'm Laura's husband, and I'm— well, I guess you could say I'm a recovering codependent. My parents were alcoholics, and I married a woman—a wonderful woman—who has been through a tough struggle with an addiction to alcohol. I just want to say that it feels good to have a safe place in this church where Laura and I can honestly admit who we are, a place where we know we are accepted no matter what." Brad nodded to the next person in the circle.

"My name is Paul," said a middle-aged man with glasses and salt-and-pepper hair, "and I'm—well, I don't know what you'd call me. I don't drink or anything. Fact is, I came to this Twelve-Step group because of my friend John." He nodded to a man across the circle. "I didn't know anything about the Twelve Steps until I saw the change come over John's life. He showed me the Steps and as soon as I read them, I thought, 'Wow! These Steps are not just for alcoholics. They're for everyone who really wants to get serious about living the Christian life and sharing the Christian faith.' That's what I want, and that's why I'm here."

They continued around the circle. Shirley, a woman in her fifties, identified herself as a survivor of infidelity. John introduced himself as an alcoholic. So did Fred, the college-age young man next to him. Brenda introduced herself as an adult child of a dysfunctional family, Larry as a driven workaholic, Nancy as a compulsive overeater and incest survivor.

That night, a fellowship came into being—a fellowship committed to living in reliance upon God through prayer, confession, and honest self-appraisal. Each member of that fellowship had his or her own reason for being there—and all had come together around the same Twelve Steps.

Clearly, the Twelve Steps of Alcoholics Anonymous are not just for alcoholics anymore. In fact, more and more Christians are coming to realize that the Twelve Steps are not just a spiritual plan for recovery from addiction.

The doctors of the Minirth-Meier Clinic believe that the Twelve Steps are:

1. A pattern for spiritual commitment, growth, and discipleship that *every* Christian can practice every day of the year.

2. A process to help—and evangelize—anyone who has a problem or a need.

3. A process to evangelize and help people overcome any obsessive-compulsive behavior: overeating, workaholism, and codependency, for instance, as well as alcoholism and drugs.

The Universal Significance of the Twelve Steps

1. The Twelve Steps are a pattern for spiritual commitment, growth, and discipleship that *every* Christian can practice every day of the year.

Many people believe that the Twelve Steps had their genesis with a small group of recovering alcoholics in the 1930s, men like Bill W. and Dr. Bob, the founders of Alcoholics Anonymous. But the truth is that *two decades* before the Twelve Steps were first published in the Big Book of AA, the essential principles of the Steps were already being used—not as a vehicle for recovery from addiction, but as a model for authentic Christian commitment, discipleship, and witness. Long before they were formulated as the Twelve Steps of Alcoholics Anonymous, these principles were at work in the life of a man who would later have a far-reaching influence on AA and the entire recovery movement.

His name: Sam Shoemaker.

A Spiritual Awakening

Not twelve steps—or six steps. One step. Sam Shoemaker was just trying to take one step when he had an experience that changed not only his life, but the lives of millions of Americans, from the early part of this century till today. That one step? To reach one person for Christ.

Sam Shoemaker went to China in October of 1917 as a short-term missionary. Soon after his arrival he was given a Bible class for young Chinese businessmen who were inquirers into the Christian faith. They gathered in his room around a stove. About twenty people came to the first meeting. The second meeting, about fourteen. The third, only seven. Sam panicked. He concluded that something was terribly wrong with his teaching methods.

But Sam Shoemaker was about to discover a more fundamental issue than teaching methods. The *teacher himself* needed a radical change.

Sam Shoemaker had been raised in a respected, church-going Episcopalian family. Early on in his life, he felt a call to the ministry. In his early ministry in the United States, he was vaguely troubled by the fact that he wasn't very successful in communicating his faith to other people. But as his first Bible class in China seemed about to dwindle out of existence, his self-doubts dramatically intensified.

About that time a group of Christian workers arrived in Peking, now called Beijing, bringing with them a spiritual power Sam Shoemaker had never known before. They seemed to know how to make faith live for other people, how to win them for Christ and set their hearts on fire. The leader of this fellowship was a man named Frank Buchman. The fellowship would later become known as the Oxford Group.

Shoemaker had first met Buchman a few years earlier at

Penn State University, where Buchman conducted a number of thriving Bible classes. Shoemaker went to Buchman and asked if he would be willing to help one young Chinese businessman in his Bible class. This man had become dissatisfied with Buddhism and was seeking the truth.

Sam expected Buchman to do what so many other Christian leaders had done: pat him on the back and commend him for going into the ministry. Instead, Buchman looked Sam Shoemaker in the eye and confronted him with a question: "Why don't you win this man yourself?"

Sam stammeringly replied that he had not been brought up that way.

Buchman listened patiently until Sam ran out of excuses. Then he said, "Now, what's the *real* reason?"

"What do you think it might be?" Sam asked, honestly wanting to uncover the real obstacle to his effectiveness as a Christian witness.

"Might be sin. Resentment kept me from this kind of work for a whole year." Then Buchman proceeded to share with Sam the four principles which had changed his own life some years before. These were the Four Absolutes that another Christian teacher, Dr. Robert E. Speer, had distilled as the essence of the Sermon on the Mount:

· Absolute honesty
· Absolute purity
· Absolute unselfishness
· Absolute love

Those four principles sliced through Sam Shoemaker's soul like a hot knife through butter. He knew he was not living his life according to those principles. That night, as he knelt at his bedside to pray, Sam Shoemaker felt that everything was "jammed." There was a barrier in his relationship with God, and it was a barrier of *self*. Either he would pierce that barrier, or God would not be able to use him. Would he clutch his own pride and self-will? Or would he "let go and let God"?

The Twelve Steps of Alcoholics Anonymous were almost two decades from being formulated. Yet it was at that very moment that Sam Shoemaker first took Step Three of the Twelve Steps:

> Made a decision to turn our will and our lives over to
> the care of God *as we understood Him.*

Sam surrendered to as much of God's will as he could understand at the time. For Sam that meant being willing to stay in
China for life if God willed it. He later admitted, "Some of us
have wills like a bar of iron, and it is hard to break them and let
God's will come into their place."

The life of Sam Shoemaker had reached a profound turning
point. That night, Sam Shoemaker also took Step Five:

> Admitted to God, to ourselves, and to another
> human being the exact nature of our wrongs.

Facing his sins as honestly as he could, he got on his knees and
handed his will, his sins, and his life over to God. He experienced
no waves of emotion, no bright lights, no skyrockets. But afterwards he felt light and at ease—as if his life had slipped into its
proper groove at last.

Next morning he wakened with an uneasy urge to go talk to
his young Chinese business friend. That afternoon he got into a
rickshaw and rode to the East City where the man lived. He had
no idea what he was going to say. Arriving, he paced up and
down outside the young man's door, almost praying he wouldn't
be home. But he *was* home.

As Sam Shoemaker entered the businessman's home, he
asked God to tell him what to say. Instantly, a message came to
him: "Tell him what happened to you last night."

Sam's Chinese friend invited him to sit down. Seated across
from each other in a pair of creaky wicker chairs, they began to
talk.

"I believe you have been interested in my class," Sam began, "but not satisfied with it. I'm afraid that's my fault. May I
tell you what happened to me last night?"

The businessman listened to Sam's story intently, and when
Sam had finished, the man surprised Sam by saying, "I wish that
could happen to me."

"It can if you will let God in completely!"

That day, Sam's Chinese friend made a decision to follow

Christ. And at that same time, Sam Shoemaker took Step Twelve of the Twelve Steps:

> Having had a spiritual awakening as the result of
> these steps, we tried to carry this message to
> alcoholics [others], and to practice these principles in
> all our affairs.

"This is the way I began to be interested in one person at a time," Sam later said. "After this I sought out individual after individual and asked each one to accept Christ and surrender himself to Him. Every day I would try to see one of the school-boys after hours, and every evening a young man in business or government service."[1]

Two years later, Sam Shoemaker returned to the United States and continued to use this process—one person at a time. Even after he became pastor of Calvary Episcopal Church in New York City, Shoemaker remained committed to one-to-one evangelism, spiritual growth, and the Four Absolutes of honesty, purity, unselfishness, and love.

One day, a hopeless alcoholic wandered into Calvary Episcopal Church. His addiction had such a powerful grip on his life that doctors gave him only a few years to live. But on that day in 1935, this man's life changed dramatically—just as dramatically as Sam Shoemaker's life changed in Peking in 1917. Moreover, this alcoholic's life was transformed by the very same principles that redirected the course of Sam Shoemaker's spiritual journey: the principles that would later become the Twelve Steps of AA. That alcoholic was Bill Wilson, the cofounder of AA, and we will tell you more of his story in Chapter 2.

More than two decades later Bill Wilson stood on a platform with Sam Shoemaker, introducing him to the Twentieth Anniversary Convention of Alcoholics Anonymous as "the Episcopal clergyman who in our pioneering time instructed certain of our older members in most of the spiritual principles which are today embodied in the Twelve Steps of Alcoholics Anonymous."[2]

"It was from Sam that cofounder Dr. Bob and I in the beginning absorbed most of the principles that were afterwards embodied in the Twelve Steps of Alcoholics Anonymous, steps that express the heart of AA's way of life. Dr. Silkworth gave us the needed knowledge of our illness, but Sam Shoemaker gave us the concrete knowledge of what we could do about it. One showed us the mysteries of the lock that held us in prison; the other passed on the spiritual keys by which we were liberated."[3]

Sam Shoemaker walked this spiritual journey himself, and then he codified it into the Twelve Steps so that others could replicate it. In his address at the Twentieth Anniversary Convention of AA, he said, "I believe that AA has derived its inspiration and impetus indirectly from the insights and beliefs of the church. Perhaps the time has come for the church to be reawakened and revitalized by the insights and practices found in AA. I don't know any fields of human endeavor in which the Twelve Steps are not applicable and helpful."[4]

We agree with Sam Shoemaker. Imagine how the church could be reawakened and revitalized by the realization of Sam Shoemaker's dream! Just picture the possibilities.

Imagine a support group, based on the Twelve-Step process, for businesspeople who want to build biblical principles into their personal and professional lives? Or a support group for parents who want to live more exemplary Christian lives before their children? Or a support group for evangelism-minded laypeople who want to become more effective witnesses for Christ? The options are endless.

Every Christian can walk this Twelve-Step walk. It is a walk of spiritual commitment, growth, and discipleship—not just a path to recovery. Moreover, the doctors of the Minirth-Meier Clinic believe that the Twelve Steps are a spiritual journey that can be used to help—and evangelize—anyone who has a problem or a need.

For People with Problems

2. The doctors of the Minirth-Meier Clinic believe that the Twelve Steps can be used to help—and evangelize—anyone who has a problem or a need.

In her biography of Sam Shoemaker, *I Stand by the Door*, Helen Shoemaker tells of two groups that met in New York City in the 1940s. Both groups met in the Great Hall of Calvary House; both were governed by parallel principles. One was Alcoholics Anonymous, which met on Tuesday nights. The other was Faith at Work, to which lay people could come to witness and learn; it met on Thursday nights. AA and the modern small group movement began at Calvary Church at the same time. Sam often said that the principles of these two groups were "fundamental for anyone with problems." Then he added with humorous insight, "For everyone has a problem, is a problem, or lives with a problem."[5]

Sam Shoemaker insisted that the small-group process, which he passionately advocated throughout his ministry, always started with personal counseling and continued in what is now called group therapy. Shoemaker simply called it fellowship. Social workers began using this method with drug addicts, neurotics, prisoners, and in many other specialized fields.

Experimenting in his own informal yet creative way, Sam Shoemaker helped to hammer out the principles and procedures that now permeate many specialized fields of therapy and ministry. Dr. Cotton, a leading New Jersey psychiatrist from 1890 through 1910, made a prophetic statement when he said, "If you find a principle and procedure that will operate with the most difficult cases you have a principle that will operate with the most normal."[6] Sam Shoemaker proved it each day through the Faith at Work groups in both of his churches, Calvary Church in New York City and Calvary Church in Pittsburgh, Pennsylvania. He also proved it in the Pittsburgh Experiment, which he launched in 1952 to enable people to live out a more personal and active faith in their homes, neighborhoods, and businesses.

Sam Shoemaker set the example that we at the Minirth-Meier Clinic seek to emulate. We believe that the Twelve-Step process is a powerful tool that Christians can use to help—and to evangelize—anyone who has a need or a problem.

And we also believe that the Twelve Steps can be used to help people overcome by any obsessive-compulsive behavior.

Steps to Recovery

3. The Twelve Steps can be used to evangelize and help people overcome any obsessive-compulsive

behavior: overeating, workaholism, and codependency, for instance, as well as alcoholism and drugs.

When the Twelve Steps were formally defined in the late 1930s, the only recovery organization in the world was Alcoholics Anonymous. Today there are Twelve-Step programs for just about any addictive agent you can imagine (addictive agents are persons, objects, or activities upon which we become dependent in an excessive or unhealthy way). There are half a million local recovery groups operating across the United States, all using the Twelve Steps as a basis for beating addictions. A partial list of addictions currently being treated by Twelve-Step groups includes:

- Alcoholism
- Drugs
- Workaholism (addiction to activity and achievement)
- Food addictions and eating disorders (compulsive overeating, bingeing, anorexia, bulimia)
- Sexual addictions
- Money addictions (gambling, hoarding, overspending)
- Codependency and dependency on toxic relationships
- Control addictions (a need to control the behavior of others)
- Materialism
- Perfectionism
- Approval dependency (the need to please others)
- Religious legalism (preoccupation with religious form and rules as opposed to a personal relationship with God)

More than fifteen million Americans are in Twelve-Step groups, and hundreds of bookstores across America are devoted specifically to recovery books. Recovery is the hottest topic on Donahue and Oprah. Major entertainers such as Liza Minnelli, Suzanne Somers, Charlie Sheen, Elton John, and Roseanne Arnold are talking openly about their addictions and the Twelve-Step recovery groups that saved them from self-destructing.

A 1989 cartoon illustrates the pervasiveness of this problem. It depicts a convention of the Adult Children of Normal Parents. The banner across the back of the room welcomes all ACONP

Members. The convention hall is full of theater seats—all empty except for two persons: a bearded man in a front row and a long-haired woman near the back, both apparently waiting for a meeting that will never begin.

The point is clear: It seems virtually everybody is in recovery these days. "Adult Children of Normal Parents" are becoming increasingly hard to find as addiction and dysfunctionalism continue to rise. We all have a problem. We all need recovery from experiences in our past.

Never before in the history of our society have so many people been so aware of their powerlessness and addiction—and so committed to changing the direction of their lives. Being in recovery has even become chic and fashionable in the 1990s, much as snorting a line of coke through a rolled C-note was in the 1980s. Still, the trendiness of recovery is a fringe phenomenon. Most people in recovery groups are not there to be in vogue, but to find hope and healing. The average person in any recovery group has come to a recognition of powerlessness—and even desperation—in the face of addiction.

Way back in 1955 Sam Shoemaker predicted this phenomenon at the Twentieth Anniversary Convention of AA: "I believe AA may yet have a much wider effect upon the world of our day than it has already had, and may contribute greatly to the spiritual awakening which is on the way but which has come none too soon, for the world of our time is not sitting pretty."[7] Today, recovery is one of the biggest issues in our culture—and the spiritual dimension of the Twelve Steps is at the heart of the recovery movement.

At the Minirth-Meier Clinic, we believe the Twelve Steps can be used to help people overcome any compulsive-obsessive behavior—overeating, workaholism, and codependency, for instance, as well as alcoholism and drugs. And we believe the Steps can be a profound part of the journey that leads people in recovery to a vital relationship with Jesus Christ.

The Spiritual Movement of the '90s

To anyone outside the recovery movement, the vocabulary of recovery is probably bewildering, including such buzzwords and buzzphrases as *adult child, codependency, denial, dysfunc-*

tional family, inner child, serenity, and *shame.* These catchwords serve as a kind of shorthand for very real and painful issues that plague millions of lives.

But the recovery movement is not merely focused on addiction and codependency. The recovery movement is also profoundly spiritual. William Zimmerman, an editor at *Newsday* and founder of recovery-oriented Guarionex Press, has called the Twelve-Step recovery movement "the spiritual movement of the 1990s."

The Twelve Steps form the spiritual chassis, the bare-bones vehicle of recovery. But unless the recovering person's Higher Power is truly Jesus Christ, the vehicle has no engine. Christ is the Power of recovery. You don't have to redesign the vehicle. You simply have to put an engine in it. Our goal is to put the engine—the Power of Jesus Christ—in the vehicle of recovery.

People who would never set foot in a worship service will go to a Twelve-Step group for healing. Many Twelve-Step groups meet in churches, and that gives the church a profound opportunity: Without compromising or watering down the gospel, we can present Jesus as the Power. We don't have to tamper with or "Christianize" the Twelve Steps. In fact, experience has shown that attempts at Christian Fourteen-Step groups or similar modified versions invariably fail. We can't "fix" what already works— and there's no need to. We can take the Twelve Steps exactly as written, identify the Higher Power as Christ, and suddenly the entire vehicle, both chassis and engine, roars to life, transforming not only behavior but souls.

Six of the Twelve Steps specifically refer to "a Power greater than ourselves" or "God." Two of the Steps add the phrase *"as we understood Him"* after the word *God,* and it is the only italicized phrase in the Twelve Steps. This phrase underscores the fact that the Twelve Steps are a spiritual framework for recovery —but even more it underscores the fact that the Steps represent a pluralistic and deliberately vague spirituality.

People in recovery have recognized their own need of spiritual power. They have been pre-evangelized. But people rarely become Christians as a result of the Twelve Steps alone. Someone must help them identify the Power of the Twelve Steps.

Someone must use the Steps as a starting point for sharing the gospel.

The exciting fact about sharing Christ through the Twelve Steps is that the groundwork has already been laid. If you speak the language of recovery, you automatically have a willing ear and a deep level of trust. Because recovering people already accept their own neediness and powerlessness, the barriers of pride and self-sufficiency are down. In the Twelve-Step process, there is an instant rapport that no other plan of evangelism can build. Any other approach is "cold turkey" evangelism by comparison.

Clearly, today's rapid boom in Twelve-Step recovery groups presents the church of Jesus Christ with an unprecedented opportunity and an urgent challenge. And there is also a danger. The danger is that if we do not act now, we will lose the opportunity.

The Twelve Steps are spiritual in nature. But the Twelve-Step recovery movement and its parent organization, Alcoholics Anonymous, are not specifically Christian. AA has no doctrinal statement, no formal worship, no religious affiliation. While Twelve-Step groups have a strong spiritual dimension and there are many evangelical Christian Twelve-Step groups in existence, the average AA or Twelve-Step group is completely pluralistic. Any god that works for you is okay.

When you commit yourself to the Twelve Steps, you commit yourself to a Power, to God as you understand Him. Your Higher Power can be Jesus or Buddha or Muhammad. It can be the other members of the group or some mystical conception of the group's "life force." It can be a goddess. It can be "The Force" of Star Wars. It can be the sun or the moon. It can be a doorknob. It can even be Satan.

In one Twelve-Step group for teenage alcoholics, conducted in the adolescent unit of a secular hospital, Dr. Brian Newman saw a sixteen-year-old youth come into the meeting with spiked hair, earrings, and dull, listless eyes. His black t-shirt sported a picture of the heavy metal rock group Poison. He announced to the group that his Higher Power was Satan.

Fifteen million Americans, desperate for healing and recovery, are plugging into a Higher Power. Many Christians are ready to come alongside these hurting people and guide them, gently and lovingly, to the true Power which can set them free, now and forever. But many other Christians have turned their backs on people in recovery. Those who have been turned away by the church are still spiritually seeking—and they are ripe for deception by any religious system that will accept them and connect with their newfound spiritual awareness. Many of these people are being swept up into the New Age movement and into various cults.

Lyman Coleman, founder of Serendipity House and a leader of the evangelical small group movement for three decades, told us, "The New Age is capturing the recovery movement because the church has failed to recognize the spiritual hunger of people in recovery. People walk into a bookstore and say, 'I'm in a recovery group. What books do you have for me?' And the bookstore clerk takes them to the New Age section. When the recovery movement got rolling, the New Age movement was standing in front with arms outstretched. Many in the churches were standing back with their arms folded, shaking their heads. But the church is coming around. Some churches are doing aggressive Twelve-Step outreach. It's finally starting to move, and it's thrilling to see it happening."

Leading people to Christ through the Twelve-Step process may seem new, but the principle is as old as Christianity itself. In the Gospels, we see that Jesus was always looking for common ground and a point of connection with people as he spread the good news of His kingdom. He evangelized the woman at the well by telling her about living water. He reached the hearts of people by healing their hurts. He met people at the place of their need and the place of their understanding.

In the Twelve-Step process, the place of need is the awareness people have of their problems, addictions, and powerlessness. The message is the same good news that has been proclaimed for two thousand years: Jesus is the Power that saves.

Elsewhere in the New Testament, we see that the apostle Paul, too, looked for common ground when he shared the gospel. The story of Paul in Acts 17 has profound implications for sharing Christ through the Twelve-Step process.

The Mars Hill Approach

The apostle Paul strode the cobblestoned streets of Athens in the company of the city's leading philosophers and teachers. Once Athens had been the dominant political power in all of Greece, but in Paul's day it was a "college town" and a center of pagan worship, much like the New Age-infused college communities of our own time.

The Greek intellectuals who walked with Paul had heard him speak in the marketplace. "This Jesus you talk about sounds fascinating," they had told him. "You must come to Mars Hill and lecture on this new doctrine you proclaim. We'll take you there."

So they led Paul to Mars Hill, the Athenian equivalent of the Free Speech area at U.C. Berkeley. As he walked the streets of Athens with his Greek guides, Paul was dismayed by all the idols that stood in the city square, in the windows of homes, in the alcoves of shops, on street corners and in front of temples. In all his travels, he had never seen so many false gods in one place. The thought of intelligent people offering worship to statues of dead stone turned his stomach.

At the same time, Paul had an intense love for people and a desire to tell as many as he could about the life-changing power of Jesus Christ, the One who had invaded his own life some years earlier on the road to Damascus. *How can I reach these people?* he wondered. *I don't know them and they don't know me. What would these people identify with? What can I use to open the door to their hearts?*

Suddenly, Paul stopped in the middle of the street. His guides watched in puzzlement as Paul stepped closer to a nondescript stone altar at the side of the street. Paul's eyes came alight as he ran his fingers over the inscription engraved on the pedestal of the altar.

Smiling to himself, Paul stepped back into the street and hurried on. His Greek companions had to hasten to keep up with him. A few minutes later, Paul mounted Mars Hill (called Areopagus or "The Hill of Ares" by the Greeks), just a couple of hundred yards west of the beautiful Parthenon and the Temple of Athena. Surrounded by a crowd of the leading intellectuals of Athens, Paul began to speak.

"Men of Athens," he said, "I perceive that in all things you are very religious. For as I was passing through and considering the objects of your worship, I even found an altar with this inscription:

TO THE UNKNOWN GOD.

Therefore, the One whom you worship without knowing, Him I proclaim to you."

Using the common ground of the Unknown God whom the Athenians already acknowledged in their pagan ignorance, Paul proceeded to tell the Athenians about the one true God and His Son, Jesus Christ. He told them about a God of love, who gave His only Son as a sacrifice for sin, who raised the Son from the dead, and who now called all people to repentance and faith in Jesus Christ. Some who heard Paul's message mocked him. But others believed and were saved, including Dionysius, a member of the Athenian ruling council whom tradition says later became the first bishop of the Athenian church.

Nearly two thousand years later, our message is still the same—and so is the common ground through which that message is communicated. People are still spiritually seeking (or "very religious," as Paul said on Mars Hill), and they still worship the Unknown God. But today the Unknown God is called a Higher Power.

The Greatest Force Known to Man

People in recovery are ripe to either be deceived by false religions or to receive Jesus Christ. As we have seen in the examples of Christ and the apostle Paul, our faith has a great tradition of meeting people at their point of need and nurturing their budding spiritual awareness in order to communicate Christian truth. Leading people to Christ through the Twelve-Step process is only the latest variation on a very old principle of evangelism.

Yet when we talk about the Twelve-Step process as an "opportunity" or a "vehicle" for witnessing, there is a danger that the most important dimension of evangelism will be lost. That dimension is our very motive for evangelism: love—obedient love for the Lord Jesus Christ and unconditional love for the people He died to save.

As Dave Carder says, "One of the big issues with recovery people is honesty. Brutal honesty. For a person to exploit the Twelve Steps for the sake of making converts is not really honest in the minds of most AA people. It's manipulation. They think, *You're only into this to try to convert me.*"

We dare not view Twelve-Step recovery groups as a means to be cynically exploited in order to rack up scores of converts. Recovery is a valuable and crucial end in itself. As Christians, we should rejoice whenever someone is liberated from addiction to alcohol, drugs, or some other addictive agent. But the rejoicing is even greater when another person finds liberation from what Keith Miller calls "the ultimate deadly addiction," sin itself and the separation from God which sin causes.

Only biblical Christianity can deal with the sin dimension of addiction. No other religion, psychological approach, or medical therapy can deal with sin. Only grace can conquer sin, and grace is the unique distinctive of the Christian church. God's grace—the grace of His forgiveness and the grace of His empowering Spirit—is the liberating force that people in recovery are seeking.

Our goal in the Twelve-Step process is to liberate people not only from the power of addiction but also from the power of sin and death; to unite recovering people not just with a vague, unknown Higher Power, but also with the Highest Power of All, Jesus Christ; and to enable people to live the abundant life not only now but throughout eternity. Our motivation is the same motivation that has powered every great evangelistic movement in history: Christlike unconditional love.

First Corinthians 13 is still true. Love is still the greatest force known to man. Love is greater than knowledge, greater than hope, greater than faith. This is an amazing truth, because faith is a tremendous power. A tiny grain of faith can move mountains—yet love, the Scriptures say, is even greater than faith.

Concentrated within the walls of the Minirth-Meier Clinic are scores of people with master's degrees and doctorates representing an aggregate of hundreds of years of study and experience in medicine, psychiatry, psychology, and theology. The people who staff the Clinic are people of great Christian faith. But all that knowledge and all that faith would be utterly meaningless if the people at the Clinic were not also people of great Christian love.

Love is a much greater power than our intellectual prowess, our schooling, our experience, our insight. The measure of our effectiveness as a healing community is essentially a measure of our love.

The questions that confront us as Christians at the end of the twentieth century are: Do we love people as Jesus loved people? Are we truly seeking to love people into the body of Christ and into the kingdom of God? How does our Christian love compare with the love exhibited by recovery programs such as Alcoholics Anonymous?

The fact is, nobody has done a better job of loving people and changing lives than AA. The basis of the life-changing power of AA is that people in AA know how to love.

We in the church should not just try to exploit AA and other Twelve-Step groups in order to win converts. We should learn from them how to love. Sure, the love in AA sometimes comes in a rough package. The love of recovery often wears an uncomely face and speaks a crude language. In our middle-class, white-bread, suburban churches, we are easily offended by the smoking and the cussing that is sometimes found in the AA environment.

But if you examine the life of Christ, you do not find Jesus evangelizing in suburbia. You find him among the outcasts, the prostitutes, the publicans, the sinners, and yes, the addicted. Christ healed those who were powerless and in need of a physician.[8] He was surrounded by crowds of people who acknowledged their own powerlessness and reached out to touch a Higher Power. Jesus harvested souls in the same fields where Twelve-Step groups now labor.

Today, we are surrounded by great masses of people who are essentially the same as the masses who crowded around Jesus. They are on skid row. They are in corporate executive suites. They are in homeless shelters. They are in country clubs. They are in gutters and along railroad tracks. They are in suburban homes and townhouses. They are shiftless drunks, who never work a day out of the year. They are driven workaholics addicted to money and power.

You cannot escape them, nor can you escape the responsibility for sharing the eternal hope that is within you. They are not "those people over there." They are your people. They are all around you. They are your neighbors, your coworkers, your friends, your family. They are waiting for you to love them.

Throughout the remaining pages of this book, you will learn how you can grow spiritually through the process of the Twelve Steps; how to bring the honesty and the accepting, unconditional love of the recovery movement back into the Christian church where it all began; how to use the Twelve Steps as an open door to witness to anyone who has a problem or need; how to draw recovering people into a relationship with Jesus Christ; and how to lift the veil from the Unknown God of the Twelve Steps so that people can plug into the true Higher Power, the One who fashioned both the universe and the human heart.

Three of your authors are members of the Minirth-Meier Clinic, one of the largest psychiatric clinics in the United States, with twenty offices throughout our country: Dr. Frank Minirth, the cofounder of the clinic; Dr. Richard Fowler, clinical director of outpatient services for the Minirth-Meier Clinics of Dallas and Longview, Texas; and Dr. Brian Newman, clinical director of inpatient services at the Dallas clinic. As we mentioned earlier we use the Twelve Steps in our treatment of obsessive-compulsive behavior and alcohol and drug addiction; we wrote about this process in our book *The Path to Serenity: The Book of Spiritual Growth and Personal Change through Twelve-Step Recovery.*

The fourth author, Sam Shoemaker, speaks to us from his extensive writings—even though he died in 1963. His ministry began in 1921, and in 1925 he was appointed rector of Calvary Episcopal Church in New York City, a position he filled until 1952 when he assumed the rectorship of Calvary Episcopal Church in Pittsburgh. He was a leading force in The Pittsburgh Experiment and the host of a Pittsburgh radio program, "Faith at Work." He published the periodical *Faith at Work*, which began as the parish magazine of Calvary Episcopal Church in New York City and then went national and international. It was read in a hundred countries throughout the world, virtually anyplace people ask, "Can faith really make any difference?" Many of the stories we tell in this book, stories about laypeople evangelizing others, were originally published in *Faith at Work* magazine.

Faith at Work was also the name of Sam's evangelistic movement, which encouraged teams of people to witness to those around them. Sam Shoemaker was the author of more than a dozen books, such as *Revive Thy Church, Beginning with Me,* and many articles in magazines like *The Reader's Digest.* In this book he will be speaking directly to you from those writings. *Newsweek* magazine once named him one of the ten greatest preachers in the United States. And when Shoemaker died, Billy Graham said, "I doubt that any man in our generation has made a greater impact for God on the Christian world than did Sam Shoemaker." In these pages, Sam speaks to us from the past about spiritual principles that are as valid today as they were then.

The fifth author is Dave Carder, assistant pastor for counseling ministries at the First Evangelical Free Church of Fullerton, California. Since the early 1980s this church (which is known internationally as the home pulpit of Charles Swindoll) has offered scores of support groups and recovery groups facing such issues as chemical dependency, adult children of dysfunctional families, eating disorders, dealing with disabilities, dealing with infertility, caring for dependent adults, recovery from divorce, recovery from incest, and recovery from grief. In Part 3 of this book Dave gives the nuts 'n' bolts principles of starting and maintaining support groups and recovery groups in a church. The Twelve Steps are a pathway to emotional wholeness and to freedom from addiction and our human sin condition. When we learn how to use the Twelve Steps as a bridge to reach those who have a problem or those who are recovering from obsessive-compulsive behaviors, those Steps will become a pathway to eternal life as well.

As Sam Shoemaker said in his "apologia for my life," a poem entitled, "I Stand By the Door":

I stand by the door.
I neither go too far in, nor stay too far out,

The door is the most important door in the world—
It is the door through which men walk when they find God.
There's no use my going way inside, and staying there,
When so many are still outside and they, as much as I,
Crave to know where the door is.
And all that so many ever find
Is only the wall where a door ought to be.
They creep along the wall like blind men,
With outstretched, groping hands.
Feeling for a door, knowing there must be a door,
Yet they never find it . . .
So I stand by the door.

The most tremendous thing in the world
Is for men to find that door—the door to God.
The most important thing any man can do
Is to take hold of one of those blind, groping hands,
And put it on the latch—the latch that only clicks
And opens to the man's own touch.
Men die outside that door, as starving beggars die
On cold nights in cruel cities in the dead of winter—
Die for want of what is within their grasp.
They live, on the other side of it—live because they have not
    found it.
Nothing else matters compared to helping them find it,
And open it, and walk in, and find Him . . .
So I stand by the door.[9]

CHAPTER 2

ONE BY ONE

The tiny, silver-haired woman was crying. Beside her wheelchair, Grand Central Station porter Number 42 ruefully watched his suffering customer. As the elevator dawdled down from the balcony of Grand Central, the black porter removed his red cap and closed his eyes, as if listening to some inner voice. Presently he bent over and whispered, "Lady, that is a sure-enough pretty hat you're wearing this morning."

Amazed at this unexpected kindness, the woman looked up at the porter. He was a bespectacled, scholarly-looking black man with a warm and empathetic smile.

"And your dress, too," he went on, "—prettiest one I've seen all today."

Over the pain-wrenched mouth came the apparition of a smile, such as only women know when their taste in clothes is admired.

"I declare!" she gasped. "Whatever made you say that to me?"

"The good Lord," declared redcap Number 42 with conviction. "I just asked Him how to help you, and the answer came to me to take a look at your hat. But," he chuckled, "the dress was my own idea."

The woman was still smiling as he pushed the wheelchair

across the noisy concourse and down the ramp to the pullman. As they arrived in the drawing room she apologized, "I'm ashamed of breaking down like that—but I'm in pain all the time. Can you imagine what that is like?"

"Yes, ma'am. I had to lose an eye—and for years afterward it hurt me like a hot iron."

"How were you ever able to endure it?"

"Just praying."

"Did prayer take your pain away?"

"No, ma'am. But it brought me the strength to stand the pain."[1]

Redcap Number 42 was named Ralston Young. He stood by the door in Grand Central Station for many, many years. For a good number of those years, he conducted a prayer group in a car on track number 13. Without even being aware of it, Ralston Young was using the Twelve-Step process to lead others to Christ. He instinctively understood that people were the most open to the gospel when they were at a point of deep hurt and need.

Ralston Young's lifestyle of sharing Christ with people at their point of need is easy to understand when you realize that he was discipled by Sam Shoemaker. Redcap Number 42's life was transformed one day when he attended a small group in the basement boiler room of Sam Shoemaker's Calvary Episcopal Church. There he learned the principles of the Twelve-Step process. Then he took those principles and applied them to the people he met on the job in Grand Central Station—one by one.

Sam Shoemaker began small groups at Calvary Episcopal Church in New York City in 1926, a year after he came to the parish. He outlined his principles for evangelization in his book, *Revive Thy Church, Beginning with Me.* These principles then formed the basis for the Twelve Steps of Alcoholics Anonymous. In this book he said that people find God through six sources: the church, need, exposure to the faith of others, the preaching of the Word of God, the personal witness of Christians, and places where faith is at work.

Let's examine each of these sources in turn.

1. People Find God Through the Church

If evangelism is to happen, said Sam Shoemaker, it should happen in the obvious place where people go for religious help: in our parishes. There men and women should find the inspiration to transform their homes and the institutions in which they work. The change will come, not through different or even better parish organizations, not through new nostrums sent out by the church headquarters, and not alone through the importation of "new blood" in the form of a visiting missioner or evangelist. It will come when ministers and laymen alike admit three things:

1. that the church is not bringing to the desperate and open world of this time the answer of Jesus Christ;

2. that we are ourselves typical of the church, and as such, responsible for its being what it is; and

3. that the change has got to begin in us, and with us, before we can expect it to affect others, our parish, or our world.[2]

How does this take place? Embedded in this philosophy is Step Twelve of the Twelve Steps. It is a principle which is often stated, "Once You Have It, Pass It On." Redcap Number 42's life is an example of this principle. When Ralston Young came to New York in 1920, he wanted a life of excitement. Being a moody and dissatisfied young man, he was bored by the fleshpots and gin palaces of Harlem. For years he was restless and disillusioned.

One Sunday morning, Ralston Young answered an insistent knock at the door of his sister's flat where he was staying. An old black woman stood in the hall.

"Little girl playing down on the front stoop say she belong here," the woman said. "That right? Then why she don't go to Sunday school like the other children?"

Ralston protested that the grownups in the flat worked late on Saturday nights.

"Let me fetch the child, then. I'll take her every Sunday and I'll bring her home safe too. Rain, snow, hail, wind don't matter to me."

"How come you do that?" asked Ralston. "What's it to you? What do you get out of it?"

"The Lord's work. That's how I keep me happy."

So the old woman began taking Ralston's little niece to Sunday school. Later, Ralston began to feel pricked in his conscience that a stranger was taking more of an interest in the little girl's welfare than the little girl's own uncle. So he began taking her to church himself.

In church, Ralston learned about a Man who died to take away the sins of the world. He became convinced that any man could become fearless, compassionate, and unconquerable, and could live without grudges or prejudice if he followed the Nazarene. After joining the church, Ralston began speaking at meetings. One night a visitor invited him to a gathering in Calvary Church, near Gramercy Park where Sam Shoemaker had been rector for twenty years.

"But that's a white man's place," objected Ralston.

"Makes no difference," replied the visitor.

So Ralston went to Calvary Church. There he learned of the fifteen small prayer groups that met regularly in stores, factories, offices, and homes. The next day he started his own spiritual cell group in Grand Central Station. Redcap Number 42's life was changed—and then he proceeded to change the lives of those he touched.[3]

The life of Ralston Young proves that people really can find God through the church. Yet nine out of ten people, says Shoemaker, disregard this initial step. They want to see what "plans" and "programs" the church offers in order to bring about a spiritual awakening in individuals, parishes, and communities. They miss the point. Until something happens to us and in us, it will not happen *through* us.

The solution is not a better church program. It is radical change from within. Sam Shoemaker learned this principle in his own life in Peking, in 1917. From then on, the prayer of his life was, "O God, revive the church, beginning with me."

2. People Find God Through Their Need

The second way people find God, said Sam Shoemaker, is through need. Anyone who has a problem needs God. And as

Sam was fond of pointing out, everyone either "has a problem, is a problem, or lives with a problem."

The strains of adolescence, of a broken family, or of difficult adjustments with schoolmates may bring about this sense of need in youth, he said. However, it may not come till much later in life. The longer one lives, the more one finds that life itself is the great evangelizer. Life seems so constituted that within it are to be found the very problems and needs that set us to thinking about God—first wondering, then seeking.

Perhaps the greatest need of all is the array of deep questions life flings at us, demanding an answer: "What are you doing here?" "Where did you come from?" "Where are you going when you die?" We drift along easily for years—then death strikes suddenly and tragically and we have nothing with which to meet it.

We coast through life with our conventional religion, complacent and self-satisfied—until one of the children turns to alcohol, another is divorced, and we see that our kind of religion is not sufficient for these persons whom we love. This drives us deeper and makes us search for something more than we had before. We look for God—for a more real experience of God—from a sense of need.[4]

Remember that silver-haired woman in the wheelchair in Grand Central Station? Though he never saw her again, he did hear from her. It was almost exactly a year later. Above the station din, a voice paged Number 42. When the red cap reported to the Information Desk, he found the daughter of the silver-haired woman. She had come to deliver a message from the dead. "Before my mother died," she told him, "she asked me to find you and tell you that what you said last summer made all the difference in the world to her."

Off came the red cap, the eyelids closed, the porter listened, and then in the boldness of faith, he said, "Don't be bitter over your loss, miss, and don't be ashamed to cry. Jesus wept. Why can't we? And why don't you say a little prayer of thankfulness to the Lord?"

"Why should I be thankful?" the young woman asked incredulously.

"Because your mother lived to be a very old lady and you

had her love for a long time. I know lots of orphans mighty young. And besides, your mother's pain is gone now! . . . That's good, miss, cry real hard!"

Hundreds of travelers were helped by Ralston Crosbie Young, who made a career of toting luggage and volunteering comfort to the downcast and bereaved. This eager black servant of God specialized in faith and common sense, mixed with an unshakable fondness for people.[5]

3. People Find God Through Exposure to the Faith of Other People

The third way people find God, according to Sam Shoemaker, is exposure to the faith of other people. Other people and other traditions in the Christian faith sometimes offer discoveries and insights into the experience of God—discoveries and insights we might encounter in no other way—that have power to transform our own lives. Shoemaker suggested that every believer might well gain spiritually by supplementing his or her own church experience with exposure to groups other than his own—various groups which offer new varieties of experience, instruction, and inspiration through other Christian leaders and speakers, and fellowship with other Christian laypeople. We grow conventional and complacent and dead when we chew our own cud too long.[6]

These groups may meet in the strangest of places, like a car in Grand Central Station, for instance. Ralston Young founded what was surely one of the most unusual of Christian fellowships. He began to feel that there should be some meeting in the Grand Central neighborhood. It was his idea, and two or three white men who worked in offices nearby, and whom he came to know at Calvary Church, concurred with it.

Why not Ralston as the host? they said. But where could they meet amid that swirling, noisy human tide that passed through Grand Central Station? Ralston remembered the idle cars which stood empty in the yard. There might be better places for a meeting than a day coach, but a single coach could hold quite a few people. He approached the company, and they gave him permission to use a car on Track 13.[7]

At noon on Mondays, Wednesdays, and Fridays, thereafter, Ralston appeared at Track No. 13 to welcome his friends. As few as four or as many as twelve, might come: executives and clerks; professional men and jobless wanderers; rich and poor; from the teeming district of Pershing Square and beyond. All of them believed that wherever two or three were gathered together in the Master's name, there He was also.

The red cap unlocked the gate and led the way down to an unlighted day coach, where for the next fifteen minutes they held a prayer meeting. Above the rumble of trains and the clangor of bells, they recited the Lord's Prayer and went on briskly to pray for the peace of the world; the ending of industrial warfare; the settlement of racial and religious strife; and the resolution of their own personality problems. They confided in each other their successes and failures as they sought to pattern their lives after that of the Master. If Ralston brought some troubled traveler along, they talked of his problems, too. Finally, they offered thanks for the help God had given them in the last twenty-four hours. Then they scattered to offices, stores, and sidewalks, feeling strengthened and invigorated.[8]

4. People Find God Through the Preaching of the Word of God

To combat biblical and spiritual "illiteracy," which Shoemaker saw as epidemic in our century, he advocated preaching that was a balance of learned teaching and realistic application to the needs of everyday life. People grow weary, he said, of religious essays musty with book learning but empty of practical, contemporary meaning.

Henry R. Luce, founder of *Time* and *Life* magazines, once said, "We are thirsty for the truth! But we will be bored by stale moralisms or inept attempts to comment on current events. Do you know about God? That's what we, in the church and out of it, want to know." You can tell when a person has thought through the deeper problems of the faith, and when that person is merely groping; you can tell whether someone is communicating to others a living, active faith, or merely spinning out ideas about religion.

5. People Find God Through the Personal Witness of Others

The fifth way people find God, said Sam Shoemaker, is through the personal witness of others. This is how the co-founder of Alcoholics Anonymous came to be rescued from his raging alcoholism. His full name was William Griffith Wilson, but the men and women of AA remember him simply as Bill W. His is the story of a man who found God through the personal witness of an ex-drinking buddy.

When Bill Wilson returned home from the trenches of the First World War, he was a battle-seasoned veteran and a leader of men. Just twenty-two years old, he had his whole life ahead of him. He knew exactly what he wanted out of life: success, prestige, and money—lots and lots of money.

Bill had the drive and the savvy to achieve whatever he set his mind to. He was a quintessential yuppie—except that he was born fifty years ahead of his time. He studied law and economics at night and worked as an insurance investigator in New York City by day. At the same time, he made a careful study of the stock market.

While most market-watchers were content to read the *Wall Street Journal* and play their hunches, Bill put a rolled-up tent and a change of clothes in the sidecar of his motorcycle, then straddled the bike with his wife riding behind. Together, Bill and his wife spent an entire year two-wheeling up and down the eastern seaboard of the United States, visiting factories and corporate headquarters. At the end of that year, Bill returned to New York as the most knowledgeable business authority on Wall Street. He made a fortune, both by investing and by selling his investment advice.

Rich and respected by the age of thirty, Bill was living the good life. The Roaring Twenties were in full swing. Booze was illegal yet plentiful, and Bill was a two-fisted drinker. He spent hundreds, even thousands of dollars a night making the rounds of the speakeasies and jazz palaces, drinking and buying rounds of drinks for the house.

By 1929, Bill had become a man of leisure, living off his investments. With so much time and money on his hands, he soon became an avid and highly skilled golfer. It was around this time that he realized his nightly drinking was continuing into the day—and sometimes around the clock. He was getting jitters in the mornings, but after downing a couple of shots of whiskey he felt steady enough to play his usual eighteen holes.

In October of '29, the stock market crashed—and so did Bill's fortunes. No more plush Manhattan apartment, no more golf, no more money. All that remained of his pre-Crash lifestyle were his faithful wife and his booze habit. He landed a job for a few weeks, but lost it after getting into a brawl. By his own account, it would be five more years before Bill would again hold a job or draw a sober breath.

Alcohol was no longer a luxury to Bill. It was his life's blood. The better bootlegged variety was beyond his means, so he settled for bathtub gin—a quart a day or more. In 1932, a stock-buying opportunity came along that would have restored him to prosperity, but he chose instead to go on a drinking binge.

Through it all, his wife stuck by him. Bill promised and resolved and swore he would stop drinking—and he meant it every time. But alcohol was stronger than his will. Soon he was reduced to panhandling, stealing money from his wife's purse, and hiding bottles of gin around the house. Over the next few years he went through cycles of quitting, then bingeing, then being hospitalized, then quitting, then bingeing, and back to the hospital, around and around in an endless downward spiral.

In November 1934, Bill received a phone call that changed —and saved—his life. It was one of his old drinking buddies, Ebby Thatcher, and he wanted to stop by for a visit. *Good old Ebby!* thought Bill, remembering the time the two of them had chartered an airplane just so they could say they had once been drunk as skunks at 20,000 feet! As he waited for his buddy's knock on the door, Bill set a bottle and a couple of glasses on the kitchen table.

When Ebby arrived, Bill was shocked at his friend's appearance: Gone was Ebby's usual stubble and red-rimmed eyes. He was clean-shaven and there was a contented glow on his face. Bill offered his friend a drink, but Ebby politely declined.

"What's this all about?" Bill asked.

"I've got religion," Ebby replied with a smile.

Bill's jaw dropped and his heart sank. He had anticipated a good, long jag with an old friend, and instead his friend had become a Bible-thumper! The very last thing in the world Bill wanted to hear about was God!

But Ebby Thatcher didn't preach or pound on a Bible. He simply sat with Bill and shared with him about the change that had taken place in his life. A few months earlier, Ebby had been jailed for public drunkenness. While in jail, he was visited by some men from a Christian fellowship called the Oxford Group. They prayed with him and, right in his jail cell, Ebby yielded his life to Jesus Christ. From that day forward, his thirst for alcohol was gone.

Bill listened sullenly to Ebby's story, but he wanted nothing to do with his God or his sobriety. Fortunately for Bill, Ebby was too good a friend to be put off. He visited Bill several times over a period of weeks before finally coaxing him into attending a meeting of the Oxford Group—which leads us to the sixth and final way people find God.

6. People Find God in a Place Where Faith Is at Work

People can find God wherever biblical faith is being actively lived out in the lives of Christians. It might be in a Christian support group, a neighborhood Bible study, an inner city ministry, or a Christian home. A church service may be the right place, if authentic worship, biblical preaching, and warm Christian fellowship are there. Or a rescue mission where down-and-outs find Christian love and acceptance may mark the turning point for someone who once considered himself "above" that kind of thing. Once the Holy Spirit shows us that, apart from Christ, we are all down-and-out inside, true redemption can invade our lives.[9]

That is how AA founder Bill Wilson finally came to God. He told this story in *Alcoholics Anonymous Comes of Age,* a book commemorating the twentieth birthday of AA:

"Remembering that Sam Shoemaker's Calvary Church had a mission where Ebby's Oxford Group friends had lodged him, I thought I would go and see what they did down there. I left the subway at Fourth Avenue and Twenty-third Street. It was a good long walk along Twenty-third Street, so I began stopping in bars. I spent most of the afternoon in the bars and forgot all about the mission. At nightfall I found myself in excited conversation in a bar with a Finn named Alec. He said he had been a sailmaker and a fisherman in the old country. Somehow that word *fisherman* clicked. I thought again of the mission. Over there I would find fishers of men. Oddly enough it seemed like a wonderful idea.

"I sold Alec on coming along, and soon we reeled in the front door of that mission.

"Just then Ebby turned up, grinning. He said, 'What about a plate of beans?' After the food, Alec and I had slightly clearer heads. Ebby told us there would be a meeting in the mission pretty soon. Would we like to go? Certainly we would go; that's why we were there. The three of us were soon sitting on one of those hard wooden benches that filled the place. I had never seen a mission before and I shivered a little as I looked at the derelict audience. There was a smell of sweat and alcohol. I could well imagine how much suffering was represented in this gathering.

"There were some hymns and prayers. Then Tex, the leader, exhorted us. Only Jesus could save, he said. Somehow this statement did not jar me. Certain men got up and made testimonials. Numb as I was I felt interest and excitement rising. Then came the call. Some men were starting forward to the rail. Unaccountably impelled, I started too, dragging Alec with me. Ebby reached for my coattails, but it was too late. I knelt among the shaking penitents. Maybe then and there, for the very first time, I was penitent, too. Something touched me. I guess it was more than that. I was hit. I felt a wild impulse to talk. Jumping to my feet, I began.

"Afterward I could never remember what I said. I only knew that I was really in earnest and that people seemed to pay attention. Ebby, who at first had been embarrassed to death, told me with relief that I had done all right and had 'given my life to God.' "[10]

That night Bill Wilson went to bed sober. The next day, however, he took a drink as he watched the sun come up. By six o'clock that night his wife, Lois, found him lying on their bed dead drunk. For the next two days he drank himself into a stupor —a non-stop three-day bender that landed him in the hospital. As the pangs of withdrawal began, he experienced hallucinations —symptoms of delirium tremens. In those days, the standard treatment for advanced alcoholism was to lock people up for "alcoholic insanity." Bill realized that his next stop was an insane asylum—unless he could beat the bottle.

While in the hospital, Ebby visited Bill. "You're licked, Bill," said Ebby. "Admit it. Let go of your life and let God take over."

His pride crushed, his defenses shattered, Bill had to recognize he was powerless. He had bottomed out. Twenty years later, he described what happened next:

"My depression deepened unbearably and finally it seemed to me as though I were at the very bottom of the pit. I still gagged badly at the notion of a Power greater than myself, but finally, just for a moment, the last vestige of my proud obstinacy was crushed. All at once I found myself crying out, 'If there is a God, let Him show Himself! I am ready to do anything, anything!'

"Suddenly, the room lit up with a great white light. I was caught up into an ecstasy which there are no words to describe. It seemed to me, in the mind's eye, that I was on a mountain and that a wind not of air but of spirit was blowing. And then it burst upon me that I was a free man.

"Slowly the ecstasy subsided. I lay on the bed, but now for a time I was in another world, a new world of consciousness. All about me and through me there was a wonderful feeling of Presence, and I thought to myself, 'So this is the God of the preachers!' A great peace stole over me and I thought, 'No matter how wrong things seem to be, they are still all right. Things are all right with God and His world.' "[11]

Some people experience conversion as a slow budding of faith. Others experience it as an explosion. Bill's conversion was the explosive kind, not unlike Paul's dramatic conversion on the road to Damascus. In an instant, Bill realized he had been liberated from his enslavement to alcohol. Not that he instantly lost the craving, for there were many times in the months that followed that he came perilously close to drinking. But he never touched another drop from that day in 1934 until his death in 1971.

After his release from the hospital, Bill joined the Oxford Group meeting at Sam Shoemaker's Calvary Church in Manhattan. For the first year and a half of his newfound sobriety, Bill struggled unsuccessfully to find work. Bill's wife continued to be the sole wage-earner, as she had been for years. Plagued by self-pity and despair, Bill was often tempted back to drink. Whenever he felt despondent he would go to the alcoholic ward of the hospital where he experienced his conversion and he would find a drunk to talk to. Helping other alcoholics would always set Bill on his feet again.

The Oxford Group, a Place Where Faith Was at Work

When Sam Shoemaker became the rector of Calvary Episcopal Church in New York City, he began two outreaches: a rescue mission in an old unused East Side chapel (the mission where Bill W. first found God), and a chapter of the Oxford Group, which Shoemaker's friend and mentor Frank Buchman had founded a few years earlier.

Frank Buchman originally called his organization "A First Century Christian Fellowship," a name which strongly suggested its evangelical, Christ-centered, grass-roots character. Under Buchman's leadership, the Group had held revivals at the campuses of Princeton, Yale, Harvard, Smith, and Vassar. In 1926, it became known as the Oxford Group, taking its name from the University of Oxford, England, which lent its support to Buchman's evangelistic efforts after the group was banned from the Princeton campus.

Buchman's vision for a new kind of Christian fellowship came to him while he was attending the 1908 Keswick Convention in England. At the time, he was harboring bitter feelings toward a colleague at a Christian hospice, which he had founded and from which he was later forced to resign. During his Keswick experience, he was confronted with the pride, resentment, and willfulness of his own heart. He realized that until he was able to release these selfish feelings, there would be a barrier between himself and God, which is what he meant when he told Sam

Shoemaker, "Resentment kept me from this kind of work for a whole year." Many of the Oxford Group's founding principles came out of Buchman's personal experience of spiritual renewal, including principles of surrender, humility, acknowledging sin, and making amends for wrongs done to others.

Alcoholism was only one of many human problems addressed by the aggressively evangelical Oxford Group. In cities and towns across the country, Oxford Group chapters met in small groups in private homes. The goal was to reach all spiritually seeking people, even people who were antagonistic toward traditional churches. Therefore, church buildings, liturgy, and religious jargon were avoided. A typical meeting consisted of testimonies, confession, prayer, Bible study, and informal talks. Members were encouraged to work through their own problems by helping others with similar problems. The Oxford Group model was thus an ancestor of the modern support group concept.

In 1938 Frank Buchman envisioned a broader goal for his movement—to change the world spiritually and morally—and a new name—Moral Rearmament—which would include more people. At first Sam Shoemaker was a leader of the new movement in the United States, but he resigned in 1941.[12] Shoemaker felt that the movement had become too political and its leadership too dictatorial and divisive.[13]

Though Shoemaker and the Oxford Group/Moral Rearmament parted company, the founding principles of the Oxford Group continued to live on in the ministry Shoemaker subsequently founded, Faith At Work, and in the small group meetings within the Calvary Church parish.

This was the spiritual environment that gave birth to Bill W.'s new and dramatically changed life. Yet by the late 1930s, Bill W., Dr. Bob, and many other recovering alcoholics in the Oxford Group began to feel the need for a fellowship focused squarely on the problem of alcohol addiction. They wanted a program without religious dogma, and which welcomed alcoholics of all persuasions—even atheists.

As mentioned in Chapter 1, two groups were spun off from the Oxford Group: Alcoholics Anonymous, the prototype of all recovery groups, and Faith at Work, an outreach to laypeople.

The principles that governed both groups paralleled. By trial and error, the early pre-AA pioneers learned what worked and what didn't in the treatment of their addiction. Then they told the world what they knew.

Bill W. Meets Dr. Bob

In 1935, Bill W. made a business trip to Akron, Ohio, hoping to close an important business deal. The deal fell through, and Bill—feeling disillusioned and lonely—was engulfed by an overwhelming urge to drink. In desperation, he phoned churches all over Akron, trying to find a member of the Oxford Group who could support him during his trial of temptation. Finally, he reached a woman with ties to a local chapter of the Oxford Group. She gave him the name of an alcoholic surgeon, Dr. Bob Smith. The Oxford group had been talking to Dr. Bob and praying with him, but he was a hard case. All the talk and prayer in the world seemed to have no effect on his compulsive drinking.

The next day, Bill called on Dr. Bob. The two men were complete opposites in temperament: Bill was outgoing and gregarious while Dr. Bob was quiet, reserved, and even severe in his manner. But there was an instant rapport between them that quickly ripened into friendship. Bill shared the story of his new spiritual awareness and his liberation from alcohol. Over the next few evenings they had more talks—long, rambling discussions that ranged from private emotional struggles to heady philosophical issues.

Finally, Dr. Bob decided to give up the bottle. He simply quit. He was amazed to find he could go a day, then a few days, and even a whole week without a drink! Three dry weeks passed, and Dr. Bob felt confident enough to take a train to Atlantic City for a medical convention. But something went terribly wrong on that trip.

"I drank all the scotch they had on the train," Dr. Bob later recalled, "and bought several quarts on my way to the hotel. This was on Sunday. I got tight that night, stayed sober Monday till after the dinner and then proceeded to get tight again. I drank all I dared in the bar, and then went to my room to finish the job. Tuesday I started in the morning. . . . I bought some more liquor on the way to the depot. I had to wait some time for the train. I remember nothing from then on until I woke up at a friend's house."[14]

Bill picked up Dr. Bob and took him back home and put him to bed. Bill even gave him a bottle of beer the next morning to get his friend through the throes of a massive hangover. That bottle of beer was the last drink Dr. Bob ever had. The date was June 10, 1935, and Alcoholics Anonymous marks that day as the founding of AA. At that moment, neither Bill W. nor Dr. Bob had any inkling what the future would bring.

They only knew one thing: To stay sober and to survive, they must devote the rest of their lives to helping other alcoholics in any way they could.

The Big Book and the Twelve Steps

In 1939, this small fraternity of former Oxford Group members pooled their resources to publish a book. The text of the book was written by Bill W. himself, then hashed out and debated into final form by the recovering alcoholics of the Akron and New York groups. This close-knit fellowship of recovering alcoholics had no name before the book was published. But after the book appeared with the title *Alcoholics Anonymous* emblazoned on the cover, the name of the new organization seemed obvious. More than fifty years later, that book—the legendary "Big Book" of AA—still sells over a million copies a year.

The Big Book is a straightforward collection of testimonies and counsel on the subject of drinking. It contains no profound medical or clinical insights. Instead, it comes across with a kind of raw power and persuasiveness that has endured for more than half a century, and has changed millions of lives. One of the most powerful aspects of The Big Book is tucked away in Chapter 5, "How It Works." It is a set of principles called The Twelve Steps.

Even after AA broke away from the Oxford Group, the practices and traditions of the Oxford Group remained the foundation of the AA program and the Twelve Steps. The Steps themselves are profoundly Christian in character, and each Step is rooted in Christian truth. The AA tradition of having people share their stories with the group is a continuation of the Oxford Group practice of sharing testimonies in house meetings, which is in turn a continuation of a sharing and witnessing tradition dating back to the first century church.

One of the most controversial aspects of the Twelve Steps—the vague reference to God as "a Power greater than ourselves" or "God *as we understood Him*"—is also handed down from the Oxford Group. Though Sam Shoemaker uncompromisingly preached the Christ of the Bible, he also encouraged spiritual inquirers who did not believe in Christ to pray to God however they conceive Him.

The need for religious pluralism in AA was recognized in those early days before the Twelve Steps were written and The Big Book was published. Alcoholics were streaming into that early fellowship from many religious backgrounds. A substantial number of them were atheists and agnostics. A few others were followers of non-Christian religions. Some had been raised in the church, but had since rejected Christianity after being judged as "moral degenerates" by religious—but uncaring—people.

If a Christian shared in those early pre-AA meetings how his relationship with Christ kept him sober, others in the group often felt they were being preached to. The result was that some meetings degenerated into religious debates. Vague "Higher Power" terminology helped head off arguments and kept the focus of each meeting on sobriety and recovery.

In their wildest dreams, Bill W. and Dr. Bob could hardly have imagined that their early efforts in the 1930s would grow to become the cultural phenomenon of the 1990s. AA alone has gone from two members in 1935 to roughly two million members today. And AA is just one among scores of Twelve Step recovery programs. Today, millions of people are finding liberation from addictive agents ranging from alcohol to food to relationships to legalistic religion—

And all are working the same Twelve Steps.

PART 2

THE TWELVE-STEP PROCESS

CHAPTER 3

WE CAME TO BELIEVE

The First Five of the Twelve Steps

The other people in the airport pretended not to notice the long-haired young man with the backpack. But Rick and Jerilyn Fowler couldn't help noticing him. He was as conspicuous as a neon sign—and not just because he was the only other American in the small San Jose, Costa Rica, airport. He was conspicuous because he was weeping softly but openly, his face buried in his hands.

Rick Fowler and his wife were seated a short distance from the young man, awaiting the boarding call for their return flight to Dallas. The plane was not scheduled to take off for another hour. Their hearts went out to this young American who sat alone, depressed and crying. Richard looked inquiringly at his wife. She nodded and replied, "Let's go talk to him." They got up and walked toward him. On closer inspection, Rick noticed a book and several pamphlets on the seat next to the young man, all dealing with the problem of drug abuse. The topmost pamphlet was *The Twelve Steps of Narcotics Anonymous*. Seating themselves on either side of him, the Fowlers introduced themselves. "I'm a counselor," Rick said. "I see you're feeling depressed and I'd like to help you."

"Thanks, but I don't think anyone can help," the young man replied in a quavering voice. He was about twenty-five, lean and tanned, with a wholesome, friendly face, brown eyes, and lanky brown hair. He tried to smile, but the combination of smile and tears made him seem all the more pitiable.

"What's your name?" asked Rick.

"Eric," the young man replied.

Lord, Rick Fowler prayed silently, *give me wisdom and the words to keep this conversation going!* Aloud he continued, "I notice you're reading the Twelve Steps, Eric."

"Yeah," said the young man, dabbing self-consciously at his eyes. "I'm in an NA group back home. I've had a lot of trouble with, like, cocaine and stuff."

As Eric talked about his struggle with addiction, he reached into his backpack and pulled out a battered and dog-eared daily recovery journal. "I've been trying to work the Twelve Steps while I've been on this trip," he said, "but it's been hard, man. Been times I've wanted to get coked up so bad. Like, I could use a blow right now."

There's more to Eric's story—much more. But first let's take a closer look at the Twelve Steps that Eric was struggling so hard to work and to walk.

Twelve Powerful Steps

There is nothing particularly elegant about the Twelve Steps. They are not poetry. They are not even particularly well written. When you reprint them in a book, the publisher's copy editor is tempted to touch up the wording a bit. But the Steps have endured and changed millions of lives in exactly the form in which they first appeared in 1939. It is risky to tamper with what works.

Of course, now that so many different forms of addiction are being treated by the Twelve-Step approach, the Steps themselves have been altered slightly to fit each particular setting. For example, in Emotions Anonymous, a Twelve-Step program is devoted to helping people who struggle with anger, depression, grief, shame, and other painful emotions, Step One reads:

We admitted we were powerless over our emotions—
that our lives had become unmanageable.

Except for such minor changes, the Steps remain the same,
and they are worked in exactly the same way in each recovery
group, by each recovering individual. The Twelve Steps are blunt
and inelegant, yet they are also profound in their assessment of
the brokenness of the human condition.

Most important of all, the spiritual dynamic of the Twelve
Steps is just as important in support groups, such as single parent
groups or widow/widower groups or step-family groups or Bible study and prayer groups, and in non-alcohol-related recovery
groups, such as Emotions Anonymous or Overeaters Anonymous, as it is in Alcoholics Anonymous. Shirley M., a member of
an Overeaters Anonymous (OA) group in the Midwest, told us,
"The spiritual side of the Steps is very important to us in OA. We
rely on a Higher Power just as the AAs do. For me, that Power is
God. A lot of people join OA because they want to lose weight,
they want results, and they don't really care about the spiritual
side. But after they're in OA for a while, they realize it can't be
done without the spiritual side."

Shirley told us about one woman who was in Overeaters
Anonymous for five full years before she grasped the importance
of the spiritual side of the Steps. "Janie said that God just wasn't
really important to her. She just wanted to get her weight under
control. After five years of trying to get by on willpower and the
support of the group, she finally saw that she couldn't control
her compulsive overeating without God's help. As long as she
was trying to lose weight by her own willpower, she was fighting
the first Step. She paid lip service to it, but deep down she was
denying the fact that she was powerless.

"After five years of struggle, Janie finally hit bottom. Then
she understood what the first Step really means: she was really
completely powerless! At that point, she began to rely on her
Higher Power instead of her own willpower. Only then did she
really find victory over her compulsive overeating."

It doesn't matter what the addictive agent is—alcohol,
food, rage, pornography, toxic relationships, or even an addiction to religious legalism: the spiritual side of the Twelve Steps is

an indispensable key to liberation from addiction. There is no magical power in the Twelve Steps themselves or in the recovery groups that use the Twelve Steps. The power of the Steps comes from the fact that they are rooted in scriptural truth and they point people back to God. Our goal at the Minirth-Meier Clinic is not to "Christianize" the Twelve Steps but to return the Twelve-Step process to its original roots: biblical Christian faith.

The Twelve Steps and Christianity

Ruth is a missionary in Europe. After being overseas for three years, Ruth returned to the States for a visit with family, including her sister Marie, who is agnostic. As Ruth visited with Marie, she was delighted to learn that her unbelieving sister had read C. S. Lewis' fantasy series *The Chronicles of Narnia*. In fact, Marie had enjoyed the series so much that she read all seven books to her children.

Ruth eagerly asked Marie what she thought of the Christian message in the books, hoping that the truths embedded in Lewis' fantasy might have made a dent in Marie's shell of unbelief. But Marie just looked blankly at Ruth. She hadn't detected any Christian themes in the books at all.

"Well, didn't Aslan remind you of Jesus?" asked Ruth, listing a few of the comparisons between the Lion of Narnia and the crucified and risen Lord.

"Well," Marie replied hesitantly, "now that you mention it, I guess I can see some similarities."

The Twelve Steps are a lot like Lewis' Narnia stories. Aslan and the Higher Power are Jesus Christ, and Christians have no trouble making that identification. Keith Miller writes, "For me, having studied the Bible for years, there is no question that the 'Higher Power' of the Twelve Steps is the same God revealed in the life, death, and resurrection of Jesus Christ."[1] Yet there are great numbers of people in recovery groups who have never studied the Bible before and who need someone to point the way to Jesus. That is our task.

If you are new to the Twelve Steps or if you have a friend or family member who is in a Twelve-Step group, you may be wondering what the Steps are all about. You may wonder, What am I

getting involved in? What is my friend or family member involved in? What does the language of the recovery movement
mean? Are the Steps biblical? Are they compatible with my
Christian beliefs?

The fact is, most evangelical Christians tend to be institu-
tionally and objectively oriented. We like to evaluate whether a
person's faith is valid or not according to certain tests: Does this
person belong to the "right" denomination? Does this person
affirm the "right" creeds and doctrines? Does this person "correctly" interpret certain passages of Scripture? In other words,
we apply cognitive, information-laden tests to determine
whether or not this person's faith is "orthodox."

Certainly, the evangelical church has always affirmed the
importance of sound doctrine and objective biblical truth.[2] But
there was a time, during the first few centuries of Christian history, when the church was much more experience- and relation-
ship-oriented than it appears today. Since the New Testament
canon was not even formally recognized until late in the fourth
century A.D., the issue for most new converts in the early church
was not so much "What do these Christians believe?" but "How
do these Christians live?"

The early church was a community that expressed the personality of God to a fallen society by means of its love, its humility, its pursuit of righteousness and holiness, and its radical commitment to God. Many churches of our own day have tended to
ignore these experiential elements of church life in favor of cognitive elements such as doctrinal orthodoxy. While sound doctrine is crucially important, a church can have orthodox theology
yet be cold and lifeless. We in the evangelical church can learn a
lot about the experiential side of our faith from people in recovery.

This is not to say that recovery groups should in any way be
viewed as alternatives to the church. But Christian Twelve-Step
groups can be a bridge not only to recovery but to fellowship
and belonging in the church. In fact, Richard Peace, professor of
evangelism and ministry at Gordon-Conwell Theological Seminary, uses exactly that analogy, calling Christian Twelve-Step
groups "bridge groups." He told us, "I think it's dangerous to
create separate Twelve-Step 'churches.' Instead, we need the

kind of structures that enable people to bridge the gap. Christian Twelve-Step groups stand between the secular world and the community of faith, providing a bridge over which recovering people can walk into the church."

The Minirth-Meier Clinic uses the Twelve-Step approach as one important feature of its recovery programs. We have found the Steps to be a powerful tool for recovery from all forms of addiction. The profoundly Christian character of the Twelve Steps will become increasingly clear as we examine each Step in turn.

Step One: We admitted we were powerless over alcohol— that our lives had become unmanageable.

It is a truth as simple and profound as the line from the children's hymn "Jesus Loves Me": "They are weak, but He is strong." We are all weak, we are all powerless, we are all addicted in our own way, and only Jesus is strong enough to save. The tragedy is that most of us cling to the notion that we are in control and that our lives are manageable if we just summon the willpower to master our problems.

The key truth that confronts us in Step One is that willpower cannot conquer our problems and addictions. Only our own brokenness coupled with God's strength can free us. The reason willpower cannot save us is that human will changes from moment to moment. Sometimes it agrees with God's will, sometimes not. When it doesn't, it yields to depression or addiction. That is why we must humbly recognize our own powerlessness— to "let go and let God," as they say in AA. Our will is unstable, but God's will is unchanging.

Step One is the biggest and hardest step for many people. No one likes to admit utter helplessness and defeat. In our American culture, we pride ourselves on our self-reliance and rugged individuality.

Yet the fact remains that we *are* powerless, completely powerless, over so many factors in our lives: the economy, the weather, aging, illness, and even our own emotional impulses. The recognition and acceptance of our powerlessness is a crucial step in our spiritual and emotional journey toward wholeness.

Many who enter Twelve-Step groups are appalled by Step One. Some cling to their own pride and willfulness right to the last gasp. This barrier of pride and willfulness is called denial. Denial blinds us to the truth about ourselves. It is one of the biggest enemies we face on the path to recovery. Some of the most common denial messages people use are "I can stop any time I want to"; "I'm doing okay"; "When things get better (or worse) I'll give up my addiction"; "I only practice this behavior because I want to." The person in denial usually avoids responsibility for his own addiction and projects blame on someone else: "If you were a better spouse, I wouldn't have this problem!" People in denial are not just lying to other people; they are lying to themselves.

Sometimes people can be made to see through the veil of their own denial just by counseling and praying with them. But all too often denial can only be broken when the addict is confronted with the consequences of his addiction. He must feel the pain of his addiction before he will admit he is licked. This experience is called "hitting bottom." Anyone who is in the grip of obsessive-compulsive behavior or addiction—such as a codependent, a drug addict, a workaholic, an alcoholic, or a control addict—may hit bottom upon experiencing a crisis. It may be a marital crisis, a health crisis (such as a heart attack or hospitalization), a vocational or financial crisis, a legal crisis, a spiritual crisis (feeling lost or alienated from God), or a confrontation by a family member or loved one (often called an intervention). Many people must reach a point of total despair and unendurable pain before they can begin the upward climb to recovery.

It's important to understand that the Twelve Steps are not sequential. That is, you do not do Step One, then move on to Two, then Three, and so forth, until you have "completed" the Steps. People in recovery work all the Steps all the time. We must return to Step One again and again, continually remembering and admitting our own powerlessness. Surrender must be continual and progressive as God gradually reveals deeper recesses of our lives. As each hidden area comes to light, it must be surrendered to God.

There is no such thing as progressing "beyond Step One." We are always at Step One. Until we raise the white flag of our own powerlessness, until we abjectly surrender to God, spiritual growth or recovery from addiction remains beyond our grasp. Why? Because without the foundation of Step One, there is nothing upon which to build the other eleven Steps.

As long as you can get by on your own power, why would you need to rely on a Higher Power? Why would you want to confess your faults to other people? Why would you want to make amends for harms you've done to other people? And why would you sacrifice time and energy carrying the message of recovery to other sufferers? It would be so much easier to live the way our society says we should live: gratify yourself; do your own thing; look out for number one!

Our problems and our addictions beat and bruise and lash us into confessing the truth about ourselves: We are powerless. We need God's power. Without Him we are helpless and lost.

The apostle Paul foreshadowed Step One when he wrote to the Corinthians, "And He said to me, 'My grace is sufficient for you, for My strength is made perfect in weakness.' Therefore most gladly I will rather boast in my infirmities, that the power of Christ may rest upon me. . . . For when I am weak, then I am strong."[3]

Step Two: Came to believe that a Power greater than ourselves could restore us to sanity.

Step Three: Made a decision to turn our will and our lives over to the care of God *as we understood Him.*

Step One broke us and left us empty and powerless. Recovery from that brokenness—both spiritual recovery and recovery from addiction—begins with Steps Two and Three, as we turn our lives over to a Power greater than ourselves. If Step One did not lead immediately to the God of Step Two, then Step One would be a statement of despair, a confession of powerlessness without any hope of change or recovery. Fortunately, the Steps point the way to a Higher Power, and the name of that Power is Jesus Christ.

The Power of Steps Two and Three invades our lives from

without. It is the Power that made the universe, a Power beyond human comprehension. As the Psalmist writes,

> The LORD is my rock and my fortress and my deliverer;
> My God, my strength, in whom I will trust;
> My shield and the horn of my salvation, my stronghold.[4]

The recovering addict knows better than anyone else that only a rock, a fortress, a Power greater than himself can restore him to sanity and save him.

That's where Eric found himself the day Rick and Jeri Fowler encountered him in that airport in Costa Rica. Eric knew he was powerless over his own addictions and problems. He knew he could do nothing to save himself. He knew that only a Power greater than himself could save him. But he didn't know who that Power was or where that Power could be found.

And *that* is why he was alone and lost in an airport far from home, weeping openly.

Once the Fowlers realized that Eric was familiar with the Twelve Steps, they had a connection, a point of common reference so that they could talk to him. "You know," Rick said, "Step Two says we believed 'that a Power greater than ourselves could restore us to sanity.'"

"Yeah, I know," Eric said despondently, "but I just can't seem to get control over my habits, man. Whatever that Power is, I just can't seem to plug into it."

It was an invitation inscribed in gold—almost as if Eric was begging Rick and Jeri to share the gospel with him! Rick silently thanked God for having prepared Eric's heart in advance. "Eric," Rick replied, "there really is a Power greater than ourselves. Jeri and I are plugged into that Power, and we want to share it with you."

The three of them continued talking. Within the first few minutes Eric opened up the most pain-ridden places of his heart —his addiction issues, his family history, the struggles in his sexual relationships. There was a bond of trust between them because Richard knew the language of AA, the language of the Twelve Steps.

Eric told Rick and Jeri about being raised in a family with

strong moral values—and how he had violated almost every moral precept he had been taught. He had gone to a Christian school as a youngster, but while he was in high school his parents divorced. His security shattered, he started along a path of rebellion, abusing alcohol and drugs to retaliate against his parents.

For the past year he had been living with a young woman named Celia, who was also a drug abuser. Since joining NA, Eric felt a growing conviction that he should sever his relationship with Celia. He loved Celia, but she kept a stash of drugs around the apartment and continually pressured him to "get piped on the stuff" along with her. If he stayed with her, she would drag him down, perhaps even destroy him. He had decided that upon his return he would break off the relationship—and that decision was one of many factors that were tearing him up inside.

Adding to his hurt, his trip to Central America had knocked the emotional props from under him. He had been hired to deliver a car from Dallas to San Jose and had spent two weeks driving alone through Central America. He was besieged by beggars, stopped at military checkpoints, searched by gun-toting soldiers, ripped off by extortion-minded mechanics when the car broke down, and tormented by insects and vermin in crowded immigrant facilities.

Driving through Guatemala, he had seen hundreds of street kids with dirty faces and vacant eyes, many of them addicted to drugs or to glue sniffing. He shook with anger as he told Richard and Jerilyn of these homeless children being rounded up and shot by the Guatemalan authorities for being a "public nuisance." He felt an intense bond with those doomed young souls. "Why do I walk around free when those little children get shot just for being beggars and addicts?" he asked bitterly. "Like, who am I, man? Just a beggar and an addict like those little kids."

He continually struggled to stay clean during his two-week tour of Central America. Once he even yielded and bought a bag of questionable-quality stuff from a teenage boy who approached him in a hotel lobby. In his room, he came *so close* to using. His body was shaking with a combination of dread, guilt, and hunger for the chemical high—but he finally made the decision to flush the whole bag, unused, down the toilet.

Even though Eric's journey was nearly over, Rick and Jeri could see the fear and loneliness lingering in his eyes. Of all his fears, the worst came from within: the fear of his own addiction. His look could only be described as *haunted*.

As they continued talking, Rick took a book called *Serenity* out of his briefcase and placed it in Eric's hands. "I want you to have this, Eric," he said. "It contains the entire New Testament, Psalms, and Proverbs. See those highlighted verses? They're keyed to the Twelve Steps. You're feeling like you're stuck at Step One right now, aren't you? Want to know what God's Word says about you right now? Turn to Romans 7:18 and 19, and read what it says."

Eric turned to the passage. " 'For I know that in me (that is, in my flesh) nothing good dwells,' " he read. " 'For to will is present with me, but how to perform what is good I do not find. For the good that I will to do, I do not do; but the evil I will not to do, that I practice.' " Eric paused for a moment as the words sank in. Then he said, "Wow! It's like God was reading my mind. That's my life in those two verses."

"And what does Step Two say about your life?" Rick asked.

"It says," Eric recited, " 'Came to believe that a Power greater than ourselves could restore us to sanity.' "

"Now read one of the Step Two verses, John 6:69."

" 'We have come to believe and know,' " Eric read, " 'that You are the Christ, the Son of the living God.' "

"Jesus is that Power greater than ourselves, Eric," Rick continued. "Jesus is the Power that can restore us to sanity. He's the Power that brought you and Jeri and me together today."

Rick and Jeri saw the light come on in Eric's eyes. "They never told me this in NA," Eric said. "The Power never seemed real. This is the first hope I've ever had."

Even in his despair and depression, Eric had been edging closer to the truth. During the past two weeks of loneliness and fear, his heart was being carefully prepared by God. Finally, in the last few moments as he awaited the flight home, someone had come into his life with just the right words to say.

Eric, Rick, and Jeri prayed together in that airport, and Eric accepted Jesus Christ as the Lord of his life. After they prayed, Richard and Jeri could see a powerful change in their new friend's face. There was hope and joy in his expression. "I just want to thank you both for coming over and talking to me," Eric said.

Looking back on his encounter with Eric, Rick Fowler reflected, "One of the most powerful experiences you can ever have is when God sends you to talk to someone He has prepared for the good news of Jesus Christ. That experience with Eric gave me just a taste of what the New Testament evangelist Philip must have felt when he led the Ethiopian man to the Lord in Acts chapter 8. Eric reminds me so much of that Ethiopian gentleman, sitting in his chariot, reading the Scriptures, hungry for spiritual truth. The Ethiopian needed someone to come alongside him and reveal Jesus to him, and so did Eric.

"If I hadn't known anything about the Twelve Steps, I wouldn't have had any inroad into Eric's need. But with the Steps as our common ground, I was able to meet this fellow right where he was. We spoke the same language. I knew the spiritual side of the system he was already plugged into."

Couldn't Eric have been reached for Christ by someone who had no knowledge of the Twelve Steps? Rick Fowler replies, "Perhaps. But other evangelistic tools such as Evangelism Explosion or the Four Spiritual Laws—as effective as they are—do not focus on this man's special needs. God had prepared Eric for a message that would meet his sense of powerlessness. Because Eric was immersed in the Twelve Steps, he was pre-evangelized. He just needed someone to tell him who the Higher Power really is."

Dr. Richard A. Fowler's experience in a Central American airport was one of many incidences he and Dr. Frank Minirth and Dr. Brian Newman and Dave Carder have witnessed that have demonstrated the power of the Twelve Steps as a vehicle for Christian witness.

Steps 2 and 3 begin with the declarative statements "[We] came to believe . . ." and "[We] made a decision."

Without question, the subject of Steps 2 and 3 is conversion. For the biblical Christian, however, the question arises: "Conversion to what?"

Sincere evangelical Christians divide in their opinion of the phrase "God *as we understood Him*." On this point, some would accuse the Steps of being spiritually wishy-washy. As historian Ernest Kurtz observes, the fundamental message of Christianity is "Jesus saves," but the fundamental message of the Twelve Steps is "Something saves."[5]

Other sincere evangelical Christians, however, consider the fuzziness of the phrase "God as we understood Him" to be part of the genius of the Twelve Steps. As Keith Miller writes,

> Hearing this is often very disturbing to Christians, who think that the spiritual life begins with a willingness to believe in Jesus Christ. But a little thought reveals that long before a person makes a specific commitment to Christ there has been some sort of awakening of the desire to believe. Authentic Christian conversion is similar to joining a Twelve-Step group, in the sense that first comes the awareness of one's powerlessness to solve the most basic problems one is facing. Then, perhaps, one meets a loving Christian, hears a speaker, reads a book, or sees a movie in which faith plays a part.[6]

Whatever side of this issue you take, there is one fact that simply cannot be argued: The Twelve Steps have stirred the spiritual responsiveness of millions who were once spiritually dead. People in recovery may not always speak in evangelical jargon. Their doctrine (if they have any) may not be orthodox by our standards. Their language, as they describe their relationship with God, may even be sprinkled with coarse words. But their eyes are turned toward God. They are spiritually hungry. They are eager to go farther on and deeper into a personal knowledge of God.

We accept the fact that the spiritual fuzziness of the Steps is an issue with many Christians—and understandably so. The Scriptures warn against those who have a form of godliness but deny its power.[7] That is why we feel so strongly that Christians need to be involved in the Twelve Steps, pointing people in recovery to the true Power of the Steps. How can we allow needy people to come so close to the Truth, yet remain so far away?

To use the Twelve Steps as a vehicle to reach others for Christ we do not have to take sides on whether the spiritual fogginess of the Steps is right or wrong. It simply is. Like it or not, it is the religious tolerance and pluralism of the Twelve Steps that draws such great numbers of people into the recovery net. Therein lies the great opportunity for the gospel in the 1990s. The budding spiritual awareness of millions of recovering people is a wide open door for witness.

Sam Shoemaker used to encourage atheists and agnostics to try a "thirty-day prayer experiment." He suggested that they simply pray daily for thirty days without worrying about believing in God. What should they pray for? That God would meet them right where they were and give them the strength they need. Literally hundreds of atheists and agnostics took Shoemaker's challenge—and thirty days later, many had become *ex*-atheists and *ex*-agnostics. Their doubts and objections were overcome by simply doing the act of faith—and they were gently, gradually brought into a relationship with God the Father and His Son, Jesus Christ.

Step Three calls everyone in the Twelve-Step process to make a decision to "turn our will and our lives over to the care of God." It is impossible to overstate the radical, transforming power of that statement in the lives of those who seriously, diligently apply it to their lives. In talking about the day his life was forever changed so long ago in Peking, Sam often said he saw four elements in that decision. One of them was the need to put life's major decisions in God's hands. It was not enough merely to decide to be a minister, he said. The bigger issue is the question of who shall be in ultimate control: Where does God want me? How can I serve Him? Am I willing to go anywhere He sends me?

To turn our will and our lives over to the care of God means that we evaluate every decision in life by God's standards —from the big questions of choosing our vocation and our marriage partner to the moment-to-moment choices: Shall I read the newspaper or have my quiet time with You? Do You want me to say something to that person who seems lost and alone? Lord, shall I admit my fault, or shall I tell a little white lie? Every corner of our lives must be yielded to His control.[8]

We know a middle-aged woman who is familiar with the Twelve Steps, although she has never attended a recovery group or been in counseling. Each morning she turns her life over to God for that day. As she says grace in the morning, she prays, "Dear, Lord, I give my life to You for this day. Help me to live today as You would want me to live. Help me to serve You, to obey You, to glorify You. In Your name, in the name of Jesus Christ, I cast out all fear—fear of failure or disease—which blocks my ability to do Your will. Help me this day to make decisions in light of my relationship with You, doing nothing that would interfere with my love for You and for other people." This Christian woman believes that the principles of the Twelve Steps are a part of her daily walk. She turns her life over to God each day. She lives "One day at a time," which is both an AA slogan and a scriptural principle.

Steps Two and Three are not just Steps to recovery. They are Steps that every Christian can and should walk. These two Steps call us to recognize that for many people, conversion is not an event; it's a process. These Steps are the key to appropriating God's power to continue that process throughout our lives.

Step Four: Made a searching and fearless moral inventory of ourselves.

Relentless self-examination is one of the cornerstones of both the Christian life and Twelve-Step recovery. Jesus set forth the principle of Step Four in the Sermon on the Mount: we should fearlessly, honestly dislodge the plank from our own eye before attempting to pluck the specks from the eyes of others.

Our natural human tendency is to shrink in denial from the truth about ourselves. We would rather clutch our illusion of adequacy than admit to ourselves that we are poor, naked, and sinful. But as long as we clutch our illusions and deny the truth, we keep ourselves from growth and recovery. As psychiatrist M. Scott Peck puts it, "We become evil by attempting to hide from ourselves."[9]

"But if we walk in the light as He is in the light," says 1 John 1:7–9, "we have fellowship with one another, and the blood of Jesus Christ His Son cleanses us from all sin. If we say that we have no sin, we deceive ourselves, and the truth is not in us. If we confess our sins, He is faithful and just to forgive us our sins and to cleanse us from all unrighteousness." The willingness to walk unflinchingly in the light is one of the keys to victorious Christian living—and to recovery from addiction.

Sam Shoemaker saw "the break with conscious wrong" as one of the elements in his initial decision in Peking. Either sin controls us, or God controls us, he said. And *pride* is the root sin. Even when we call out to God for help—even during the very act of prayer itself!—the deceptive power of pride can be so strong that it stubbornly attempts to wrest control from God and hand it over to self. Shoemaker used the Four Absolutes, which Dr. Robert E. Speer derived from the Sermon on the Mount, as his own yardstick when he took his own Step Four inventory in Peking: absolute honesty, absolute purity, absolute unselfishness, and absolute love. Frank Buchman adopted these absolutes and made them a fundamental part of the Oxford Groups.

As he compared himself against the standard of absolute honesty, Shoemaker confessed, "I had not lied or stolen in any shocking fashion, but neither had I ever been honest about myself with any other human being." From that moment on, he committed himself to an uncompromising truthfulness in all of his dealings, whether momentous or trivial.

"Absolute purity," Shoemaker said, "means to find some all-consuming and high faith and purpose which takes up and uses one's energies. It is partly because Christ offers just such an all engulfing program to anyone that he can call for such a high standard of living.

"Absolute unselfishness—that catches us all in a hundred places, but for me the main place was in the whole matter of life work." Part of Sam's Step Three self-surrender had been giving his life and ministry to God, even if that meant staying in China for the rest of his life.

"And then absolute love. There were many minor irritations, but the cleavage between my father and me, due to our inability to communicate, was a deep one. I say in the diary, 'I wrote a letter to Father, a very hard one to write, saying I was sorry for anything hard I had said or thought of him.' "[10] This letter, which Sam Shoemaker wrote in 1917, was the first of many letters that millions of people have written to loved ones they have wronged, in obedience to Steps Four and Five.

In describing the moral inventory Shoemaker took in 1917, he later wrote,

> I just knew that basic dishonesty, impurity, selfishness, want of love, and withal a kind of pervasive inferiority, were holding me down. One by one I tried to release them, like a lot of black birds out of a crate. There was no emotion or elation about it. I felt only a sense of release as I went to bed that cold, crisp January night. But—to change the figure—it was as if something that had been out of joint had slipped back again where it belonged. I felt forgiven and free. The ways seemed open to God through Christ. . . . Without some decisive, comprehensive facing of ourselves and our sins at the outset, I do not think we ever make even a start of overcoming our sins. For me the best test has proved to be whether God could use me in the life of someone else.[11]

The Big Book suggests that the process of taking moral inventory be done in writing. Why? Why can't we just take a *mental* inventory of our lives and offer those thoughts to God? The answer is that this moral inventory is for our information, not God's. He already knows our every defect and sin. It is we who tend to have blind spots concerning our own lives, not God. When we write down an inventory of our character defects and sins, they become concrete. We must look at them. We must acknowledge them. A written inventory is a powerful tool for penetrating denial.

Dave Carder suggests yet another benefit of a written inventory. "A written inventory," he says, "reduces mental and emotional confusion. Guilt and bad memories have a tendency to stay in the brain and just keep buzzing round and round. Amazingly, when you pull those memories out of your head and put them on paper, you actually begin to purge them out of your system. People are always apprehensive about doing a Four Step, but once you have it out on paper, your mind can finally start letting go of it. It's a crucial part of the healing process."

Step Five: Admitted to God, to ourselves, and to another human being the exact nature of our wrongs.

Step Four, moral inventory, leads naturally to Step Five, confession. In Step Five, you meet in a confidential setting with a trusted friend and verbalize to that person what you learned about yourself in Step Four.

Sam Shoemaker learned that taking a moral inventory was not a one-time event. There comes a day, he said, when you realize that total victory over all sin would take you right out of the world. You must learn to expect some failures. Be honest about them, with yourself, with God, and with any persons they concern when they come. This creates a continuing, renewing, grace-oriented process by which we are forgiven, we begin again, and we grow in an ongoing way.[12] "Many Christians do not make this step decisive enough," he added, "and it accounts for their falling by the wayside later. Nothing can be tolerated that interferes with God's pouring His power into and through us."[13]

Confession is an essential principle of Christian living. "He who covers his sins will not prosper,/But whoever confesses and forsakes them will have mercy," says Proverbs 28:13. Not only is confession at the heart of the Christian faith, but it is also a key to healing and recovery. "Confess your trespasses to one another," says James 5:16, "and pray for one another, that you may be healed."

Both the Bible and the Twelve Steps encourage us to live honest, transparent, fully illuminated lives. Step Five calls us to find a few close friends to whom we can disclose ourselves in safety. We confess not only our sin, but our grief, pain, and weakness. Confession cleanses the soul, purges shame, and brings a healing sense of forgiveness and a new beginning into our lives. Confession is also an escape valve for toxic emotions that threaten the spirit. When we name our hidden sin, shame, fear, or bitterness to another person, we reaffirm our commitment to growth as we enlist the prayers of others.

What kinds of issues does Step Five call us to confess?
- Our addictions.
- Pain that we carry from childhood (in recovery language, pain from our "families of origin").
- Multi-generational issues (areas of brokenness in our families of origin that have hurt us; this may be expressed as a need to understand, accept, and forgive our parents or other family members).
- Pain or toxic emotions arising from the major relationships in our lives.
- Wrongs we have committed against others as a result of our addictions.

AA founder Bill W. once said that Step Five is the hardest Step of all because it makes us vulnerable and demands our humiliation before another human being. We naturally fear that the one who hears our confession will condemn us. After confession has been made, however, we discover that people in recovery are the most accepting people on earth. They listen without judging, even to our darkest secrets, for they have already faced and confessed their own dark secrets to others. And when our darkness has been confessed, then God's light can come flooding in.

In Shoemaker's book *Faith at Work*, Norman P. Grubb, American Director of the Worldwide Evangelization Crusade in the 1950s, warned evangelical Christians about the danger of taking the act of confession too lightly. "We evangelical Christians," said Grubb,

> have usually experienced some dynamic and often clearly dated meeting with the Spirit. There has been this conviction of sin, repentance and confession, forgiveness through Christ, and regeneration. The Spirit has moved vitally upon us. But our spiritual "birthday" has been so outstanding and so clearly marked, and its benefits for time and eternity are so immeasurable, that it casts its shadow, like a giant peak, too much upon our dusty pathway and tends to obscure the white light in which we are to walk as constantly and openly as on that first day in which we responded to it. In other words, conviction,

repentance, confession, and cleansing are to be
continuous (1 John 1:7), if the movings of the Spirit
are to be continuous in us. . . .

We don't mind admitting that in the past (in a
general sense, maybe) we were sinners and came to
the Saviour; but for me to admit today, in a specific
sense, that I was caught out by the devil in
irritability, or untruth; in hard or critical thoughts; in
selfishness, or sloth, or sensuality—that I could never
do! Why? Because I am too proud. I say I glory in
no righteousness except Christ's imputed to me, and
have no plea except His blood shed for me; but
actually I am most sensitive about my own
righteousness before men. Pride, in fact, is my root
sin, underlying all the rest.

This has one most serious effect on me: I
become insensitive to sin. It is easy enough for me to
admit sin in a sort of a way to God; that doesn't cost
too much, for He is very merciful, and I am not too
ashamed, because anyhow He knows all about me. It
is when I am honest before men that the thing hurts
and shames; that is what makes it real to me, and
equally makes the forgiveness of God wonderful to
me. . . .

When I was on a visit to Central Africa . . . I
found myself among companies of African Christians,
and some missionaries, who lived 'walking in the
light' with each other. I had never before experienced
such free, open, and happy fellowship; but it was
completely honest. If jealousy, criticism,
covetousness, impurity, coldness of heart had a hold
on any, as they met together, they would quietly say
so, and praise would ascend from all for Jesus'
cleansing.

I was often smitten in heart that the same kind
of things went on within me, but I was not *saying* so.
Then one day a man unexpectedly arrived whom I
had met in England and had disliked. He gave me a
warm greeting and I gave him the same; but in a

second the Spirit said to me, "You hypocrite; you know you don't mean that!"

I recognized my sin of dislike and hypocrisy and confessed it in secret to God. But did I get rid of it that way? Indeed not. Every time I saw him, I felt the same towards him.

Then God showed me that my repentance was not genuine; I wanted to repent in secret and save my face in public. My respectability meant more to me than the fact that I had sinned and needed cleansing. I had to tell the man right out; and, as a member of that Christian company, to be really honest, I had to tell them all. That took me two days to do!

I learned how deep inward pride is. But when I "broke" and did it, in a moment the antagonism had gone, the blood had cleansed. And I began then to see the reality and release of walking in the light, for myself and for the fellowship.

I had much more to learn. I came home wanting to walk like this with all my fellow Christians, but God soon said to me, "Start at home." I have been married over thirty years, but I found myself face to face with a sin I had slurred over, all these years, the sin of impatience and hard attitudes toward my wife. . . .

Then I saw myself a bit more really as I am with my children, and how often I would [punish] them, not out of genuine love for them, or for their improvement, but because they had annoyed me or caused me to lose face. And so on, in my mission relationships, too, until today, two years later, there is a whole new plane of living relationships, and honest, open fellowship, with my fellow workers. It is like a new world. It is "revival."

Sin always binds—that's its nature—and the worst of it is that we are so often bound just because we have not seen sin as sin. What release, as sin is squarely recognized, confessed to God, forgiven, and the facts frankly spoken of, as God guides! What new bonds of understanding and love are forged as fellow Christians meet "down at the Cross!" . . .

One of Satan's favorite weapons is to whisper to us that we are the only Christians who ever do a thing like that and not ever to let anyone know. And what release to find that we are all "men of like passions," and none of us has anything to boast of, in our wretched flesh—but only in the Cross! How frank and practical we can be in speaking to others "outside," when we can tell them of what we are even now without Christ, and what a difference He makes![14]

These are the first five steps of the Twelve Steps. Their focus is to reunite us with God, our Father. The last seven steps are a designed as a pathway of spiritual growth and the basis of a continued walk with Christ.

CHAPTER 4

WALKING THE WALK

The Last Seven of the Twelve Steps

His name is Stephen W., and he's an alcoholic.

One Friday evening in June 1984, Stephen unlocked the door of his small North Hollywood apartment and stepped inside. In his hand was a long, narrow paper bag, and in the bag was a 750-milliliter bottle of Popov vodka, cheap and potent. He set the bottle on the counter that separated the kitchen from the living room.

When Stephen first rented the place, he noticed how close and stuffy it was, how a nasty and not-quite-definable odor seemed to emanate from the stained carpet. But he didn't notice such things anymore. These days Stephen seemed to sleepwalk through his life, through his minimum-wage job at a daycare center, through evenings alone in his apartment with nothing to do.

As he did every evening when he got home from work, he closed the olive-green drapes in the living room. There being no other window in the apartment, the entire place instantly filled with gloom. Then, as usual, he unplugged the phone and poured himself a drink. It burned going down and hit his empty stomach like napalm.

As the alcohol seeped into his system, Stephen's mind

turned to thoughts of self-destruction—a recurring theme in his life for the past few years. Though he had done nothing about it, he had often considered killing himself. *Maybe tonight's the night*, he thought as the deadening spirits coursed through his bloodstream and seeped into his brain.

Every night, he drank till he passed out. It was always lousy waking up the next morning. Sometimes he got himself so badly toxed he couldn't go to work. *After tonight*, he decided, *I won't have to wake up at all.*

His mind made up, he went to the bathroom and took all the bottles out of the medicine cabinet. He lugged them into the bedroom and uncapped the bottles, making a pile of capsules and tablets on the bedspread. It was all there, everything from over-the-counter allergy pills to heavy-duty prescription stuff. He proceeded to swallow them by the handful, washing them down with vodka.

Fifteen minutes passed. As he waited, he thought about why he was killing himself. It wasn't that he felt so depressed. There were many times in his life when he'd felt much worse than this night.

Before taking the job at the daycare center, he had been involved with a mission in downtown LA. There he had seen so much suffering, so many broken lives, so many wasted minds and bodies that he was in constant emotional pain. He identified with all the people he met, taking their misery into himself. Soon he realized he was becoming just like those he had set out to help: lonely, depressed, bitter, defeated. When he could no longer stand his pain, he began numbing it with alcohol. Trouble was, alcohol numbed everything, both the bad feelings and the good. Now he hardly felt anything anymore—not even regret that he was about to die.

Just then he realized he did feel something after all. Something bad. It started in his stomach and rose into his throat. But it didn't matter. He could tell he was about to pass out. A minute later, he did.

Then he woke up again. *I'm not dead*, he realized as he drifted back to consciousness. *I'm just real, real sick.* Even worse, he was afraid. Suddenly, he didn't want to die anymore.

God, please let me throw up, he thought. But he couldn't. He could only heave and heave.

He crawled to the phone and plugged it back into the jack, then punched the number of an acquaintance at work. "Beth," he moaned into the receiver, "I'm real sick. Can you get me to the hospital? . . . Yes, right now. I—I took some pills. . . . I dunno what kind. Every kind. I took 'em all. . . . Yeah, I can hold on till you get here. But hurry, okay?"

A few minutes later, Beth picked Stephen up and took him to the hospital, where the doctors pumped him out and kept him overnight for observation. The next morning a social worker came by and asked him a lot of questions. After they had talked awhile, the social worker asked, "Has it ever occurred to you that you might be an alcoholic?"

This question came as a shock to Stephen. Even though he drank himself to sleep every night and woke up sick every morning, it had never even crossed his mind that he might be an alcoholic. "An alcoholic?" Stephen said, turning the idea over in his mind. "I just thought I was crazy."

The Turning Point

An alcoholic. Stephen had to get used to the idea. He had been raised in a strict, legalistic church. His parents had taught him that alcoholics were the dirtiest, most despicable creatures on two legs. How could he be one of *those?*

The social worker suggested a hospital program for alcoholism. Fortunately, it was covered by his insurance at work. For the next few days, he underwent the hospital detox program; then he was referred to an AA group that met in a church basement about a mile from his apartment.

"They talked about God in that AA group," Stephen told us, thinking back to his first encounter with Alcoholics Anonymous. "I wasn't ready to go back to church at that point in my life, but I could handle the idea of God as a Higher Power. I knew I wasn't making it on my own. I needed God's help. The longer I stuck with AA, the more I realized that the real Higher Power was Jesus Christ. As I got more sober, Christianity made more sense."

That experience—his near-suicide and his first few steps toward recovery—was the turning point in Stephen's life. "It really shook me up," he recalls. "I was looking at the logical conclusion of the way I was living: total self-destruction. I didn't finish the job this time, but I figured I would the next time."

We asked Stephen if it was the alcohol that drove him to the edge of destruction. "Alcohol was a major factor," he replied, "but I had a lot of other emotional problems. The alcohol really interacted with who I was. I was drunk when I tried to kill myself, but I eventually would have attempted it even if I was sober."

About six months after joining AA, Stephen lost his job at the daycare center, so he hitchhiked up the coast of California. He stayed with some friends in Monterey for a while and got involved with an AA group there. "Around that time I started getting crazy again. I really wanted a drink. But Chuck, a friend I met in the group in Monterey, stuck by me and kept me sane. In fact, I probably owe my life to Chuck."

Chuck, a strong Christian and an elder in a Monterey Presbyterian church, introduced Stephen to other Christian friends. Chuck never preached to Stephen; he simply befriended him and shared the story of his life, including the story of his own struggle with alcohol and his recovery through the power of Jesus Christ. Stephen's faith, which was first rekindled in an AA meeting in North Hollywood, now began to deepen and grow.

Today, Stephen W. has a master's degree in social work. He is married with two children, and he lives in a city about fifty miles south of Monterey. He serves as the director of a Christian ministry to poor people, street people, and transients in the central part of town. A lot of the people who pass through the doors of the mission remind Stephen of his younger self.

"I'm real involved in AA, and in a small group Bible study," he says. "I've never been real comfortable in churches, but I go to church when I can. I can't point to one moment where I had a lightning-like conversion or where I came back into the fold, but I do know that I used to be on the outside and now I'm in.

"Most AAs are not theologically sophisticated. Their faith tends to be real simple. They may read AA literature more than the Bible. Only God knows the heart, but I believe most of the guys in my AA group worship the same Lord I do. I've found a real easy balance between AA and Christianity. I've seen a lot of people find God in AA. Some have experienced a resurrection of a faith that wasn't working for them before AA."

We asked Stephen why the Twelve Steps work, and why people are able to discover faith in God through the Twelve Steps. "One of the reasons the Twelve Steps work," he replied, "is that the essence of the Steps is the essence of the early church. Everything that makes for a healthy Christian life is there in the Steps—admitting powerlessness, confession of sin, making amends for wrongs, taking moral inventory, asking God to remove your shortcomings, prayer and meditation, and passing the message along. The Twelve Steps are really nothing more than orthodox Christianity in a nutshell. The Steps are real simple, and that's one of the reasons they work."

The next Steps—Steps Six and Seven—are the steps of confession, which brings us even deeper into an intimate relationship with God.

Step Six: Were entirely ready to have God remove all these defects of character.

Step Seven: Humbly asked Him to remove our shortcomings.

Steps Six and Seven take us even deeper into the process of sanctification, of surrendering our entire lives to God. The psalmist anticipated these Steps when he wrote,

> Search me, O God, and know my heart;
> Try me, and know my anxieties;
> And see if there is any wicked way in me,
> And lead me in the way everlasting.[1]

And Hebrews 12:1–2 concurs: "Let us lay aside every weight, and the sin which so easily ensnares us . . . looking unto Jesus, the author and finisher of our faith."

Steps Six and Seven look easy enough because at a superficial level we all want to have God make us into "better people."

But when we examine those sins and defects one by one, it becomes clear that change must involve pain. Our natural tendency is to shrink from the pain of God's healing, surgical knife. No matter how much we want God to reshape our character, a part of us clutches grubby little sins and habits like a miser grasping at every last farthing.

Step Seven inserts the all-important word "humbly" into our thinking. To be humble is to see ourselves accurately, in all our powerlessness and sin. Whereas society tells us to be our own gods, Step Seven reminds us of the humility of Step One: we are powerless. The strength for our recovery comes not from within us but from a Power greater than ourselves.

Step Eight: Made a list of all persons we had harmed, and became willing to make amends to them all.

Step Nine: Made direct amends to such people wherever possible, except when to do so would injure them or others.

Steps Eight and Nine, which involve making amends or restitution to those we have wronged, reflect a crucial biblical principle. They are also one of the distinctive traditions of the Oxford Group, the forerunner of all Twelve-Step groups. This is the same principle Jesus set forth when he said, "If you bring your gift to the altar, and there remember that your brother has something against you, leave your gift there before the altar, and go your way. First be reconciled to your brother, and then come and offer your gift."[2]

People in recovery are encouraged to make amends to all those who have been hurt by their addictions, parents, children, spouses, friends, employers, employees—in other words, our families of origin, our families of marriage, our work families, our church families, our community, and even the family of man (for many people, their addictive behavior has included intolerance toward other political, religious, and ethnic groups).

Even though these two Steps are directed outward to relationships with our fellow human beings, a potent benefit comes back to us when we make amends to those we have wronged.

The memory of wrongs we have committed against others carries a toxic residue of guilt and shame. Making amends enables us to expunge those emotions and memories so that we can be restored to emotional and spiritual wholeness.

Steps Eight and Nine also pull us deeper into the process of sanctification and surrender to God. They help to restore our sense of responsibility for our own actions. The sin addiction is deceptive, regardless of the form it takes. Our addiction corrodes our sense of responsibility—even to the ones we love, the ones who love us. Making amends restores us to sanity and wholeness in our relationships with others.

There is another chapter from the life of Ralston Young—Grand Central Station's Redcap Number 42 in the 1940s—which vividly demonstrates the importance of making amends, both in relationships between believers and in our witnessing lifestyle. As Ralston Young and a fellow redcap named Edgar were chatting near the information booth in the terminal, a man approached Edgar for assistance. "My daughter's taking the Yankee Clipper," the man said to Ralston's friend. "Can you see her safely aboard the train?"

Edgar agreed to look after the girl and told the man to wait with his daughter at Gate 27. He would be with them in twenty minutes. So the man took his daughter to the gate and waited. Ralston and Edgar continued talking for a while; then when it was nearly time for the Clipper to board passengers, the two of them walked toward Gate 27. That's when Ralston Young noticed that the man who had approached Edgar for help was holding a dollar bill in his hand.

Instinctively, Ralston sped up his pace, reaching the man ahead of his friend Edgar. In a low voice, so his friend couldn't hear, Ralston told the man, "I'll wait on your daughter," and quickly palmed the tip.

Instantly, Redcap Number 42 felt a pang of guilt and shame. Edgar was not only a friend, but a man Ralston had been witnessing to. *Here's a man who doesn't even profess to be Christian,* he thought, *yet he always acts generously to me. And I, who talk about serving Christ, turn around and knife him in the back!*

Ralston Young carried the conviction of that sin for three days. Finally, in the terminal locker room, he took his friend

Edgar aside, and said, "Edgar, I want you to forgive me." He extended a hand to Edgar, and in that hand was a dollar bill. He explained to his friend what he had done and that he could not live with himself until he had made amends.

Edgar grinned and waved the money away. "Forget it, Ralston," he said. "I admire your honesty in 'fessing up to it, but this is a competitive job. It's survival of the fittest."

"Nothing excuses a person like me acting as selfishly as I did," Ralston countered. "I hope you'll forgive me." From that moment forward, Ralston and Edgar enjoyed a much closer friendship than ever before.

Later, in the regular group meeting Ralston hosted in the car on Track 13, he felt a sense of conviction midway through the meeting. He sensed a degree of superficiality in the sharing of the group and felt God prodding him to confess to his fellows what he had confessed to Edgar. So he repeated the whole story.

"Well sir," Ralston later recalled, "just being honest about that dollar bill did amazing things! Suddenly several of the others realized that they also had recently been guilty of questionable acts, and when I stopped talking it was just as if a plug had been pulled—and three people in succession . . . admitted their failures to the group and outlined what they were going to do to put things right."

Honesty about our own faults also lends a reality and vitality to the group process that superficial sharing bleeds away. "People wonder why fellowship groups sometimes get weak and die," Ralston Young reflected. "It's because we hide dollar bills and won't admit we've been wrong! There's no substitute for being honest about oneself."

Redcap Number 42 also recognized that admitting wrongs and making amends is a powerful force for both recovery and evangelism. "We've got to pass on our faith to other people," he said. "We've got to win a man's friendship before Jesus Christ can capture his life."

There's no record of whether Ralston's friend Edgar ever made a decision to follow Christ. But we do know that Ralston's act of confession and making amends enabled him to win Edgar's trust and friendship at a deep level—an important first step in the process of winning Edgar's soul.[3]

At this point in the Twelve Steps, we come to another shift in focus. Steps One through Five forced us to recognize our need of reliance upon God. Then Steps Six through Nine performed "major surgery" on our souls, reminding us of our need to have our defects and shortcomings cut out of us, while we sought to make amends to those we had harmed. Now, in Steps Ten, Eleven, and Twelve, we come to the "maintenance Steps," the Steps that show us how to stay on the path of recovery and authentic Christian discipleship for life.

Step Ten: Continued to take personal inventory and when we were wrong promptly admitted it.

AA members never graduate from AA. No one in Alcoholics Anonymous says, "I used to be an alcoholic," not even the AA old timer who hasn't touched a drop in forty years. AAs see themselves as alcoholics for life. The same is true for every other addict and every other addiction: Temptation always hovers nearby. We are never more than one choice away from succumbing to our addiction.

And the same thing is true of any Christian. We are all sinners, the Bible says. Each of us needs to take a personal inventory each day—and when we are wrong, to promptly admit it.

The Christian life and the recovery lifestyle both require lifelong daily maintenance. It is part of the deceitfulness of the human heart that we want to say to ourselves after a time, "I'm well now. I don't need my recovery group or Christian fellowship. I don't need accountable Christian relationships. I don't need to work the Steps anymore. I'm cured." Steps Ten, Eleven, and Twelve point us to our need of continuous renewal.

Hebrews 3:12–13 admonishes us, "Beware, brethren, lest there be in any of you an evil heart of unbelief in departing from the living God; but exhort one another daily, while it is called 'Today,' lest any of you be hardened through the deceitfulness of sin." And Jesus warned His disciples, "Watch and pray, lest you enter into temptation. The spirit truly is ready, but the flesh is weak."[4]

Step Ten concurs with the diagnosis of God's Word: We are prone to wandering, prone to self-deception and denial, and we must continually take personal inventory in order to guard against moral and spiritual drift. Surrender is not a once-for-all event. Surrender is a lifelong process—and a moment-by-moment choice.

Step Eleven: Sought through prayer and meditation to improve our conscious contact with God as we understood Him, praying only for knowledge of His will for us and the power to carry that out.

Whereas Step Ten focuses on daily maintenance of our integrity, right behavior, and right relationships with others, Step Eleven focuses on daily spiritual maintenance. Christian fellowship, prayer, and meditation in God's Word are indispensable tools for our spiritual growth.

Sam Shoemaker saw daily time for personal devotions as another of the four elements in his initial decision. "I had struggled with the old 'morning watch,' " he admitted,

and found prayer dry and the Bible like sawdust. Somehow my new experience made prayer live, for prayer became seeking God's will afresh, not trying to change it.

The Bible opened up as a living record of those who tried to live in obedience to God's will. I shall never forget how it helped me to read every reference I could find to Simon Peter; he had so many weaknesses, yet God greatly used him.[5]

Since the earliest stirrings of the recovery movement, prayer and Bible study have been viewed as crucial, indispensable elements in the recovery process. AA founder Bill W. devoted himself to the spiritual side of the Twelve Steps. He prayed daily, immersed himself in Scripture and Christian literature, and often said that Oswald Chambers' classic devotional *My Utmost for His Highest* was his favorite book aside from the Bible.

Step Eleven is a commitment to pray and meditate in order to "improve our conscious contact with God." Counselors at the twenty Minirth-Meier clinics in the United States have written many of the books in the Serenity Meditation Series, and we often recommend them to our patients.

In Philippians 4:5–8, the apostle Paul gives us five ingredients for making prayerful contact with God. Those ingredients are:

1. We should quiet our anxieties. "Be anxious for nothing," writes Paul. Or as Psalm 46:10 says, "Be still, and know that I am God."

2. We should give thanks to God for the good things in our lives. Paul continues, "but in everything by prayer and supplication, with thanksgiving . . ."

3. We should be honest, sincere, and candid with God as we lay our needs before him. Paul adds, "let your requests be made known to God."

4. We should wait expectantly as we pray for the infilling of God's peace, which passes human understanding. Paul writes, "and the peace of God, which surpasses all understanding, will guard your hearts and minds through Christ Jesus."

5. We should meditate on the things of greatest significance and value—"whatever things are noble, whatever things are just, whatever things are pure, whatever things are lovely, whatever things are of good report, if there is any virtue and if there is anything praiseworthy—meditate on these things."

Twelve-Step groups encourage people to experience a natural dialogue with God. There is no pressure for a person to pray "the right way." It's a moving and powerful experience to be with people who are truly encountering the Almighty for the first time, pouring out their thoughts and feelings in simple, unpretentious sentences, sometimes with quaking voices and tears and always with genuine feeling.

A clergyman in Sam Shoemaker's Faith at Work groups in the 1950s, Robert M. Man, told how the power of prayer transformed his ministry and his life. As a young clergyman in his first parish, Pastor Man was frustrated by his inability to comfort people in the sickroom. He planned out his words of consolation beforehand, yet he always seemed to get tongue-tied in the presence of a suffering person.

One day, as he made his rounds at the hospital, he entered to room of Mrs. S., a member of his parish who was in a coma.

The bedside nurse told him she had suffered a cerebral hemorrhage and wouldn't even recognize him.

But he went to her side nevertheless and began praying for her. As he silently prayed, her eyelids fluttered open, and her hand reached for his and took it. "Would you like me to pray for you?" he asked.

"Yes," she replied softly, "I would."

He prayed aloud for her, and as he finished, she whispered, "Amen." The nurse's eyes were wide in astonishment as Pastor Man left the room.

On his return the next day, he found Mrs. S. conscious in her bed and her husband weeping quietly at her bedside. "The doctors told us," said Mr. S., "that my wife will never recover."

Pastor Man bent close to the woman, took her hand, and said, "I have a prayer group meeting at five o'clock this afternoon. We are going to pray for you by name, and I want you to join in prayer with us." She weakly nodded her agreement.

That evening, Pastor Man prayed for Mrs. S. with the prayer group, and the next day he returned and found her remarkably improved. A few weeks later, she left the hospital, completely well. She left behind an amazed and befuddled team of doctors and nurses.

"When patients are seriously ill," Pastor Man concluded, "I learn their given name and then, one night a week, our prayer group meets and we pray for each of them by name. It is amazing what great things have been accomplished through this regular, persistent prayer effort."[6]

People who are working the Steps are people in search of a miracle. The source of miracles is the same today as it ever was. We meet God and access His transforming power through the discipline and persistent effort of prayer.

Step Twelve: Having had a spiritual awakening as the result of these steps, we tried to carry this message to others, and to practice these principles in all our affairs.

People come into a Twelve-Step group feeling pain and seeking relief from their addictions. But in the process, they discover more than just recovery. They receive the gift of a profound spiritual awakening. Their suffering and their healing have just been way stations on a road to a more sublime destination than they had imagined possible: intimacy with the infinite God of the Universe.

There is a phrase that AA old-timers often use when they introduce themselves in Twelve-Step groups: "Hi, I'm _____, and I'm a grateful recovering alcoholic." What are they grateful for? For their recovery, certainly, but there's a lot more to it. Most are grateful for the fact that they have discovered joy and deep meaning in life. Having passed through the fire of their addiction, they emerge with a profound sense of God's presence. Before their recovery, they were spiritually asleep; now they have been awakened.

This is an experience that all Christians, addicts and nonaddicts, can share. We have all known pain in our lives—the pain of losing a job, losing a loved one, suffering a serious illness, going through financial crisis, enduring conflict, or being unfairly robbed of a good reputation. Having passed through the fiery trials of life, we all emerge with a deeper and more profound sense of God's presence.

Next, notice the evangelistic dimension of the Twelfth Step: "We tried to carry this message to others." People in recovery are like Christians of the first-century church: they have a mission field—fellow addicts and codependents like themselves— and they have a sense of urgency about carrying their message of recovery and spiritual renewal to this mission field. Clearly, the goal of sharing Christ with others through the Twelve-Step process is embedded in the Twelfth Step itself. (We will discuss the implications of the Twelfth Step for evangelism in greater depth in the next chapter.)

In AA witnessing is called "Twelfth-Stepping." It simply means telling your own story. In the first few decades of Alcoholics Anonymous, most AAs were aggressive "Twelfth-Steppers," going into the alcoholic wards of hospitals and talking to any drunk who would listen. The goal of "Twelfth-Stepping" is two-fold: (1) to reach out and rescue other addicts, and (2) to enable the "Twelfth-Stepper" himself to stay sober. In the 1990s AA witnessing is less aggressive, but the principle of the Twelfth Step is the same: This message must be carried to others.

One of the oral traditions of AA is, "You can't keep it unless you give it away." Or, as one Christian recovering alcoholic told us, "I know I can't stay sober unless I'm helping some other guy stay sober. And it's the same with my Christian faith: I'm not living it if I'm not sharing it." People in recovery have good reason, as the psalmist wrote, to "proclaim the good news of His salvation from day to day."[7]

Sam Shoemaker saw "the need to learn how to witness" as the fourth element in his initial decision. Yet he realized that most Christians are tongue-tied. Many of us, he said, do not witness because we have nothing to witness to! We have no experience of authentic conversion, of genuine prayer, of an experience of God's transforming power! We call it shyness, but it is really spiritual poverty.

Shoemaker was fond of saying, "Until something happens *to* us and *in* us, it will not happen *through* us." A witness, Shoemaker reminds us, is simply someone who reports what he has seen with his own eyes. Once we have experienced a spiritual awakening, we have an event that we can witness to others about. Through the Twelve-Step process, we can make friends and listen to our friends tell their stories; and we can share our own stories and tell how our lives have changed since God began living with us, in us, and through us. In the process we are witnessing to them, helping them to begin living with God, in God, and for God.[8]

The last phrase of Step Twelve, "and to practice these principles in all our affairs," closes the circle of the Twelve Steps. All of these principles, from Step One to Step Twelve, must be fully activated in every area of our lives, in all our affairs—our finances, our relationships, our career and community involvement, our sexual conduct, and on and on. The radical transformation of every aspect of our lives is the most convincing witness of all. This type of witnessing was encouraged by Sam Shoemaker in the Faith at Work and Fellowship of Witness programs. An attorney in a large American city told the story of how he witnessed to a client in *Faith at Work*:

> One evening a young married woman brought me a
> familiar story: her love for her husband had turned to

loathing and she had twice asked him for a divorce. As she rehearsed her grievances there appeared in clear outline the picture of a life which had gone hollow. The center was without motivation. Even caring for her children—she had two: eight and ten—had lost its meaning and she had come to the place where she was merely existing in a kind of desert—an arid life without love, faith, or hope.

When I could, I asked her a few questions: what she thought a divorce would solve, what problems it would raise, what the effect would be on the children's personalities and futures.

She'd thought of all those angles, she assured me, and had considered the children's welfare before all else. They would be better off, she maintained, with a mother who could live happily, rather than growing up in an emotional vacuum—better off in the fruitful atmosphere of love than under the tension of a home that "resembled an armed camp."

Then I asked her what she had tried to do to prevent a divorce and if she had tried to cope in any way with the sterility of her life. Yes, indeed, she replied, that was just where the desperation had come in; she had tried "everything"—even prayer—but nothing had worked. "Except perhaps those prayers" —she had wanted to ask me about them—what did I think about prayer?

"Before I answer," I found myself saying, "I want to ask you two more questions: first, do you think there's any possibility of your husband, or you, changing, so that you can be happy?"

"No, people don't change," she replied. "After reaching a certain chronological maturity," she went on, "they're stuck with whatever psychological immaturity they may happen to have; they settle into their respective ruts, and live out their lives in loneliness, never really understanding each other, or themselves, and raising children that they do not understand." She was sure of it. That's why she had to have a divorce.

I proceeded to my second question, "What do you believe about God?"

She didn't know. She'd had two "peculiar experiences" when she prayed. Both times she seemed to be relieved. Was it possible that God answered prayers?

At this point in the discussion I remember clearly pushing back from the table and silently praying myself. I believe I said something like this: "Father, you see this child of yours. You know her needs better than I, better by far than she does. Direct my words to her needs and to your will for her. Let them penetrate so that they will have meaning and direct her life to you, and to your Kingdom. Use me—use my words—make them yours."

Then I felt guided to remind her of the biblical injunctions *against* divorce; and this made a visible impression upon her.

We talked for about three hours; I tried to invoke divine aid constantly. I spoke first of changes that had occurred in the lives of people that she had known, dramatic flip-flops from past conduct, unpredictable changes. Then I brought up some of the miracles of the New Testament. She had always questioned these but agreed with me that, as far as we knew, if they had happened, they had been performed always with prayer. I mentioned the miracle of Pentecost, when twelve unlettered, ignorant, diverse personalities—bound together only by their memories of Jesus and their prayerful dedication to Him—had been transformed through His Spirit. I talked of St. Paul and of his transformation on the Road to Damascus. These were miracles that not only had changed the lives of the men involved, but also the face of history. And I told her I had seen some others happen first-hand myself.

"God has never stopped intervening in human life," I insisted; "but He's a polite God—He's got to be invited."

There was a pause. Then, "How do you invite Him in?" she asked.

"Through prayer, dedication, and devotion. Prayer can do it."

At 12:45 A.M. I took her to her car. She thanked me, drove off, and I didn't hear from her again for nearly seven months. But on December 14, a letter lay on my desk which was one of the finest Christmas gifts I've ever had, and which meant more to me than a ten-thousand-dollar fee. It read:

"I'm returning these books in hopes that they may help someone else as they did me. . . . Miracles can happen, can't they? Perhaps some day the time and place may present itself to tell you more of my little private one and to thank you as profusely as I should like for the impact of that evening last May. . . .

"Thank you, sounds utterly inadequate, but I have never said it more reverently. God bless you. Dorothy."⁹

Dorothy wanted a divorce. Instead she found Christ. All because a man took that Twelfth Step.

These, then, are the Twelve Steps. They are powerful. They are biblical to the bone. Handled with love, with care, and with prayer, these Steps are a workable, livable guide on our spiritual journey—and they are a powerful tool for leading spiritually hungry people to God.

CHAPTER

5

TAKING THE TWELFTH STEP

Passing On Your Spiritual Awakening

Carol J. was tired. It was the end of the day and she had big plans for the evening. A classical music devotee, Carol intended to spend two hours in a darkened recital hall with Chopin. She could imagine nothing better than taking the weight off her tired feet while listening to a masterful rendition of the *Polonaise-Fantaisie*, opus 61. But as she got in her car, a feeling came over her. A feeling of indecision. No, stronger than that.

A *compulsion*.

She wanted so much to hear the music, but something was telling her she needed to go home. Arriving at her apartment, she found her roommate, Fran, sitting alone and depressed. Poor Fran! She was hungry, but so tired from school and work that she hadn't bothered to fix anything to eat. Seeing her roommate sitting on the sofa, seeming so aimless and directionless, Carol suddenly caught a glimpse of Fran's life from an eternal perspective. It seemed to Carol that here, compressed into this one moment, was Fran's entire spiritual existence in microcosm: an aimless, rudderless life, spent simply marking the time from her birth until her death. Throughout the previous summer, Carol had wanted to help Fran—a sweet girl with a generous personality and numerous friends, bright and gracious, but with a melancholy side that came out when she was tired, as she was this evening. Now, as Carol J. entered her apartment and shut the door, she felt that *this* was the reason God had changed her plans. *This* was the reason God had deflected her from an evening with Chopin, choosing instead to send her home.

Over the time they had been roommates, Carol had tried many times to talk with Fran about spiritual things. Fran had never been hostile toward Carol's beliefs, but she had never been particularly open either. On *this* night, however, Carol sensed an opportunity that had never existed before—and that might never come again.

Carol J. was not a recovering substance abuser. She was not a member of AA or Al-Anon. She was a member of Sam Shoemaker's Faith at Work groups in the 1950s—just an ordinary Christian seeking to live out her faith in God to the best of her understanding. Yet she was about to take the Twelfth Step. She was about to pass on her spiritual awakening to another human soul.

Sam Shoemaker told the story of Carol J. and her roommate Fran in *Revive Thy Church, Beginning with Me,* where he related his plan for sharing our spiritual awakening with others. There is more to Carol's story—and Fran's—and we will learn more about what happened that night as we explore the meaning of that all-important Twelfth and final Step:

> Having had a spiritual awakening as the result of
> these steps, we tried to carry this message to others,
> and to practice these principles in all our affairs.

The Step of Evangelism

The Twelfth Step is the Step of evangelism. It sets forth the missionary imperative of the Steps: "Having had a spiritual awakening . . . we tried to carry this message. . . ." The message of our spiritual awakening is not just a message for alcoholics, not just a message for people who are broken and bruised by addiction. It is a message for every human being on the planet.

"Carry this message." Or, "Pass it on." Or, "I will make you fishers of men." Or, "Go therefore and make disciples of all the nations, baptizing them in the name of the Father and of the Son and of the Holy Spirit," as Jesus said.[1] However you say it, the intention is the same.

"Passing it on" was a necessary part of Sam Shoemaker's spiritual growth. The first thing he did so long ago in Peking was to go to see a Chinese businessman, to carry the message to another human being. That act of commitment helped to confirm the life-changing decision he had made the night before. In April of 1918 he wrote, "I begin to think my mission in life is to be something like Frank Buchman's, to spread the gospel of personal evangelism. Would I might do it in my own Church throughout every land where she is at work!"[2]

"Passing it on" was also a necessary part of Bill W.'s spiritual growth. In The Big Book, Bill W. recalls how his friend Ebby Thatcher explained to him that he needed to give away his recovery in order to keep it:

> My friend . . . [said it was] imperative to work with
> others as he had worked with me. Faith without
> works was dead, he said. And how appallingly true
> for the alcoholic! For if an alcoholic failed to perfect
> and enlarge his spiritual life through work and self-
> sacrifice for others, he could not survive the certain
> trials and low spots ahead. If he did not work, he
> would surely drink again, and if he drank, he would
> surely die. Then faith would be dead indeed. With us
> it is just like that.[3]

Bill W. also told the story of talking about his awakening to Dr. Bob on one business trip to Akron:

> I was pacing up and down the hotel lobby,
> wondering what I could do. The bar at one end of
> my beat was filling rapidly. I could hear the familiar
> buzz of conversation. . . . I was seized with a

thought: I am going to get drunk. Or no, maybe I won't get drunk; maybe I'll just go into that bar and drink some ginger ale and scrape up an acquaintance. Then I panicked. That was a real gift! I had never panicked before at the threat of alcohol. Maybe this meant that my sanity had been restored. I remembered that in trying to help other people, I had stayed sober myself. For the first time I deeply realized it. I thought, "You need another alcoholic to talk to. You need another alcoholic just as much as he needs you!"[4]

"Passing it on" was a necessary part of Dr. Bob's spiritual growth. When Bill W. and Dr. Bob had their first meeting on Sunday evening, May 12, 1935, Dr. Bob noticed that Bill had acquired the Oxford Group's idea of reaching out to others. "I had not," he later admitted, even though he was an Oxford Group member.

I had done an immense amount of reading they had recommended. I had refreshed my memory of the Good Book. . . . They told me I should go to their meetings regularly, and I did. . . . They said that I should affiliate myself with some church, and we did that. But I got tight every night. . . .

I couldn't understand what was wrong. I had done all the things these good people told me to do . . . very faithfully and sincerely. And I still continued to overindulge. But the one thing they hadn't told me was the one thing that Bill did that Sunday—attempt to be helpful to somebody else.[5]

And that's what Dr. Bob did next. And for the first time in his life, he stayed sober.

Thus the chain was forged. From Sam Shoemaker to Bill W. to Dr. Bob to the early AA members to the millions of Americans today who are alcoholics or overeaters or workaholics or codependents or. . . .

The early AAs realized that Step Twelve was essential to the transforming power of the Twelve-Step process. Many of them had been members of the Oxford Group, but a large number of these repeatedly failed to maintain their sobriety through these meetings—that is, *until* Bill W. and Dr. Bob and Sam Shoemaker discovered the importance of "passing it on."

Shoemaker's Evangelistic Steps

The message of recovery, it is often said, is something that we keep only if we are giving it away. The same is true of the Christian gospel: if we are not giving away the message of Jesus Christ to others, can it truly be said that we even have that message in our own lives? By giving away our strength and hope, we keep strength and hope alive. We carry the strength of Christ to those who are weak. We carry the hope of Christ to those who are afraid and filled with despair.

In *Revive Thy Church*, Sam Shoemaker showed how ordinary people like Carol J. could pass on their faith—their spiritual awakening—to others. Shoemaker offered six steps for taking the Twelfth Step of reaching people for Christ:

1. Make Friends

Sam Shoemaker advised, "Don't begin talking about religion till you have won the other person's confidence, and he is taking some initiative in the conversation. This may come in the first five minutes, or you may have to wait months or years for it. You can not force the issue, nor push too fast without disaster. Keep living out a real friendship and relationship all the while."[6]

Carol J. had done just that in her friendship with her roommate Fran. Their relationship had grown, slowly and gradually, until the evening when God seemed to be showing Carol that Fran had tired of wandering aimlessly through life, getting nowhere. Fran was prepared to hear the gospel, as shared by a close and trusted friend.

2. Find a Point of Need

Finding a point of need was a theme in Sam Shoemaker's process of evangelism. This need may be an outward trouble or sorrow, he said.

There are times when, in sheer mercy, God picks us up like a ball, and tosses us whither He will—rolls us like a stone in a stream till the rough edges are worn off—lets us suffer contempt and agony if it will restore our souls and bring us back to Himself.

Now such times are open times for His Spirit to work in men's lives. If we come to people at these times with genuine sympathy, we can go on to the expression of real faith, and they are specially sensitive to the need of it when their lives are in difficulty.[7]

Sometimes this need is more universal. "Many well-adjusted people, with little sense of personal need," said Shoemaker, "will best be reached by their concern for the need of the community, the nation, the Church, the world—or even a person in trouble. If this concern is more than an emotional one, they will be doing something about it, and we may find them already teammates with us in some cause that needs help."[8]

Sometimes the need is addiction or compulsive-obsessive behavior, which is not all that different, Shoemaker said, from anyone's powerlessness over anger or self-centeredness. "One does not say to an alcoholic, 'Of course, I have never had your problem.' One says rather, 'Well, you get drunk on gin and whiskey; I am more apt to get drunk on fear, or criticism, or gossip.' "[9]

Carol J. was sensitive to her roommate's point of need. As she related to Sam Shoemaker, "I knew she was tired . . . so I suggested dinner at home—not solely for her benefit, for I was tired too. At dinner we began talking rather seriously about her feelings of discouragement and aimlessness. She has known all along what my religion means to me but has never inquired much about it. Nor did she take the initiative that night."[10]

3. Be a Good Listener

Sam Shoemaker pointed out that it is more important that others hear what they need to hear than that we say all we have to say. For people to hear, their minds must be open. There must be a bond of trust and caring, the kind of bond that is built up when we truly listen to what others say and show them that we understand their feelings and hurts. That is why it is just as important that we listen to others as that they listen to us.

"The old adage says, the best way to stop a runaway horse is to run with him," observed Shoemaker.

> Somewhere we must say enough to intrigue them about faith, and open up a need; after that, once the interest is roused, we do well to be silent for much of the time, only putting in a word here and there. There is an immense healing in letting the story come out as it will, as every psychiatrist, good counselor, and well-versed priest or pastor knows; if it were allowed to come out earlier with some of the family, a trusted minister or other friend, it might never need to get to a psychiatrist at all.
>
> It is sometimes difficult for people to talk about what concerns them most, and we must be creatively attentive, unsentimentally sympathetic, and at times almost impersonal, as though we happened to be a kind of listening-post for life. . . . Others will need to be helped about "total recall" who should not, at least more than once, be allowed to go over the whole story in detail, though we shall sometimes find that deeply troubled persons need to say what is on their hearts no matter how often this has to be done, for it is the only mode of relief and of healing.
>
> This time of listening should give us opportunity for two things: (1) continuous prayer to God that we may be led by Him in every move we make, every thought and emotion we have, and (2) the chance to understand what kind of person this is, watching for characteristics like ambition, temper, neurotic tendencies, willfulness, insecurity, self-indulgence.[11]

4. Speak About Your Own Faith

Personal witness and testimony were at the center of both the Faith at Work groups in Sam's churches and the Alcoholics Anonymous groups. "We must learn to discover the universal elements in our own and others' experiences and emphasize them, rather than the merely individual factors," Sam Shoemaker said.

> In discussing St. Paul's conversion, for instance, we would not emphasize the blinding light and the loss of sight and the supernatural vision of Jesus which was given to him, but rather that when he lay prostrate in the dust of that Damascus Road he said something we all need to say in some terms or other, "Lord, what wilt thou have me to do?" That was his self-surrender [his Step Three], his part in his own conversion; and it indicates ours.
>
> Professor Hocking says a profound thing, "We find that religion becomes universal at the same time that it becomes most peculiarly personal." We must not fear, then, to say what is real and personal to us.[12]

That's just what Carol J. did. She told Sam Shoemaker, "I merely began to point out that I had once reached the same place she was reaching right now, and that the only thing that seemed to make sense was finally getting in touch with God, finding out that He is personally interested in every single thing about me, and wants to help me much more than I ever sought to have His help.

"I told her various reasons why I came finally to believe in and know the power of prayer. That talk began about 8:00 P.M. and at 2:30 A.M. we were still talking. I read her several stories of transformed people and told her how one girl had come through to real faith. Well, a glorious thing has happened. She had always thought it would be so complicated to find God. I simply suggested that she turn over as much of her life as she could to as much of God as she could understand."[13]

5. Suggest the Answer

Sam Shoemaker counseled that a person's point of need gives us the opportunity to suggest *the* answer to that need.

We may want to point out that there are always two factors in every problem: there is the situation, and there is the way we meet and react to that situation. The second is more important than the first. . . .

Whether an event shall bless or curse us lies, not so much in the nature of the event, as in the nature of our [response to that] event. Faith mixed with a problem is what often turns a mess into a miracle.[14]

Carol J. suggested the answer to her roommate's problem. It was the same answer that she had found: a living faith in Jesus Christ.

6. Encourage the Decision

Many a conversation about spiritual matters vaporizes into an inconclusive haze, said Sam Shoemaker, because the Christian does not take the step of encouraging the decision.

There will be some moral decisions which should be reached. A man living in sin with a woman not his wife must be prepared to give her up—not to throw her off irresponsibly, for he ought to seek to make his new decision a challenge that she make the same one—but the relationship will be wholly different. A financial debt will be acknowledged, and a promise made to pay it off as rapidly as possible, the dates and amounts being agreed upon. A relationship in which bitterness has existed needs honest confession all around, and this somebody must start who sees the moral point, taking the risk of confession whether the other person reciprocates or not.[15]

Decision, he said, should also include taking on steady devotional habits—as in Step 11 of the Twelve Steps. "We need to continue and deepen the New Life which we are beginning. Time must be set aside for this, the first half hour of the day being the best time to begin. It will include the Bible, some other devotional reading, and prayer. It will include linking up with the church of our choice and loyalty, going regularly, and taking full responsibility in its life and work."[16]

That decision should also mean examining the way one is investing one's life, with a view to fulfilling the great command, "Seek ye first the kingdom of God, and His righteousness."[17]

That's what Frank Buchman asked Sam Shoemaker to do after he gave God control of his life in 1937. Shoemaker said, Buchman

> knew, as do few spiritual leaders, the value of getting a young convert on his feet to begin witnessing about what has happened to him, and bringing him in contact with other persons on a team in action; and also of keeping in touch with him by letters. He wrote me dozens of them in the ensuing weeks and months. I hooked up again with him whenever he was within striking distance. In those days he sometimes called himself a "missionary to the missionaries," and heaven knows most of us needed one.[18]

And that's just what Carol J. did too. She told Sam Shoemaker, Fran "made the experiment. Her nerves which earlier in the evening were completely 'shot' were just as completely relaxed later. We have several fine books around the apartment, some of C. S. Lewis's. Up to this time she had no desire even to look at those books. But she said, 'I have a million things to do to get ready for school, but right now all I want to do is to read one of those books.' I found her in bed reading when we stopped talking. She said, 'I think talking to you and reading this may well be the most important thing I've ever done.' Next morning, even after so few hours of sleep, we both felt wonderful, and she told me she never had such a good outlook before—she thinks things will never bother her again as they used to.

"Funny, isn't it?—I thought I had been slipping on Fran—because I hadn't been able quite to reach her need. It all proves that God has His time for doing things, and all we can hope to do is to trust and obey.

"P. S. Suppose I had gone to the recital?"[19]
After telling this story Sam went on to ask,

Will you note several things about that story which
are of general usefulness and importance in making
faith real to individuals? She let God guide her to the
place where He wanted her to be, by natural factors
like "tired feet" and by the inward prompting. She
had been wanting to help her friend, waiting for an
opportunity, and was alert to it when it arose. She
had sensed the need before. She did a natural, human
thing like suggesting they have dinner together.[20]

After that night Carol J. introduced Fran to other people
who were finding the same adventure of faith so that she might
have fellowship in her new life and begin to take her share in the
life and work of the church.

Sam Shoemaker was a pioneer in recognizing the lay ministry, particularly in an ecclesiastical denomination like the Episcopalian church. "The recognized channels for the spread of our
religion—the services and sacraments of the Church, the Bible
and other books of spiritual truth, the campaigns of a great evangelist such as Billy Graham—cannot by themselves generate full
Christian awakening," Sam Shoemaker said. "They must always
be supplemented, undergirded, brought home by the rank-and-
file men and women who themselves possess a vital faith and can
speak of it intelligently to the needs of the individual nearby."[21]

That's the Twelve-Step process of evangelism. That's the
process Sam Shoemaker used so long ago. And that's the process
that the heirs of Sam Shoemaker and Bill W. and Dr. Bob continue to use to change lives—the lives of alcoholics and drug
addicts, overeaters and overspenders, workaholics and codependents, and people who are just plain empty inside, wandering aimlessly through their lives.

Fran, who found Christ through Faith At Work, is not all
that different from Scott and Darcy Jennings, who found Christ
through Alcoholics Anonymous.

Sobriety Wasn't Enough

Darcy Jennings lives in Ridgewood, New Jersey, a quiet suburban community west of New York City. She is a widow now, and as she speaks of her late husband, there is a note of affection and gratitude in her voice—gratitude to God for the privilege of sharing some of life's journey with a very special man. "Scott left a powerful legacy in AA—and he left a powerful legacy through his Christian faith," she told us. "It was very low-key, the way he shared it, but there was no doubt that he walked with Jesus."

Scott and Darcy Jennings didn't always have a close walk with Jesus. Scott had been raised in the Mormon church, and as a young man had rebelled against the religion of his upbringing, finding its rules restrictive and its doctrines hard to accept. Darcy had grown up in a nonspiritual home where God was never mentioned.

Scott was a raging alcoholic before Darcy married him in 1964—but Darcy didn't realize it. "I was not familiar with alcoholism," she said. "I knew his drinking was out of control, but I didn't have a clue that he was an alcoholic until 1968, when he told me he was joining AA."

The transformation in Scott Jennings was apparent from the moment he joined AA: He sobered up immediately and never touched a drop of liquor for the rest of his life. A few months after Scott joined Alcoholics Anonymous, Darcy entered Al-Anon. "Al-Anon was my first introduction to anything spiritual," she recalled. "The idea that there was a real Higher Power in the universe was something I had never considered before."

They were living in an apartment in Teaneck, New Jersey, at the time. The first year of Scott's sobriety was a rocky one for their marriage. Scott was miserable with his sobriety. He went to the meetings, he stayed sober, but he didn't work the program wholeheartedly. Darcy was surprised to discover that Scott's sobriety made her miserable too.

This is a classic pattern that was recognized in the earliest days of AA: When a person becomes sober, that person's loved ones tend to believe the problem has been solved. Yet problems and conflict almost always increase during the first year of that person's sobriety. During that year it becomes obvious that alcohol was just the symptom, not the root cause of the problems in the alcoholic's personality and relationships.

The turbulent first year of Scott Jennings's sobriety was complicated by a relocation from New Jersey to Philadelphia. He still attended AA, but he wasn't working the Steps. Darcy was attending Al-Anon, too, but the meetings in Philadelphia were so big that it was easy to get lost. She had no friends, either in the brownstone apartment building where they lived or in the program. What's more, neither Scott nor Darcy was working on taking personal inventory, admitting wrongs, or making amends. Abruptly, Scott announced he was leaving. "I finally figured it out," he told his stunned and tearful wife. "You are the cause of my problems!"

In Search of a "Specific God"

"I was totally alone and friendless in that big city," Darcy told us. "I was scared. I had to really take a hard look at where I was with God. I had never hit bottom before. Scott had done so well staying sober in AA that I never felt a need to fix myself in any way. I sort of hung around Al-Anon because Scott was in AA and that was the thing to do back then. But when Scott left me, I suddenly realized I needed a spiritual way of life."

Darcy struggled in her first steps toward the God of her understanding. Her first spiritual experience came about three months into her separation from Scott. "I was so miserable," she said. "I had not heard from Scott since the day he walked out. I didn't know where he was. Some friends in Al-Anon told me that if I would just surrender my marriage and turn it over to God's care, He would act. I remember getting on my knees and praying, 'Okay, God, my marriage is in your hands. I surrender it all to You.' And once I finally surrendered, something happened."

It happened less than twenty-four hours after Darcy prayed that prayer of surrender: Scott called for the first time in three months! "Honey," he said, "I really think we should try to get back together." In the same moments Darcy was surrendering her marriage to God, Scott was sensing the conviction that he needed to be living out the Steps—examining himself, admitting his wrongs, and making amends to the person he had hurt, his wife, Darcy.

"That was the first moment I really believed in God," Darcy said. "My friends had told me that if I would just surrender, then God would enter my life—and He did! It was a genuine miracle. Scott came home and we started all over."

Years passed. Scott received an offer of a good job with an insurance company in Connecticut, so they moved. During those years, Darcy drifted into a spiritual slump. "I was very involved in Al-Anon for the first ten years," she told us, "and I understood the Steps. But I didn't keep up my program. I wasn't honestly working the Steps. I talked the program but I didn't live it." After ten years in Al-Anon, Darcy realized she either had to "fish or cut bait"—to identify her need for the program or to leave it. "I don't think you can stand still in the program," she added. "You either move backward or forward. Standing still was making me miserable."

Scott was feeling a similar sense of unrest, so the two of them together embarked on an intensive search for God. They had bought a beautiful home in a Hartford suburb, and were very involved with AA and Al-Anon. Darcy was pregnant with their first child. Though life was going very well for them, they were both very dissatisfied with a concept of God as nothing more than an ambiguous "Higher Power."

"We were really looking for a specific God," Darcy said. "I knew God was real because of the miracle in my marriage, but I didn't know who God was. Scott and I were really searching. He knew he didn't want to go back to Mormonism. And since I'd grown up without any spiritual preconceptions, I was open to anything. So we began investigating the Christian faith."

Scott chose an unusual approach to investigating Christianity: He stole a New Testament from a church! One night after an AA meeting, Scott arrived home with a J.B. Phillips translation of the New Testament in his hands. The two of them read it eagerly, hungrily. They had never seen a modern English translation of the Bible before.

"It was so readable, we couldn't put it down," she said. "That was the first time I had read the Bible and been able to understand it. Before that, Scott and I wanted nothing to do with the Bible. After our first child was born, a relative sent a New Testament as a gift to her and we just threw it away. All our lives Scott and I had been fighting the Bible, but when we began to read it for ourselves it suddenly became very precious to us."

Soon afterward, Scott and Darcy were attending church and going to Bible studies. "In the process," said Darcy, "we came to believe that our Higher Power was Jesus Christ. That was really the turning point in both Scott's recovery program and mine. I really needed a very specific God to turn my life over to. The God in the Bible is so specific, and there was no question in my mind that He was the God who had already been involved in our lives through the Twelve Steps. I am grateful my husband was a member of AA," she told us, "because that was my entrance into the kingdom."

Darcy Jennings's story resonates with our own conviction, based on having seen hundreds of people walk across that Twelve-Step bridge which leads to a relationship with Jesus Christ. For millions of people, the Twelve Steps have been a path to recovery and emotional wholeness. And for some, the Steps have also been a path to Jesus Christ.

The Same Old Steps

The Twelve Steps are a powerful, highly specific tool for recovery from addiction—and Twelve-Step groups are the wave of the future. Even more importantly, the Twelve Steps are a distillation of profound Christian truths. The question is, How can we as Christians learn to use the Twelve Steps to help people and to bring them into a relationship with Jesus Christ?

We put this question to Bob Bartosch, director of Overcomers Outreach, an organization based in Southern California which has helped to establish Christian recovery groups in nearly a thousand churches in the United States, Canada, and several other countries. "All we've done," he replied, "is take the Twelve Steps of AA and apply the Word of God to them. And we clearly identify our Higher Power as Jesus."

There are many Christian organizations that minister to people in recovery. Some of these organizations have rewritten the Twelve Steps in an effort to "Christianize" them and make the Steps more compatible with their doctrinal viewpoint. From our experience, however, we have concluded that the Steps serve their purposes exactly as written—both the purpose of recovery and the purpose of evangelism and spiritual growth.

Bartosch agrees. "If some groups want to change the Steps, that's fine," he says. "But at Overcomers Outreach, our mission is to reach people in Twelve-Step groups. We've found it best not to tamper with the Steps because the Steps are very dear to people in recovery."

One thing that happens when you "Christianize" the Steps is that they cease to project a feeling of openness and acceptance toward people who are spiritually seeking. For example, one "Christianized" version contains the following rewritten Steps:

Step 2:
We come to believe that God through Jesus Christ can restore us to sanity.
Step 3:
We make a decision to turn our lives over to God through Jesus Christ.
Step 11:
We seek to grow in our relationship with Jesus Christ through prayer and meditation and obedience, praying for wisdom and power to carry out His will.
Step 12:
Having had a spiritual awakening, we try to carry the message of Christ's grace and restoration power to others who are chemically dependent and to practice these principles in all our affairs.

These are certainly accurate, orthodox statements of Christian belief. They are fine statements for Christians in church groups and in recovery. But for non-Christian people who are spiritually seeking—including those who would like to know more about Jesus but have not reached a place where they can commit to Him yet—these "Christianized" Steps are like a door that is shut and bolted. They seem to say, "Come back when you have your doctrine straight. Come back when you believe the way we do."

We are not criticizing groups that "Christianize" the Steps, providing their intent is purely to design support and recovery groups for people who are already Christians. But we have to point out that changing the Steps in this way blunts their effectiveness as a vehicle for evangelism. As originally written, the Steps are a bridge. Altered for the sake of orthodoxy, they become a closed door.

At the Minirth-Meier Clinic, we believe in the same old Steps that have been changing lives, promoting healing, and drawing people to God for over half a century. In our programs, we present Christ as the only Power who can change lives and bring true healing, and we present the Steps exactly as written. We don't want to tamper with what works.

Different Needs, Different Groups

Regardless of the issues that people face, there is power and healing wherever people gather in groups to face those issues together. The recovery movement began with a few alcoholics who realized they were powerless over their addictions. But now that the truths of the Twelve Steps are being applied to a vast spectrum of addictions and hurts, we see the group process taking a variety of shapes and sizes. For purposes of clarity, we divide these groups into three basic categories.

1. Sobriety Groups

Sobriety groups aggressively seek to stop addictive behavior, such as drinking and drug abuse. Examples of sobriety groups include AA and Narcotics Anonymous. People in sobriety groups need intensive support in their effort to abstain from their addictions. Some are fresh from a hospital or a detoxification facility, and a sobriety group is their only hope of staying clean and sober. It is not unusual for newcomers in sobriety groups to attend several meetings a week—or even every day.

Sobriety groups often focus more on the obsessive-compulsive disorder itself, rather than on underlying causes such as "adult child" issues. Once sobriety is achieved, the person can then proceed to work on recovery issues in a group that encourages the expression of those feelings that fostered the substance abuse in the first place.

"Some people in AA don't like that distinction between sobriety and recovery groups," says Dave Carder. "They feel threatened when you suggest that there should be more to AA than just sobriety. But if you go to some AA meetings, you quickly encounter what are called 'dry drunks.' They have their sobriety, but they are a long way from recovery. They don't drink, but they're still raging, they're still sleeping around, they're still into pornography. When you see these people, it's clear that sobriety is not enough. Once people get sober, they have to begin their recovery. They have to work on their issues of pain and the lack of nurturing they never received in childhood."

2. Recovery Groups

These groups focus on the underlying issues that feed into the addiction and compulsive behavior. People in recovery groups are, for the most part, working on childhood issues— abuse, incest, dysfunctional family relationships, love hunger. In one sense, the "recovery" in recovery groups suggests a return, a release, or a rescue from wounds and pain. But in another very real sense, "recovery" suggests getting back that which was lost. For many, the recovery group is a place to recover lost childhood, a childhood that was taken from them. The group is a place to be nurtured and reparented.

3. Support Groups

These groups tend to deal with transitory hurts rather than the wounds of childhood (although the crises of adulthood and the wounds of childhood often become intertwined). Support groups focus on issues such as illness, grief, divorce, caring for disabled children or dependent adults, blended families—issues that arise and provoke intense but relatively impermanent crises. The Twelve Steps are not used in all support groups. Many support groups center discussion and sharing around a book or workbook study.

Sobriety groups, recovery groups, and support groups all

have a place in the church and can be used as a sanctuary and a refuge for people with spiritual and emotional needs.

Where Does the Evangelism Take Place?

The odds are that at least one person close to you—a neighbor, a family member, a coworker, a fellow church member—is in recovery for an addiction. When that person begins working the Steps, his or her Higher Power might be anything from God to a doorknob. So as Christians we have an opportunity—and an obligation—to move into that spiritual vacuum and introduce that person to the Highest Power of All.

But how do we do that? At what time in the Twelve-Step process do we share the good news of Jesus Christ?

The answer: At all times. We share the Good News quietly and gently. At times we even share it nonverbally. The crucial concept to understand is this: sharing Christ in the Twelve-Step process is not an act. It is a process.

Certainly there will be situations such as Richard and Jerilyn Fowler's encounter with the troubled young man in a Central American airport. There may be times when, because you know the Twelve Steps, you will have an instant connection with a complete stranger, and you will be able to spring into action and share the gospel.

But for the most part, the Twelve-Step process takes place over time, in the context of relationships. Within Christian support and recovery groups there is freedom to share in the meeting itself and in fellowship times after the meeting. Even in a traditional AA or Al-Anon group, where you may be restricted to talking about God in terms of a vague Higher Power, there are still plenty of opportunities to witness to what God is doing in your life.

Scott Jennings used to state boldly in AA meetings, "My Higher Power is the Carpenter." During his twenty years in the program, he had earned the right to make that claim—and no one ever challenged him on it. He also witnessed to his Christian faith in sponsoring relationships and when he received a call to be with someone who was struggling with temptation. He didn't merely witness with his words. He witnessed with his life.

In recent years, there has been a gradual but profound shift in the way the church views the issue of evangelism. Indeed, our whole definition of evangelism is undergoing a quiet but important revision. Richard Peace, professor of evangelism and ministry at Gordon-Conwell Theological Seminary, describes that change this way: "It is a shift away from the old marketing-oriented approach to evangelism, which is informed by the principles of salesmanship. The old paradigm was: 'I have a product. You need the product. It's free. To signify that you've accepted the product, please pray this prayer and sign on the dotted line.' In point of fact, there's a certain irresponsibility that has emerged because of that approach. We have paid a lot of attention to making converts but very little attention to making disciples, which is the spiritual process of the Twelve Steps and what Jesus really called us to do in the Great Commission."

Sharing Christ through the Twelve-Step process is not, for the most part, cold-turkey evangelism. It is lifestyle evangelism. It takes place as we meet people in the trenches of life and make ourselves available to them over the long haul. "This approach to evangelism," says Richard Peace, "sees witness and conversion to Christ as a process. You can see this process approach to evangelism in the way Jesus evangelized his disciples over a period of three years. The New Testament doesn't just present us with dramatic Damascus Road conversions as in the life of the apostle Paul. It also informs us how to do evangelism in a much more process-oriented way."

As we examine the conversion stories in the New Testament, we do indeed find that people experience conversion in a variety of ways. Someone once used this analogy: For some people, conversion is like the budding of a flower; for others, it is like the sting of a bee. Most evangelistic efforts, such as Evangelism Explosion or the crusades of Dr. Billy Graham, are of the "bee-sting" variety. They call people to make a decision. These are excellent approaches, which God has used—and which He continues to use—to bring millions to Himself.

But some people will never respond to such approaches. For these people, a quite different but equally biblical approach is in order. This approach is lifestyle evangelism, and people who come to Christ through this vehicle experience conversion as the budding of a flower rather than the sting of a bee. For them, conversion is not an event but a process.

"With that kind of process thinking in the back of one's mind," adds Peace, "you have to ask, 'How do people become Christians?' Because there is a difference between a person who is a Christian and a person who is not a Christian. How does a person who is not a Christian become a Christian? And my experience in small group evangelism—which has been my area of specialization for the past thirty years—is that over the course of a small group experience, whenever people are open to sharing their stories with one another, two things happen. First, people in the group realize they have decisions to make along their spiritual journey. And second, some people realize they have never really accepted Christ. And people accept Christ in a variety of ways."

Sometimes people make a decision for Christ in a very open way, and they announce that decision to the group. Their eyes are alight. Their faces beam with joy. They have obviously had a dramatic encounter with God. At other times, people make a quiet, almost imperceptible change. Perhaps the person who has always said, "I don't believe in God," suddenly begins to pray or to share what God is doing in his or her life. Still others experience a gradual dawning of spiritual awareness as they work the Steps, doing their personal inventories, seeking daily contact with God as they understand Him, inviting God to remove their defects of character.

Is there ever a place for a point-blank evangelistic message in a Twelve-Step meeting? Our experience, and the experience of others in the recovery field, says no. "I've seen groups destroyed by evangelistic presentations," says evangelism professor Richard Peace. "The group may be going along well for seven or eight weeks of sharing and mutual support; then the leader abruptly gets up and gives an evangelistic presentation, which just doesn't feel integral to what has been going on in the group." Genuineness and trust are key components of the Twelve-Step process. If the presentation of the gospel appears to be preprogrammed or artificially imposed, it will certainly fail.

There is a saying that "the ground is level at the foot of the cross." Sharing Christ through the Twelve-Step process is the essence of ground-level evangelism. It is humble, it is authentic, and it takes place at eye level. It calls us to recognize that the world is not divided between sinners and nonsinners, but between sinners and recovering sinners.

Sharing Our Experience, Strength, and Hope

Many old-timers in traditional secular Twelve-Step groups are suspicious of the word evangelism. If there is one thing that dyed-in-the-wool AAs abhor, it's proselytizing. The premise of this book could easily be misunderstood or misinterpreted by those who do not read it carefully.

So let us be absolutely clear: We are not advocating exploitation of Twelve-Step groups as a way of building church membership rolls. Nor do we advocate that anyone should try to "sneak" the gospel into an AA meeting by subterfuge. We sincerely believe in the Twelve Steps as a potent tool for recovery and spiritual growth, and we respect the traditions of AA, believing them to be time-tested, well-founded, and wise.

The concept of evangelism does not violate the Steps or the traditions of AA. Rather, we believe that when we share Christ through the Twelve-Step process, we are fulfilling the truest goals of the entire recovery movement. When we use the word evangelism, we are simply talking about carrying this message to others. Evangelism is "Twelfth-Stepping"—a concept as integral to Twelve-Step traditions as admitting our powerlessness, taking inventory of ourselves, and making amends to others. The Big Book of AA devotes an entire chapter to Step Twelve—Chapter 7, "Working With Others." It contains a carefully formulated plan for sharing the good news of AA with other alcoholics— what to say, what not to say, how to say it. We encourage you to study that chapter.

Of course, the good news of AA (liberation from alcohol) and the good news of Jesus Christ (liberation from sin and death) are not the same thing. But there is no question that belief in God is integral to the Twelve Steps and that Step Twelve entails carrying to others the message that (a) God exists, (b) He is able to heal us, and (c) He wants to have a relationship with us. Whenever we carry to others the message of a God who is there, who wants to heal us, and who reconciles us to Himself through Jesus Christ, we embody the spirit of Step Twelve.

How, then, should we carry this message to others? Sharing Christ through the Twelve-Step process is not about preaching on street corners or passing out tracts or buying radio and television time. It is perhaps the most simple, nonprogrammed, and utterly natural form of evangelism there is. AAs have a phrase for it. They call it "sharing our experience, strength, and hope."

Our experience is what our lives have been, both apart from God and since we have been reconciled to God through Christ. Our strength is the power of God himself. Our hope is the recovery we now experience—not only recovery from the power of addiction, but from the power of sin and death. Sharing Christ through the Twelve-Step process means nothing more and nothing less than telling our own story—the story of what our Higher Power, Jesus Christ, has done in our lives.

This is the story Carol J. carried to her roommate Fran back in the 1950s. And this is the same story the early Christians carried to their neighbors in the first century world.

The Christians in the early church had no global strategy of evangelism, no textbooks on church growth. All they had was the story of their own experience, strength, and hope—the story of what Jesus had done in their own lives. They told that story again and again, and the world was transformed. The world can be transformed again as we follow their example.

Someone once described evangelism as "one beggar telling another beggar where he found some bread." This is certainly a fitting description of the Twelve-Step process. There is no room in Twelve-Step settings for one person to preach from a platform of superiority. All we can do is share our stories.

Authenticity and Identification

One reason many people in the recovery movement have a problem with the word *evangelism* is that it conjures up the idea of persuasion and coercion—and even of arguing and haranguing. But authentic evangelism does not rely on verbal arguments or intellectual persuasion. Our goal is not to straighten out the recovering person's theology, but to introduce that person to the spiritual reality of Jesus Christ.

People in recovery have already begun to experience God as their Higher Power. They have already been persuaded of their need for God by their own powerlessness and pain. All they need is to find a face and a name for this vague, cloudy conception of the Power in their lives. Many people in recovery are stuck in the same place Darcy Jennings described when she told us, "I was really searching. The concept of an ambiguous 'Higher Power' was not enough for me. I really needed a very specific God to turn my life over to."

There are essentially four avenues by which we express the tangible, living reality of Jesus to others in recovery:

1. In Christian recovery meetings, we can share our own stories, openly naming Jesus Christ as our Higher Power (this is rarely permitted in secular groups such as AA and Al-Anon, but we can witness with total freedom in Christian recovery groups).

2. In one-to-one settings, we can share with people who have recognized their addiction. Whenever we talk to people who are in pain, who are experiencing defeat, or who have hit bottom, we have an opportunity to carry the message by sharing our experience, strength, and hope.

3. In sponsoring relationships (which we will discuss in the next chapter), we can share our stories and our faith with newcomers in the program. Sponsors act as mentors to newer members of recovery groups, who are usually at a teachable and receptive point in their lives.

4. Through acts of supporting, serving, and helping, we can carry the message without even saying a word. The person who carries the message in a Christlike life can often do more to exalt Christ than all the eloquence in the world. This life includes being available to talk to people at odd hours of the night; showing hospitality to a person in need; setting up chairs or making coffee before a meeting; offering to baby-sit so that people can attend a Twelve-Step group; providing transportation to meetings, church, or the hospital; or even mowing someone's lawn or cleaning house as an expression of Christlike caring and servanthood. Actions, it is said, speak louder than words—and this is certainly true of the Twelve-Step process.

The key dynamics in the Twelve-Step process are authenticity and identification. You tell your own authentic story, and the person listening identifies and responds. People in pain do not respond to preaching. They do not respond to theological reasoning or logical arguments. They certainly do not respond to condemnation and blame.

There will be people who, after you tell your story, will not identify with you. They may be too saturated with emotional, spiritual, or chemical toxins to sense your genuine love and acceptance. They may not want your God. They may spit at the name of Jesus, just as people spat at Jesus two thousand years ago. You can't persuade such people. Only their own pain can ultimately persuade them. When they are hurting enough, they will listen.

Jack B., who has been a recovering alcoholic for twenty years, told us, "Alcohol will make you willing to change. It'll take everything away from you so that you are willing. That's the beauty of it. The more miserable you become, the more receptive you are to change. When you hit that bottom, whatever it is, boy, the only way is up. You have to be rendered totally helpless. If there's any ego left in you, you've just got some more drinking to do."

The Twelve-Step process requires patience and a willingness to step back from the person who is simply not ready to change. Many of us who tend to evaluate our own service for God in terms of "results" will have to redirect our focus. Instead of "results," we will have to concentrate on obedience. Our motivation for evangelism must be doing God's will, not seeing results. Certainly the results in the lives of Scott and Darcy Jennings occurred over a long period of time.

"Joy Comes in the Morning"

The experience of a personal relationship with Jesus Christ transformed the Jenningses' marriage. "Even after we got back together after a three-month separation, we had a lot of problems, and a lot of healing to do. With Jesus at the center of our relationship, the healing began to take place," Darcy told us.

From Connecticut they moved to Houston, where they

were very happy and comfortable for over ten years. Then, when the Houston area fell on hard economic times in the late 1980s, Scott lost his job. He soon found another job—but it was in New York City, half a continent away. They moved to Ridgewood, New Jersey, a quiet suburb of New York City, and Scott took the train to work every day. It seemed that Scott and Darcy had again achieved "the good life"—a good job for Scott and a stable, comfortable lifestyle for the whole Jennings family.

But "the good life" didn't last long. Within a year after their move, Scott was diagnosed with terminal cancer. But Scott would not let his spirit be beaten, even by this deadly enemy. He continued his ministry with AA—traveling and speaking in AA gatherings around the country, while mentoring young men who came into the program in need of a sponsor. During the last months of his life, his walk with the Lord grew closer and closer.

"He lived on two or three hours of sleep a night," Darcy recalled. "During the first six weeks after his diagnosis, the Lord would wake him up throughout the night, making him aware of people he needed to talk to, things he needed to take care of in his work, issues he needed to deal with regarding his family—all these details. In those days, Scott accomplished a lot for AA and for the people he sponsored and counseled in the program. There was no doubt in people's minds that he knew Jesus in a personal way. His spirit touched a lot of people. Even though he was undergoing radiation therapy and getting very little sleep, he never seemed to tire."

After Scott's death, Darcy grieved her loss deeply. She went through it with the love and support of close friends in her church and in Al-Anon. "There's a Scripture verse I've been claiming since Scott died. It's Psalm 30:5—'Weeping may endure for a night, but joy comes in the morning.' God has been faithful. He has given me a support group and hundreds of friends. The church sanctuary was filled at his memorial service, even though we had only lived here a year."

Looking back over her life with Scott and her life with Christ, is there one factor in Darcy's life that God used to lead her to Himself? "Yes," Darcy told us in a voice filled with firm, quiet conviction. "Without the Twelve-Step program, I would not have Jesus Christ in my life."

Taking the Twelfth-Step—In order to keep the message alive in ourselves, we carry the message to others—we carry the Gospel of Jesus Christ to our roommates and loved ones, to our neighbors and to those at work, to those who are in the hospital, to those who are newcomers to a recovery program, to those who need a ride to the meeting, to those who have hit bottom and cannot see the light beyond the tunnel of their despair. We carry the message to others because we cannot keep it unless we give it away!

CHAPTER 6

THE ONE-TO-ONE CONNECTION

Sponsoring and Mentoring

To this day, Jack B. has no idea whom to thank for giving him back his life.

"I had a wife, kids, a good job, and I gave it all up for drinking," he told us. "By the time I hit bottom, I was forty-two years old, living on the streets, drunk all the time, no money, running with another guy who was in as bad a shape or worse than I was. I couldn't help myself. I couldn't think my way out of my soul-sickness. There's no way I can describe how awful it is to be in that condition, how much it hurts. I didn't even realize what a pit of despair I was in because at that point in my life, I didn't know how good life could be."

Not until Jack had sunk as low as he could go did his life suddenly change. It happened around midnight on Halloween 1968. "I had drunk myself into unconsciousness," said Jack. "Totally passed out. While I was unconscious, somebody picked me up and put me in a car and drove me to a place on top of a mountain, about thirty miles outside of the city. It was a Catholic retreat, San Damiano's."

Jack woke up sick and hung over the next morning. He

never learned who took him to San Damiano's. "It was a gift of God—that's all I know," he said. "And if someone hadn't picked me up and taken me to that mountaintop—who knows?"

The priests at San Damiano's let Jack stay until he was well enough to get on his feet. They told him about Alcoholics Anonymous—an organization Jack had never heard of before—and helped him find an AA chapter near his home. He has not had a drink since he joined AA in November of 1968.

"I didn't do anything to become sober," he said. "God did for me what I was not able to do for myself. He picked me up out of that hole I was in and placed me on a path. I've been walking this path, and God has given me specific instructions that say, 'Jack, you have to stay on this path, because I have made the way for you.' I thank God for that from the bottom of my heart. Every day, I tell him how much I love Him."

In AA Jack started working the Steps. Step Eleven made him aware of a need to develop conscious contact with God. At first it was hard. He prayed every morning for weeks even though he didn't feel like praying. He prayed because Step Eleven told him to pray, and he was working the Steps to stay sober. He developed a routine of making his bed first, then kneeling in prayer beside that freshly made bed. Finally, after about three and a half months of praying without feeling any contact with God, Jack just had enough.

"Part of me just rebelled," he said. "Something inside me said, 'You're wasting your time, Jack! None of it is true! There's no God out there listening to your prayers!' I started to walk out of the house without making the bed. But as I was walking down the hall, another part of me said, 'Hey, what about that commitment you made?' It was a voice I couldn't argue with, so I said, 'Okay, I'll go back and make the bed.' But I was really mad about it. I was swearing and kicking the bed and throwing the covers on there—I was really mad! I made that bed and it was a terrible job."

Angry as he was, Jack knelt and began talking to God. "Father, here I am," he said. And that's when everything changed and Jack experienced a spiritual awakening. "Right at that moment," he told us, "I saw my immaturity, my denial, my character defects absolutely exposed, just staring me right in the face. I couldn't believe I was that screwed up. It became almost comical to me! I thought, 'Who am I to think that God is going to come when I call him?'

"So I prayed and I said, 'Oh, Father, I'm really sorry.' And that's when I felt God saying to me, 'Jack, I love you. I'll never leave you. We will be together forever.' It was as clear as if an audible voice had spoken to me. And from that day to this, I have never had a problem with prayer and meditation.

"I love Jesus. I love to visit my God. Sometimes he fills the room with the Spirit. Sometimes goosebumps jump out on me. Sometimes I cry. Sometimes I'm so happy I can't stand it."

Today, Jack is an AA old-timer with more than two decades in the program. With his winning smile and his upbeat attitude, he has earned the nickname "Happy Jack." He is a mentor to young men coming into AA with drug and alcohol problems, looking not only for recovery but for the key to unlock their own spirituality, their own relationship with God.

"That's how I carry the message," said Jack. "God wants me to be a mentor to the young fellas in Twelve-Step groups. God has given me my life back, and it's just about the greatest life anybody could have. These guys in the program see how happy I am, and they want what I have. Most of them are kids in their twenties. They want to know God; they want guidance; they want help with the Steps. So they come to me and say, 'Jack, how do I do this? How do I do that?' I say, 'Go to the Father every morning and love Him. The rest of it will be taken care of.' A lot of them say, 'What if I don't feel like praying?' I tell them, 'It doesn't matter what you feel like. Just do it and everything happens for you.' My experience has taught me that, and it's my experience I share with these young fellas."

The Sponsorship and Mentoring Principles

The Twelve-Step process involves living by a set of disciplines which include

1. Attending recovery group or support group meetings;
2. Making conscious contact with God through prayer and meditation;

3. Reading the Bible, recovery literature (such as the Big Book), and Christian books; and

4. Carrying the message to others.

All people in recovery should keep these disciplines, even those who have been in the program for years. Newcomers, however, are advised to maintain one additional discipline:

5. Becoming involved in a sponsoring relationship, in which an old-timer in the program mentors the newcomer.

This last discipline is very important to the recovery of newcomers to the program. Having a sponsor or mentor is a principle of spiritual growth practiced since New Testament times. Jesus mentored the Twelve. Barnabas mentored Saul, who was later known as the apostle Paul. Paul, in turn, was the sponsor of Silas, Timothy, John Mark, and many others.

Whether you call it sponsoring, discipleship, or mentoring, this principle of both AA and biblical Christian faith calls us to walk beside other people as they make their spiritual journey through life. After taking the Twelfth Step and carrying the message to them, we are to walk the walk *alongside* them.

In the favorite poem, "Footprints in the Sand," the writer asks why there is only one set of footprints during the tough times in life. Christ answers, "That's because I carried you." And Christ often uses sponsors and mentors to support us during difficult times. The sponsoring-mentoring principle is embodied in Paul's counsel to the Corinthians to imitate him as he imitated Christ.[1] The recovery dimension of a sponsoring relationship is also strongly implied in Galatians 6:1: "Brethren, if a man is overtaken in any trespass, you who are spiritual restore such a one in a spirit of gentleness, considering yourself lest you also be tempted."

At the Minirth-Meier Clinic, we believe Twelve-Step sponsoring and mentoring relationships will become one of the primary focal points for spiritual growth in the 1990s. The closing days of this millennium will be the era of the lay evangelist, quietly sharing his experience, strength, and hope with others on a one-to-one basis.

We believe that the vital, alive churches of the 1990s will largely be churches that have discovered the power of the Twelve-Step process for emotional recovery and spiritual renewal. The cutting edge of evangelism will be wielded by ordinary laypeople who have been equipped and motivated to share their own experience, strength, and hope in a one-to-one connection with people who are hurting and seeking recovery.

Bringing Sponsor and Newcomer Together

There are at least three important motivations for becoming involved in sponsoring, mentoring, or discipling relationships. First, as recovering people and as sinners saved by grace, we can find in sponsoring relationships an opportunity to share our experience with others and to further their recovery and spiritual journey. Second, sponsoring relationships provide the ideal atmosphere for sharing Christ through the Twelve-Step process— a relational, lifestyle-based form of evangelism. A third and often overlooked motivation for becoming a sponsor is that sponsoring others is an important part of the sponsor's own recovery and spiritual growth.

Sponsoring and mentoring relationships are as important in Christian recovery settings and in the church as they are in AA and other secular programs. Christians are a family, brothers and sisters in Christ, and we have a biblical responsibility to lift each other up, pray for one another, encourage one another, and bear one another's burdens. It is a privilege—and a solemn responsibility—to place our own shoulders under another person's burden and help him or her carry that load.

How do sponsors and newcomers get together in a recovery or support group setting? The AA model applies to recovery and support groups in the church. From time to time, the leader or facilitator of the meeting should mention the importance of sponsoring relationships and encourage newcomers to find a sponsor. Newcomers do not have to find a sponsor at their very first meeting; they should feel free to sit through a few meetings, listen to different people share, and see if they sense rapport and understanding in a particular individual. After the meeting, the newcomer can seek out the other person and ask if he or she would be willing to be a sponsor. If the answer is no, the newcomer should keep trying. Also, old-timers in the program should keep an eye out for newcomers and be willing to make the first move if that newcomer seems alone and in need of a sponsor.

When the sponsor and newcomer meet for the first time, both should share their own stories—their addictions, how they came to recognize their powerlessness, how they came into the program. This is the first among many opportunities for the sponsor to share his or her own experience, strength, and hope— and particularly the gospel of Jesus Christ as it has affected his or her own life.

What Does a Sponsor Do?

There is no such thing as a job description for a sponsor or mentor. Sponsoring is not just a job; it is a human relationship, and every sponsoring relationship is unique. That's why it's so applicable to the discipleship process. The sponsoring role is encompassed not by written rules but by traditions, most of which originated in the Oxford Group and Alcoholics Anonymous. The Big Book of AA contains numerous stories of alcoholics whose sponsors encouraged and supported them along the road to recovery, and these stories embody the sponsoring traditions.

Here is a summary of some of the ways Twelve-Step sponsors can encourage the growth and recovery of newcomers to the program. We have derived this list of ideas from the traditional practices of AA, and we have adapted them for Christian recovery and support groups. These are only suggestions, not hard and fast rules:

The sponsor can check on the newcomer's progress and attendance at meetings and can encourage him or her to read recovery literature and stay involved in the program.

The sponsor can act as a coach and an encourager for the newcomer who is learning to work the Steps or learning the Christian faith. A sponsor has a particularly important role to play in easing the newcomer through the painful processes of taking moral inventory, admitting wrongs, and making amends.

A sponsor can be available to the newcomer in times of crisis or temptation. The newcomer should be given the sponsor's phone number, plus the numbers of other available people in the program and any twenty-four-hour hotlines, and be encouraged to carry those numbers at all times. (A note of caution: Recovery groups often attract dependent personalities who may fixate on a sponsor in an unhealthy way. You may want to consider whether you feel safe with a person before you give him or her twenty-four-hour access to your time and emotional energy.)

A sponsor can encourage the newcomer to ask questions. A sponsor who doesn't know the answers can point the newcomer to other people or resources where the answers can be found.

A sponsor can serve as a sounding board. A newcomer who is uncertain or apprehensive about sharing a certain issue in a meeting may first bring the matter to sponsor for advice.

A sponsor can counsel a newcomer with regard to personal issues that cannot be raised in meetings and can help that person to make wise choices about lifestyle and relationships. A sponsor should always be ready to give honest, peer-level feedback to the newcomer's issues and questions.

A sponsor can watch the newcomer's life and behavior, and confront that person whenever patterns of sin, addiction, or denial become apparent.

A sponsor can help the newcomer deal honestly with emotions. "You just told me you're not angry," a sponsor might observe, "yet I couldn't help noticing that you tore the phone book in half while you were talking. I would suggest you are not being honest with yourself about your feelings."

Ultimately—and this is a rule, not a suggestion—the sponsor should continually strive to model the character qualities and lifestyle embodied in the Twelve-Step process.

Are there requirements for being a sponsor or mentor? Yes, but the qualifications for sponsorship are no more stringent than the requirements of the Steps themselves. They are:

1. A sponsor should have spent a lot of time in the program. How much is "a lot"? There is no hard answer. However, the key ingredients are maturity and experience.

2. A sponsor must be seriously working the Steps on an ongoing basis. His or her life must reflect the fact that recovery is literally a matter of life and death.

3. A sponsor must be seriously committed to an ongoing, daily relationship with God through prayer and meditation.

4. A sponsor must have a humble, loving, accepting heart

toward other people, and a desire to see other people find recovery and a relationship with Jesus Christ.

Sam Shoemaker gave five principles for our relationships with other people, which apply to both the mentoring and the sponsoring relationship:

1. Deal Always in the Truth

Truth is the salt of sound human relations, as love is their sweetness, Sam Shoemaker said. We need both at all times. When a relationship is all love, and no truth, it becomes squishy and sentimental, and the health goes out of it. If we fear to speak the truth, we will go around in circles and get nowhere. "The truth shall make you free"—the whole truth, and nothing but the truth. Not one side of it, not the truth that supports your side, but the truth as it really is.

The truth always includes our own shortcomings, Shoemaker said. We do well to begin by confessing them.

> When I confess my own sins, I tend to make peace, and when I confess the other person's sins, I tend to make war. You may have to say a very strong word to someone about something he has done that is wrong; begin by saying you have done something at least analogous yourself.
>
> If we will begin with what is wrong in us, the other person will generally follow suit with what is wrong in him; and even if he doesn't, our honesty has given us both a right and an opportunity to ask a like honesty of him. It is this which Christ means by "turning the other cheek"—expose yourself to the other person by frank admission of where you have fallen down. It will take the wind out of his sails, when he thinks you are coming to criticize him, if you will first criticize yourself.[2]

2. Speak the Truth in Love

Most of us speak flattery in love, and we speak the truth in resentment, Sam Shoemaker said. He cautioned against this. "There should be no anger in our eyes or voice as we speak it; we need to get our 'righteous indignation' dealt with before we come face to face with the person. We are not out to get our own way, or win our own point; we ought to be out to change the person and the situation. If we have bathed it all in prayer before we come to talk about it, we shall find God has come there before us, and a miracle is ready to begin, if it has not already begun."[3]

3. Take Responsibility, Not Sides

Hardly a conversation will take place in which one does not hear of some conflict with another, Sam Shoemaker warned.

> Listen interestedly, and draw out the facts. Though the teller might be injured innocence itself, do not take sides. There is another to be heard, also, and only as one knows both sides, and is trusted by both, can he bring the truth that will set the relationship on the right basis. We must watch and control our emotions, or they will betray us. We need enough sympathy to hear the story out, enough objectivity to hear some of the things the other person is saying *in absentia*. We may heal it all by helping the person before us to go to the other party with an honest admission of where he has been wrong, which may start the solution of the situation. Or we may need to see and hear both sides. Our capacity for objective judgment, for suspending judgment, for helping the individuals concerned to make up their own quarrel, is the measure of our maturity, and of our capacity to realize how much more important it is to act wisely than it is just to sympathize or "emote" all over the place.[4]

4. Don't Let People Down

A sponsor or mentor may have to confront the newcomer or deal with a person who is under a deep conviction of sin, Sam Shoemaker warned.

He wants sympathy and an easy way out. He will try
to get it from another counselor. A man died in his
sins because, after the challenging advice of one
counselor, who told him frankly his relations at home
were utterly self-centered and wrong and needed to
be changed, the man called in his minister, who
buttered him up and flattered him, and told him the
other counselor was too stern and should not have
spoken to him that way! I do not know what the sin
against the Holy Ghost is, but I think this is one of
the sins: when a man has been used by the Holy
Ghost to bring genuine conviction of sin in the life
of another, a third comes in who lets the whole
situation down. Let us honor the work of the Spirit
who 'shall convict the world of sin' by doing nothing
to prevent the often surgical work with which He
begins His dealings with the sons of men.[5]

5. Don't Fear Opposition

The Christian message has always converted some and con-
victed others, Sam Shoemaker said:

It still does the same thing. Someone said that
wherever St. Paul went he had a riot or a revival. He
generally had both. Nobody need fight the milk-and-
water pap that is sometimes passed out as religion: it
has neither blood nor bones, and is hardly the ghost
of Christianity. But the real thing gets under people's
skins, makes them uneasy till they do something
about it, and meantime often makes them very hard
to get along with. They may for a time have a knife
out for the fellow God used to bring this conviction
to them.

One reason why some of our churches have
never got a real plan of evangelism going is that they
are trying to find something that will please
everybody—the half-converted and hypocritical
within the fold, and the pleasant pagans on the
outside—and there just isn't any such commodity.

If the gospel begins moving in power, you will always get opposition, from individuals under conviction, or from interests that are challenged about the social value of their product or their practice. We must be as loving as we can, and try not to meet them with anger and fight fire with fire.[6]

What Should a Sponsor or Mentor Not Do?

There are several traps a sponsor and a mentor could fall into which might hinder the effectiveness of the sponsoring or mentoring relationship—or dismantle the relationship completely. Here is what a sponsor should not do (we will be applying many of these to the recovery group situation, but the principles are just as valid for any mentoring or discipleship relationship):

A sponsor should not be a controller or a fixer. The person who is learning the program needs freedom to work the program as he or she sees fit. A sponsor should listen, counsel, hold accountable, and sometimes confront, but a sponsor should never try to dominate. (Sponsors who get involved in "fixing" people are often running away from their own issues.)

A sponsor should not allow other people to become emotionally dependent. The goal of recovery is maturity. At times, a sponsor may have to say, "You are calling me daily. You are asking me to make your decisions for you. You don't seem to be growing. I think I need to step back from this relationship for your own good."

A sponsor should resist the temptation to be a "rescuer." Often a newcomer has lessons to learn from his or her pain or mistakes. Some are learning responsibility for the first time. If we repeatedly bail them out when they get into trouble, we only enable their denial and immaturity.

Though sponsors may need to counsel newcomers, they should avoid giving advice. Counseling without advising is something of an art form, but it's easily learned. Counsel should begin with the words, "I would suggest . . ." or "You may want to consider . . ." rather than, "You should . . ." or "What you need to do is. . . ."

Usually, however, the most helpful form of counsel a sponsor can offer is in the form of questions: "What are your options? What possibilities do you see? How do you sense God is leading you?" People usually have the truth inside them and just need a trusted friend to draw it out of them. As sponsors, we must be wary of "fixing" others—of trying to do for people what only they can do for themselves.

A sponsor should not treat the newcomer as a child, a subordinate, or an underling. Every person in a recovery program, old-timer and newcomer alike, should be treated as an equal. As a sponsor, you may be a little farther down the road of recovery, but if you think you are qualified to be another person's "guru," you have abandoned the essential humility of the Twelve Steps.

A sponsor should never violate confidentiality. Trust and safety are absolute essentials in a sponsoring relationship. Many Christians have a bad habit of divulging other people's problems and secrets as "prayer requests." This should never be done, even in a veiled way.

The amount of suffering and damage that has been caused by gossip—including the gossip of Christians!—is incalculable, said Sam Shoemaker.

> We love to go with the tale of another's wrong, and
> be the first to tell so-and-so! Such talk is like
> spreading germs. Not alone does it increase the
> wrong by increasing the knowledge of it, but it will
> usually unfit us ever to do anything constructive
> about the person of whom we have gossiped. We
> may hear of a wrong through the gossip of another;
> take that fact in confidence, lay it before God, pray,
> and do what He says. But never divulge that to
> another, except where morally you do not see what
> should be done, and you go to some well-trained and
> mature Christian and lay the situation before him,
> anonymously and in confidence, and ask his advice.
> There is always some temptation when one is the
> recipient of many confidences to show how much
> one is trusted by letting some of the confidences slip
> out: one does not quite mean to do this—sometimes

one simply has a leaky tongue. Pray to God to stop
the leak, or you will never be fit to be entrusted with
the confidences of other people.[7]

If, for any reason, you truly feel that someone else needs to
be made aware of a situation the newcomer has shared with you,
a general guideline is that you should do everything possible to
convince the newcomer of that fact and to get permission to
share the information with the appropriate person or persons.
Only in the most extreme cases should confidentiality be
breached, such as a case involving child abuse, murder, or suicide.

"Thirteen Stepping"

We strongly believe that sponsoring and discipleship relationships should only occur between people of the same sex. The
failure rate (or perhaps we should say "disaster rate") of cross-
gender sponsoring relationships is so high that we must state it
emphatically: men should never sponsor women and women
should never sponsor men, period!

Dan Reed of Overlake Overcomers takes a very strong position against male-female sponsorships. "You have a man trying
to help a woman get clean and sober or vice versa," he said, "and
what generally happens is they get involved in each other and
both of their programs go out the window. They stop concentrating on getting well because they are so focused on pleasing
the other person."

There are too many aspects of sponsoring relationships that,
in a cross-gender situation, can easily lead to sexual involvement:
Strong emotions are stirred up. Vulnerability and hurt are expressed, often arousing protective feelings. Frequently sexual issues are shared in a sponsoring relationship, and this kind of
sharing between a man and a woman cannot help but trigger
sexual tensions.

Cross-gender sponsoring can also create tensions and conflict in the personal lives of both people. If, for example, you are
a man sponsoring a woman, how would your wife feel, knowing
you are hearing another woman's most intimate confessions?

And if you are a woman being sponsored by a man, how would your husband feel knowing that you may be discussing issues involving your marriage relationship?

There is a longstanding tradition in Alcoholics Anonymous against male-female sponsorships, and AAs even have a name for it: "thirteen stepping." The clear implication of this term is that when you sponsor someone of the opposite sex, you have gone one step too far!

Steps Four and Five: A Special Role for Sponsors

Sponsors have a special role in helping people cross the difficult and threatening hurdle of Steps Four and Five. These Steps call for a "searching and fearless moral inventory" and for admitting "to God, to ourselves, and to another human being the exact nature of our wrongs."

We suggest that sponsors encourage newcomers in the program to do what is commonly called a "Four Step"—a written inventory of their own sins and character defects. This is not easy. Many people strongly resist the idea of actually writing down their shortcomings in a journal or a notebook. But a written inventory is a much more concrete and effective tool for penetrating denial than a mere mental inventory.

The sponsor's encouragement of the newcomer to do a written "Four Step" should be affirming and positive. The sponsor may want to share his own "Four Step" notebook or passages from his journal to help the process seem less threatening. A sponsor's encouragement can help ease the pain that comes with the penetration of denial. In *The Path to Serenity: The Book of Spiritual Growth and Personal Change Through Twelve-Step Recovery*, Doctors Robert Hemfelt, Frank Minirth, Richard Fowler, and Paul Meier have given a seven-point plan for working the often daunting Fourth Step (see pp. 82–115). The sponsor might want to take this inventory with the newcomer. We also suggest that any Christian mentor take this extensive inventory or the type of inventory Sam Shoemaker took that day in Peking when he measured himself against the Four Absolutes of the Oxford Group—honesty, purity, unselfishness, and love.

When a recovering person or new Christian begins to take a

full-blown inventory of his or her life, the results can be emotionally devastating. "I'm the lowest form of life on earth!" is an often-heard cry from "Four Steppers." The sponsor or mentor can be available through that process to share his or her own experience, strength, and hope. "You think you feel like scum! Let me tell you how I felt when I did my first Four Step!" The sponsor's role in such situations is to impart grace, forgiveness, and a sense of perspective.

Not everyone responds to a "Four Step" with a sense of worthlessness and remorse. Some deny, rationalize, and blame: "Okay, I admit I did such and such, but it's not as if I killed anybody!" "Sure, I did A, B, and C, but my spouse did D through Z! Compared to my spouse, I'm a saint!" "All right, I admit I did it—but I never would have done it if my boss wasn't such a blankety-blank!"

In such cases, the sponsor's duty is to confront: "Look, a Four Step isn't graded on a curve. It's just a list of your sins and defects—yours, no one else's. You'll never get well as long as you make excuses for your behavior and try to blame it on others. Your job is not to justify your wrongs, but to write them down and turn them over to God."

Most people find doing a "Five Step" even more difficult. A "Five Step" is admitting to God, to ourselves, and to another human being the exact nature of our wrongs. Most people in recovery find that the best person to admit those wrongs to is their sponsor in the program (although some may choose to make confession to a trusted friend, a clergyman, or someone else outside of the program). Because Step Five is so difficult and painful, it is crucial that the recovering person find someone completely trustworthy, accepting, and understanding. Few people fit those conditions better than Twelve-Step sponsors.

A sponsor is a recovering person, just like the newcomer, and a mentor is a sinner, just like the new Christian. The sponsor or mentor has heard and seen it all and has personally experienced the healing surgical pain of working the Steps—including Step Five. When the newcomer admits to the sponsor the exact nature of his or her wrongs, the sponsor need only be a trusted, nonjudgmental listener, not a counselor or therapist. The sponsor need not—and usually should not—give advice to a person who is doing a "Five Step." However, the sponsor should reassure that person of God's grace, acceptance, and forgiveness.

If you are sponsoring someone and you make an appointment to hear that person's Step Five confession, here are some suggestions:

1. Allow plenty of time.

2. Encourage the person to bring the notebook or journal in which he or she has done a written "Four Step." This serves as an agenda and a reminder so that the person can confess everything he or she intended to confess—and get it all said within the time frame you have allotted.

3. Don't interrupt that person's sharing. Just offer your affirming eye contact and your listening ear.

4. Don't be afraid of your emotions. Your own tears can be a powerful expression of empathy and support.

5. Be prepared to reassure the person that you unconditionally accept him or her. Some people feel better after admitting the exact nature of their wrongs—but many feel worse. Some even regret having been so honest, especially if they have not been truly rendered powerless and humble at Step One.

By expressing your own acceptance and the assurance of God's forgiveness, you contribute powerfully to the healing of that person's spiritual and emotional pain, and you further that person's recovery in an important way.

One of the spiritual principles that Sam Shoemaker advocated in *Revive Thy Church* was restitution: "The matter is not mended until the penitent person goes to the wronged person, admits his own share in the wrong, and does what he can to right it. . . . Nothing but this gets at the pride which is almost always deeper than the immediate cause of the sin—temper, greed, jealousy, impurity, fear."

Then he told the story of a highly respectable church woman who realized in middle age that she had never really been converted. A conviction of sin came to her one Sunday morning at Holy Communion. She recalled years before having taken some money from the till of a library where she was working and not returning it. What should she do? She was well known in her small community. She decided she would send the money back, with accrued interest, of course—but anonymously!

She consulted her minister, who probably was Sam himself, as to whether this was sufficient. He replied, "Let us ask God if it is what He wants."

They prayed. A conviction came to her that she must return the money over her own signature and that anything less was moral cowardice. It was a great step forward in her life, said Shoemaker, and it launched her in the full stream of spiritual faith and discovery. We do people a great disservice when we do not hold them to such costly restitution, for nothing less than making full amends will cleanse both the relationship and the soul.[8] As you can see, most of the sponsorship principles are as applicable to the discipleship-mentoring relationship as they are to AA and recovery groups. That's no coincidence, since the principles were first established in the Scriptures, then applied by Sam Shoemaker in the Oxford Group, then transplanted to AA.

The Key to Evangelism

Twelve-Step meetings offer the opportunity to hear and to share, but Twelve-Step sponsoring relationships plunge us deeper into the recovery process than we could ever go by attending meetings alone, just as discipleship relationships contribute more to spiritual growth than just attending support group or Bible study meetings. In a one-to-one relationship, the atmosphere of accountability and human connection is tailor-made for lifestyle evangelism. Suzanne S., contact person of the women's support group at the Evangelical Free Church of Hershey, Pennsylvania, told us that she feels one-to-one sponsoring relationships are the key to sharing Christ through the Twelve-Step process.

"The women in our group are at various places in their spiritual growth," she said. "Some have a personal relationship with Jesus Christ; some do not. No one has ever announced in one of our meetings, 'Tonight, I want to accept Christ, I want to be a born-again Christian.' Rather, what we are seeing is that women are getting serious about their spiritual life. They are praying, studying the Bible, and growing in their understanding of Jesus Christ through the Steps, through the sharing in the meetings, and most of all through their sponsoring relationships.

"Twelve-Step sponsorship is really a form of discipleship. The women in our group are being discipled, and they are coming to a deeper knowledge of their faith. In some cases I believe they are coming to faith for the first time. Sponsorship is a very important aspect of the program, both for recovery and for evangelism."

The one-to-one connection of the sponsoring relationship is a quiet dimension of the Twelve-Step recovery movement. It takes place almost invisibly in out of the way places—in restaurants and coffeeshops, in living rooms and over kitchen tables—as two people come together to disciple and be discipled, to share their experience, strength, and hope with one another. It is here, in the warm and nurturing enclosure of an intimate human relationship, that recovery takes place, that lives are changed, that souls are literally loved into the kingdom of God.

Sam Shoemaker advocated the mentoring relationship in his poem, "I Stand By the Door":

There is another reason why I stand there [by the door].
Some people get part way in and become afraid
Lest God and the zeal of His house devour them;
For God is so very great, and asks all of us.
And these people feel a cosmic claustrophobia,
And want to get out. "Let me out!" they cry.
And the people way inside only terrify them more.
Somebody must be by the door to tell them that they are
     spoiled
For the old life, they have seen too much:
Once taste God, and nothing but God will do any more.
Somebody must be watching for the frightened
Who seek to sneak out just where they came in,
To them how much better it is inside.

The people too far in do not see how near these are
To leaving—preoccupied with the wonder of it all.

Somebody must watch for those who have entered the door,
But would like to run away. So for them, too,

I stand by the door.

REVIVE YOUR CHURCH

Faith at Work

The air was close and moist. The walls were cold, close-fitted stone. The steps that led down into the dark and musty place were old and worn and narrow. As such, that place—which was sunk deep beneath the edifice of Calvary Church—was as close a replica of the first century Roman catacombs as you could find in New York City in the 1940s. It was the church boiler room.

Sam Shoemaker had something weighing on his mind and conscience as he descended those steps, something he needed to talk over with another human being. The human being Shoemaker chose to talk to was the building superintendent, Herbie Lantau. Shoemaker found Lantau right where he knew he would be: laboring for God in a dark, out-of-the-way, unseen place, doing the kind of dirty work that has to be done but which brings no recognition, no glory.

There, in that catacomb-like boiler room, two Christian souls met and exchanged honesty for honesty. Shoemaker spilled the contents of his conscience on the concrete floor. Lantau did the same. Then they prayed together and spoke words of grace and peace to one another. Something came into being on that day and in that place: a bond of trust and fellowship, forged from the clean, costly metal of honest confession.

Before Sam Shoemaker climbed back up those stairs and out of Herbie Lantau's subterranean boiler room world, they made an agreement together. They agreed to meet once a week for prayer and confession. And the place they chose was that boiler room.[1]

Not too long after that a Jewish painter named Bill Levine was hired to do some repainting in the interior of Calvary House, the church office building and staff living quarters of Calvary Church. Naturally, Bill Levine made friends with Lantau, the building superintendent. One day Levine made a pilgrimage down to the boiler room and struck up a conversation with Herbie, who spoke so persuasively and passionately of his relationship with Jesus Christ that Bill began to want what Herbie had. Herbie astutely suggested that Bill join the weekly meeting in the boiler room for the sharing of experience, Bible study, and prayer.

As a member of the Calvary Church staff, Herbie had the admonition drummed into his ears, "Be a witness where you are." So he chose as his place of witness the boiler room. This became Herbie's chapel, and for a couple of years he and his friends met there.

One of the members of that boiler room fellowship was one Ralston C. Young—Redcap Number 42 of Grand Central Station. He felt so much at home in that boiler room and found such a profound stirring of his newfound faith when he was in that fellowship that he decided to start a group of his own in a car on Track 13. Ralston Young often said that Grand Central Station was his cathedral, just as the boiler room was Herbie's.

The Small Group or Cell

The group continued to grow until it became too large for the boiler room and had to move up to the second floor of Calvary House. The group met every Monday afternoon, attracting all sorts of people from messenger boys to business executives. The principles that governed the Tuesday night AA meetings, the Monday afternoon "boiler room" meetings, and the eventual Thursday night Faith at Work meetings were parallel, having descended from the founding principles of the Oxford Group. In those early days of the modern small group movement, Shoemaker referred to groups such as the boiler room fellowship and the Track 13 group as "cells." These cells were the experimental forerunners of the Faith at Work groups.

"There is an evident need today for another kind of spiritual gathering than the formal service or the parish organization," Sam Shoemaker said in *Revive Thy Church, Beginning with Me.*

> Many are finding this need best satisfied in what is often called a spiritual "cell," which is a small, informal company that meets for prayer, or fellowship, or study, or work, or all four together. . . . In England there is what is called "The Advisory Group for Christian Cells." These companies are quite numerous and so eager to learn from one another. This group says, "The cell is as old as Christianity. Our Lord called together a little group of twelve. . . . St. Paul, too, formed little groups wherever he went."[2]

Sam Shoemaker reminded the church that Jesus created three groups: the Three (Peter, James, and John) with whom He seems to have discussed the affairs of His kingdom and His mission, and who knew Him better than any others; the Twelve, who were the men whom He had called to be His apostles and who had accepted His challenge and given themselves to His work and to one another; and the Seventy, a special group called out to do a particular piece of missionary work.

> These three have become a kind of classic pattern. We often find that we need three or four who are our intimates, with whom we can pool all our needs, problems, decisions, joys, and sorrows. The best number for a regular cell meeting is about twelve: more than that tends to cause people to make speeches, instead of staying simple and personal. And again, at a conference, or in the spiritual attack on a

city, it will be necessary to call together a larger
spiritual force that will find its cohesion largely
through the one common objective. Such a company
comes together, works, breaks up, and may come
together again with some additions and some
subtractions at another time for another objective.
These teams are very essential if we are to move away
from the sterile individualism into which so much of
Protestantism has degenerated.[3]

The meetings of the early church were more the nature of
"cells" than of services, Sam Shoemaker said.

A scholar who has made special study of the primitive
Christian community, Dr. E. F. Scott, writes: "It was
only in fellowship with one another that they could
rightly live their own individual lives. . . . In the few
glimpses we have of them they are always together—
in prayer, in study of the Scriptures, at the common
meal. As in Jesus' lifetime they are not merely a
number of persons who believe in Jesus and look for
his return, but 'the brethren.' It is evident to any
close reading of the New Testament that what we are
seeing is not a string of individuals bound to Christ,
but a company of men and women bound to Christ
and to one another.

Modern psychology is moving toward the same
conception. A few years ago, psychology considered
man in himself, in his emotions, in his reactions, in
his conscious and subconscious mind. But today
psychology considers man in his relations, and is
beginning to say that he cannot be understood, nor
can he adequately manage his life, apart from those
relations. Dr. C. G. Jung says that 'the meeting of
two personalities is like the contact of two chemical
substances: if there is any reaction, both are
transformed.' "[4]

"God seems to have His own 'economy' in dealing with His world," Sam Shoemaker said.

> At different times He uses different instruments.
> Time was when the great evangelistic instrument
> seemed to be great meetings with a guest speaker.
> However, that method does not seem to be the
> characteristic method for our day. And while
> personal, man-to-man work must ever be the
> foundational work of evangelism, the "cell" is
> perhaps the characteristic instrument which God's
> Holy Spirit is using today.
>   There is a profound *psychological* reason for this
> at this particular time. People today are, on a very
> wide scale, "neurotic" and self-centered. Their
> answer will be found, not only in faith in God, but in
> fellowship with people: they will find themselves and
> begin to be themselves, when they find open, warm,
> satisfying relations with even a few people. Only a
> Christian group will give them deep fellowship
> without trying in some way to "use" them.
>   There is also a profound *social* reason for the
> emergence of cells today. We seek now, not only
> Christian persons, but Christian relationships,
> knowing that only as persons live out their lives into
> other lives do they truly live at all. The world is filled
> with social tensions—racial, class, economic, political,
> national. The sight of one bridge built between
> individuals naturally on opposite sides of the stream,
> between two men who meet democratically as
> Christians, and are not divided by any other belief or
> condition whatever, is more than welcome—it is
> hopeful, it may offer the beginning of a solution.[5]

Sam Shoemaker went on to tell the story of a brilliant black teacher who found himself in a "cell" with a varied company of men—Catholics, Protestants, blacks, businessmen, lawyers, architects, missionaries, ministers, teachers. This man listened for a time to what was said and was evidently more interested in the way these men got on with one another and in their possessing a common ground than in the fact that each of them individually had found God. Before he left he said, "I am not a Christian. My father is a minister, but I have reacted against the church and all that. I do want to say that, if what I have heard here today, coming from such a diverse company of men, is true, then Christianity may offer us the basis of human solidarity for which we are all looking."[6]

The Dynamics of Small Groups

The small groups that Sam Shoemaker encouraged could be prayer or fellowship or study groups—or all three together. Many of these groups met more for fellowship and the application of Christian principles to their everyday lives than for formal Bible study. And these groups were the ones that came from the Twelve-Step model. Today the groups that we think of as support groups, those that are created to serve a common need (parenting, divorce, loss of job, grief, Bible study, or intercessory prayer) are typical of the Faith at Work groups.

Sam Shoemaker gave his outline for small group meetings in *Revive Thy Church, Beginning With Me:*

1. The Leader

"There is usually one leader who, because he knows more, or has better qualities of leadership, or started the thing, permanently stands behind it," Shoemaker explained.

> "But he does not lead every meeting: it is his purpose to train as many others as possible to do a good job of leading also. He will not monopolize the meeting, nor make it a forum for his own pet theories, nor crack the whip too much. He will try to evoke the best from everyone, being sensitive to their needs, aware of their victories or defeats, conscious of a new man who needs to be introduced to the company, or of one who has recently had a great experience which will help the rest.
>
> The meeting will not be run like a committee:

neither will it be too go-as-you-please, for the leader will nicely stop someone who talks too long, turn a controversial subject to one on common ground, draw out the silent, include the shy, and use the spiritually creative.[7]

2. The Meeting Format

"The meeting may begin with an informal prayer," said Shoemaker.

It may proceed with a brief but relevant exposition of a passage of the Bible. It may be right for one man to tell enough of his own story, or the story of his situation, to give a flavor and set a pace. It is like leaven, and begins permeating the others. Informality, laughter, unselfconsciousness, naturalness, honesty, evident practicability—these things make strangers feel at home, and encourage others to say something who may have thought they would feel ill at ease in such a gathering. The life and vitality of the group depend upon the progressive growth and discovery of the men and women who compose it.

The progress seems to be: we listen first, then we experiment, then we tell others because it is too good to keep! "We suggest," says Dr. E. Stanley Jones, "that no one argue, no one try to make a case, no one talk abstractly, and no one merely discuss religion, but that we simply share what religion is meaning to us as experienced."[8]

A description of how one of these groups works was given by Edward J. Meeman, the editor of the *Press-Scimitar*, a Scripps-Howard newspaper in Memphis, Tennessee, in the 1950s. "Every Saturday," wrote Meeman,

a group of business and professional men meets in a private dining-room in a hotel for luncheon, religious discussion, and a quiet period, or prayer. The group consists of not more than twelve, with an average of seven or eight present at each meeting. The subject and chairman have been chosen at a previous meeting. The chairmanship rotates alphabetically, with adjustments because someone may not be able to serve because of absence from the city or other reason. The subject may be such matters as "What God Means to Me," "Effective Prayer," "How to Help Other People."

At luncheon the conversation is merry but not frivolous. After lunch we sit in a circle of easy chairs. We are not dignified; we sprawl. We may even put our feet up on a straight chair we pull from the lunch table. We find that, if we relax physically, the mind and spirit are free and active.

The chairman states the subject and makes a few sentences of comment on it. He calls for five minutes of silent meditation on the subject. Then he calls on each person in the circle to express himself, starting with the person on his left and going around the circle, clockwise. If time is limited, each person is given a definite number of minutes. If one does not wish to make a contribution, he may pass. If there is time, we may go around the circle a second time for additional thoughts that may have occurred. But there is no talk *across* the circle, no questions.[9]

This "no cross-talk" rule and the circular response is a common principle of AA and other Twelve-Step groups.

Edward J. Meeman went on to describe some of the reasons that Faith at Work groups adopted a no cross-talk rule and the circular response:

There are two kinds of people in the world—the talkative and the silent. I am one of the talkative, and I have no apology or boast because of that fact. The talkative are neither inferior nor superior to the quiet, and vice versa. It is an accidental difference of temperament, no more qualitative than the difference

between blonds and brunettes. The talkative are not
necessarily more shallow than the quiet, and the quiet
have as much to say as the talkative—if given a
chance! The technique of "going around the circle"
equalizes the talkative and the quiet, gives them both
the same opportunity to say what they have to
contribute in the same length of time.

One does not hesitate to speak candidly, or to
express a view different from that voiced by one who
has preceded him. But there is no argument, no
debate, nothing that might lead to acrimony or
rancor, though the group represents men of different
faiths, including both "fundamentalists" and
"modernists."

At the close of the discussion, the chairman
makes very brief closing remarks and we become
quiet again for fifteen minutes when we pray for each
other, for the president, for the secretary of state, and
others, prominent or otherwise. Then we go around
the circle to choose the subject for the next meeting,
which often grows out of the discussion just
concluded.

There is no pressure for attendance, though one
member acts as secretary to telephone all members
the morning of the meeting to see who will be
present. Members do not need to be urged; they
come if they can because they get so much joy and
benefit out of it.

There is value in groups which cut across
denominations as ours does. We find that a wide
range of ages in a group is not a handicap, but a
good thing. We have found that a group should
consist of not less than seven nor more than twelve.
The average attendance will always be less than the
total membership.

Our present group is the result of an earlier
group, formed in the middle thirties, which was the
result of the hunger of three different men for a
fellowship with other men for different reasons. One,

a religious liberal, said: "We need an association that cuts across denominational lines." Another, a fundamentalist, said: "Let's form an association in behalf of the underdog." A third, who had been touched by the Oxford Group, wanted a group for "quiet time" and a study of "the four absolutes."[10]

Ten Suggestions for Groups

Sam Shoemaker also gave ten suggestions for groups, which were taken from a person who was particularly successful in helping others start groups in the 1950s, the Reverend W. Irving Harris:

1. "Nothing happens while we merely think about starting a cell, so pray for God's direction and try something. Everyone makes mistakes, but he who wants to be used will find both like-minded people and a practicable plan."

2. "Keep the group *small*. If you must enlarge, then form a 'heart-beat' out of those three or four who are most spiritually in earnest and meet with them for prayer and planning at a different time from the larger meeting."

3. "Accent *friendliness*—it is a sign of love. It is emotional release which leads people to say what they think and 'this will be created largely by the leader's hospitality to them and their ideas.'"

4. "Keep the room, whether in home, church, or office, coolly ventilated and eliminate glaring lights and unnecessary noise. Avoid using a table."

5. "Welcome *silences*—they can lead to conviction and conversion when used patiently, without fear or embarrassment."

6. "A silence closed with the Lord's Prayer helps a cell to gain unity and strength and leads individuals to rediscover their voices."

7. "*Draw out* those who are moving forward spiritually, or have just made a decision of some kind, and let the meeting take flavor from them. If debates arise, suggest that those who are in disagreement talk through the points at issue privately at another time. Relate examples of God's power at work; tell how you first

came to know Christ yourself. Give illustrations of helping other people and bringing Christ's Spirit to bear on business and community affairs."

8. "Use the Bible when you find a story which relates to the life of the cell or the outreach of that life in the community and world."

9. "Keep the separate meetings short and stop on time. Those who want to linger can do so, but some must leave promptly and you will not get these back if you are undisciplined in closing."

10. "*Follow up* all meetings by talks with one or more friends individually. Get the habit of praying aloud with one other person. In your own devotions, ask God to show you what to do next for 'A' or what further step to suggest to 'B.' "[11]

How did ministers in the 1950s feel about these Faith at Work groups? Some encouraged them. Others feared them. But the ones who remained open-minded often identified with the feelings of Howard B. Haines, a Presbyterian minister in Middletown, New York.

The Minister's Role

Haines talked about the beginning of Faith at Work groups within his church and within his fellow ministers in the 1950s in Sam Shoemaker's book, *Faith at Work:*

> Daily more ministers are becoming eager for warm, deep, and growing Christian fellowship for themselves and for their people.
>
> But how? How can a minister break loose from the role of religious *leader* to which he is accustomed and which he is expected to assume, and become a *member* of a small group fellowship? And unless he does, how can he guide others into something which he has not himself experienced?
>
> Many ministers find that they can best begin where there is not the distinction between clergymen and laymen—with other *ministers*.
>
> In my own case, a start came when a

neighboring minister with whom I had attended a
Faith at Work conference, telephoned to ask if we
two could talk about and pray for a member of his
congregation who was ill. In our search for God's
way in sickness and in healing, on our knees in
common concern, we found a rich and compelling
bond that could not be dismissed. We made a date to
meet again, inviting a third minister who immediately
and eagerly responded to something he had been
longing for and did not know how to find.

For almost a year there were just the three of us.
The mutual bond was so personal and deep that we
hesitated to bring in another who might not fully
share it. Meeting on alternate Mondays from 3:30 to
5:30 P.M., we studied the Bible in what was for some
almost a new sense; what is God through Scripture
saying to me now? We prayed, sometimes with
extended silence. But most of all we shared ourselves
with each other before God: the joys that we felt
impelled to express, the sins that we hated to
mention, our concerns for each other, for our
families, for others, the way Christ was directing,
releasing, and using us. New discipline came in daily
Bible study and prayer, new discoveries of the power
and love of Christ, victories over moods and over
pride, recognition of failure that had long been
unnoticed, new willingness and ability to put into
words to others what God had done with us.

In time we felt led to include a fourth minister,
one of another race, with whom we felt a certain
common bond. More quickly then we expected, he
saw that we were not met for discussion of theology
or Biblical points of view, for planning of church
programs, or complaining and criticism about others
or the world in general, but only to let the Holy
Spirit speak and work through us. Within a month he
reported remarkable, unexpected changes in his life,
his home, his church.

Others were included as the group grew and

then divided. A minister from another state sought
and accepted a call to a church in the neighborhood
especially so that he could be part of this group.

And in the church of almost every one of us,
there has now come into being at least one small
fellowship group of lay people, because the minister
first had the experience himself.

In the church which I serve there are now nine
such groups meeting every week, at least one on each
day of the week. Each has its own story of how it
came into being and developed, but there is space
here only to hint at what has happened.

Two men, one eagerly and one somewhat
reluctantly, agreed to meet with the minister each
Thursday morning from 7:30 to 8:30—including a
simple breakfast in the church kitchen. In nature, it
was much like the ministers' group already described.
It increased, and gave birth to a second group when
one of its members, no longer able to meet at that
time, announced that he would be at the church on
Wednesday evenings at 6:30, and invited any others
to join him who would.

Another type of fellowship came with young
people, eight or ten of whom promptly responded to
a suggestion that they gather together in the middle
of the week for prayer and Christian search. They
chose the hour of 7:30 on Wednesday in a quiet
room of the church (which is a full mile from the
high school where most of them went). After the first
four months of training, they continued to meet and
to develop for more than two years with neither the
minister nor any other adult being present.

They agreed on daily plans for personal practice,
and then reported on the results. One spoke about
the results when "dates" were preceded by prayer.
They talked, prayed and worked together on the
relationships between boys and girls at their high
school, and over a period of weeks were convinced
that the entire atmosphere among the thousand

pupils had changed. They explored what it meant to be a Christian day by day at home. They prayed together for those in need, and saw results in healing of body and spirit. They became the spiritual heart of the youth program of the church.[12]

The boiler room group, the Track 13 fellowship, and Faith at Work were the early forerunners of yet another small group movement founded by Sam Shoemaker: The Pittsburgh Experiment.

The Pittsburgh Experiment

In 1952 Sam Shoemaker accepted the rectorship of Calvary Episcopal Church in Pittsburgh, Pennsylvania. In doing so, the man who had ministered so effectively to "down-and-outers" and alcoholics through the rescue mission of the New York City church turned his efforts toward the "up-and-outers" of the country club. "The Lord loves snobs as well as other people," Shoemaker said when he accepted this position.

Sam Shoemaker took this conviction right into the Pittsburgh Golf Club, where he conducted a seven-week series of lectures entitled, "How to Become a Christian." The problem, he discovered, was not snobbery but just a polite skepticism. Once a week from forty-five to seventy young married couples sat and listened to him.

Most of the men had seen service in World War II, when they had experienced some momentary sensations of religion. But in their own words they "had recovered from that." Fortified with college diplomas and family prestige, they had settled down into the comfortable life.

The story of what happened after these meetings was so significant at the time that it was the subject of a major Fortune Magazine article, "Businessmen on Their Knees," in October of 1953.

Putnam B. McDowell was fairly typical of them, the article said. "Putty," a veteran of the war in the Pacific had a minor executive job at Scaife Company (range boilers, gas cylinders).

With unusual candor he told a church meeting what happened to him at the Golf Club.

He was brought up in a family "where religion was so personal you did not speak of it," he explained. "I think the truth of it was that it just wasn't there, but no one knew which one was bluffing. I went to a nonsectarian school, rarely going to church, usually only because it was a bad Sunday and we couldn't get out on the hockey rink, or something like that. I went to college [Harvard] where I think they teach reliance on man's own endeavors, perhaps too much, and where cynicism and sophistication have a rather high, but unauthorized place on the curriculum."

Putty went to Shoemaker's Golf Club meetings out of courtesy to friends who had asked him. "None of us had any particular problem that would cause us to turn to religion," Putty said. "We were not broke or unhealthy, most of us were married, had families and good jobs.

"I think in the initial stages the most important thing to me was that I saw people like myself, my friends, begin to discuss religion in public—healthy, attractive, wholesome people, many of whom finally came across and said, 'Yes, I do pray.' For me that was quite a strange thing."

In this novel and friendly atmosphere Putty decided "to try this thing out." He committed himself to daily prayer. Soon, he found he was getting along better with people—and he was even sleeping better than before. "I work principally with older men and my job usually is to get them to do things they would rather not do or would prefer to do in another way than what is being suggested to them. And that's a hard job. When I prayed before those situations arose . . . things worked out better."

Putty entered the confirmation class at Calvary, and he and some of the others started to teach Sunday school. They realized then that you cannot simply pray for yourself. "I began to experiment with praying for other people. For the first time in my life I found that I could really like people whom I didn't know too well, or something like that. I had always been quite polite to them because I was brought up that way, but I felt no genuine liking and that had always bothered me. . . ."

In the end Putty and a number of the others found their

faith. And in the end there was a minor revolution along a highly strategic Pittsburgh social front. Sam Shoemaker's young converts (and their wives) became crusaders, quietly evangelizing among their neighbors, their friends, and their associates in business, trying to persuade them of the value of communion with God. To the bewilderment of outsiders, their cocktail parties were more apt than not to turn into religious discussions. Even their drinking habits changed. As Putty explained, "You can't go out and get plastered Saturday night and make any kind of an appearance at your Sunday school class."[13]

Another man who attended that course on "How to Be a Christian" was Dave G., also a veteran of the war in the Pacific. He worked in the power-and-fuel department of U.S. Steel's Homestead Works. This good, decent, basically kind man was slowly losing his mind, as Fred Remington, the radio-TV editor of the *Pittsburgh Press* told his story in Sam Shoemaker's *Faith at Work*:

> Pressing the man from one side were his superiors, uncompromising in their expectations of a high, continuing level of production. On the other side were the men along the assembly line, grumbling at the demands of employers.
>
> The relentless squeeze in which this man found himself was personified by a union grievance committee chairman, a man as iron-clad in his resistance to greater work loads for the men as the plant superiors were in their insistence upon production goals.
>
> "Every time I saw the grievance committeeman my stomach went into a knot and I was ready to fight," the foreman told Fred Remington. "And always there was the noise, the incessant, demoralizing roar of the industrial process."
>
> The foreman was gray with a fatigue that sleep didn't cure, tense, resentful. At a point close to despair he was invited to that course on "How to Be a Christian."
>
> Apply your Christianity to your job was one of

the themes of the workshop. The words seemed so
glib and so simple; they had the sound of having
been said so often before that at first they had little
meaning for the foreman.

But they kept recurring to him. He was, after all,
a fine, practical Christian in his family life. He was a
churchgoer, a faithful Bible-reader. *But*, he realized,
*he had never consciously tried to relate his religion to
his work.*

In his next meeting with the grievance chairman,
the foreman fought back the rancor which arose
instinctively before a word had been uttered.
Diffidently, more in curiosity as to what would
happen than in any real hope, he made some oblique
references to religion. The union man's reply was
sincere, interested. So they talked for a moment of a
matter that in previous encounters had been the
farthest from their thoughts.

The foreman was a Protestant, the union official
a Catholic, but their denominational differences were
insignificant in the face of the new respect and
understanding that marked their relationship. They
met, no longer as resistant adversaries, but as two
Christians confronting a mutual problem.[14]

"We're really about to get together now," the foreman told
Remington.

During the long steel strike of the 1952 summer, Dave G.,
in desperate financial straits due to his idleness, pondered what
one man could do to avert this ruinous industrial strife. He
talked it over with Sam Shoemaker. They decided that the answer must be a kind of dynamic and contagious Christianity in
day-by-day job situations.

Dave G. went to President Clifford F. Hood of U.S. Steel
and J. & L.'s President Austin and suggested that the matters in
dispute be submitted to the judgment of the strikers, voting by
secret ballot. Both told him the same thing: the steel companies
"for various reasons" could not advance the idea at that time.

But once Dave G. had started there was no stopping him.

When the eight-week strike was finally over, he launched a new crusade. He was convinced that only through a mutuality of faith could labor and management live in peace, and he called Hood. Griffith this time had been inspired by a story of Stupakoff Ceramic & Manufacturing Company workers in Latrobe, Pennsylvania, who had been holding a weekly prayer meeting on the assembly line ("There hasn't been a strike at Stupakoff in eleven years.") and he broached the same idea to Hood. Hood said he thought the initiative for such a novel experiment should come from the men in the plant, whereupon Dave G. began holding prayer meetings once a week in a corner of his department.

It cannot be said that the idea spread spectacularly—about twenty-five men attended the meetings—but the meetings were amplified over a public address system so that several hundred men heard them, Fortune Magazine reported. "The singing of hymns out at Homestead is an unusual sound on that old and bloody ground."[15] Sam Shoemaker described the amazing occurrences that were taking place to one of his prominent parishioners, Admiral Ben Moreell, board chairman of the Jones and Laughlin Steel Corporation. He described the exciting response to his course on "How to Be a Christian"; the new meetings that were springing up at Pittsburgh's Harvard, Yale, and Princeton Clubs; the people who were coming to study the Bible and take part in an experiment in the spiritual power of Christianity. He concluded with the words, "Here's a hunk of leaven. How can we use it?"

Admiral Moreell was so interested, he assembled a group of Pittsburgh industrialists to "put Christianity to work." The group included executives from J. & L., along with some executives from Alcoa, Blaw-Knox, and the big Joseph Horne department store. The group's discussions were put in a statement, which Admiral Moreell passed out to his employees at J. & L.: "We attempt to work out too many of our human-relations problems without asking for divine guidance. Actually, what we need is God's help. . . . We must be Christophers, 'Christ bearers.' Our lives, our words, our inspired acts, our deeds of honesty and integrity and unselfishness, must be bridges across which He walks again into our world."[16]

From that discussion the Pittsburgh Experiment was formally launched in 1955. A Pittsburgh foundation, never identified, contributed an undisclosed sum of money to get it started.

In the 1950s about 350 people actively identified with the Experiment. The workshops might take the form of a luncheon or evening meetings. So that participants could share an intimate understanding of one another's problems, the groups were composed of men in similar lines of work. There were workshops for lawyers, salesmen, insurance men, engineers, labor foremen.

In grappling with the problem of living out their faith in the context of their jobs, the men came to grips with many basic and troublesome questions. For example, engineers involved in atomic energy projects mulled over the spiritual implications of the awesome forces with which they were working.

Businessmen frankly grappled with the issues they faced in attending trade conventions far from their homes, where liquor flowed freely and other temptations abounded. Bill Cohea, who was director of the Experiment in the 1950s, said, "To me the realism with which they tackle this is amazing. Their conclusions about conventions is not to avoid them, nor to try to moralize while attending them. Go and be a part—but not a degenerate part. Set an example of decent Christian behavior."[17]

The Pittsburgh Experiment groups led to the establishment of Employment Anonymous. In the next three years the prayers and efforts of fifteen to twenty employed Christian businessmen in Pittsburgh resulted in approximately four hundred men finding employment. Most of the men found their own jobs as their experiments in prayer brought about increased confidence and a renewed faith in God's love and concern. Others found work through leads provided by those group members who were employed.

One of the leaders of Employment Anonymous told about this group in Sam Shoemaker's *I Stand by the Door*:

> As we met at lunch with unemployed men, we found
> that they often had something more than just an
> employment problem. They had lost initiative,
> aggressiveness, and confidence in themselves, and
> certainly had lost faith in their God. We encouraged
> them to try prayer, and some of them embarked on a

thirty-day prayer experiment. We suggested that they pray each day for thirty days that God would give them the will to work. This seemed to change many of the men and they found a new confidence, a new faith, and went out with a new attitude.

At later meetings they reported that when they went for interviews they seemed to be better received, and undoubtedly made a better impression. A number of "success stories" tended to reinvigorate the men who were still looking for work. Those who first found employment would come back to the meeting the next week, tell of their experiences, and testify to the power of prayer and the change it had made in their lives.

One man who had been unemployed for eight months started on a thirty-day prayer experiment to ask for the Lord's help for his situation, and twenty days later went to work in a position better than he had even hoped for. He was so convinced that prayer was the answer that he started an unemployed neighbor on a similar prayer program, and prayed with him for help in his situation. The neighbor went to work just twenty-nine days later.

The amazing thing about all of these cases was that the job each man found fitted his qualifications perfectly. The coincidences which occurred could only have been the work of the Lord in answer to prayer. None of the men who have tried to help in this work are trained in employment or personnel work, and we have no magic formula. We tried to open any doors we could and contacted people around the city to let them know of these men in need of work. The results which occurred, however, were far beyond our limited means, and came for the most part from changes in the men themselves.[18]

The Experiment Continues

Most important of all, The Pittsburgh Experiment continues to be a vibrant and growing force for social and spiritual change in these closing days of the twentieth century. Its theme for the 1990s is "Helping Individuals Develop a Faith and Confidence in God Equal to the Challenges They Face." The Experiment has expanded its ministry in new directions and now offers a Small-Group Ministry (with specialized groups for men, women, businesspeople, and executives; downtown groups, suburban groups, and groups which meet at factories and corporate offices), Seminars and conferences (everything from retreats for corporate execs to marriage enrichment seminars), counseling services ("a free ministry, a gift to the city"), and consulting services, which help outlying churches develop their own small group ministries.

The small groups of the Pittsburgh Experiment are designed to be places where nonbelievers, skeptics, and the disillusioned feel just as welcome as Christians; where people of all walks of life can come to discover how the saving power of Jesus Christ can be applied in their daily lives; where people can find acceptance and receive support; where people can pray together and work through their problems together; where people can find hope.

A typical Experiment meeting begins with a welcome and prayer from the group leader. The leader then opens the sharing time, offering some experience or spiritual discovery he or she has made in the past week. The leader then asks, "What has happened in your life this week?" The sharing proceeds around the circle (those who do not wish to share are free to say, "I pass"). After everyone has had a chance to share, the group prays around the circle. The ground rules are simple: Sharing is voluntary. You come as you are and you are accepted. You don't have to pray aloud; you may pray silently, say "Amen," and pass to the next person.

The powerful, life-changing traditions that were instituted by Sam Shoemaker in the 1950s continue to be a fundamental part of the Experiment today. The Thirty-Day Prayer Experiment is still one of the most powerful tools for transforming lives, and those who undertake the Thirty-Day Experiment continue to find Shoemaker's guarantee as valid today as it was in the 1950s: Ask God every day, in all honesty, to meet you in your need, despite your doubts, and you will receive an answer within thirty days!

The Employment Anonymous arm of the Experiment steadily advances through both boom times and recessions. Its mission continues to be one of helping men and women to find jobs—and Jesus Christ.[19]

"The book of Acts continues to be written today," says Reverend Paul F. Everett, Executive Director of the Pittsburgh Experiment. "Our goal in the Pittsburgh Experiment is to add new chapters every day through our Christian love, through the acceptance of people where they are, and through being instruments of reconciliation."

Shoemaker's dream of reviving the church continues in Pittsburgh and across the country and around the world—wherever committed Christians are honestly, lovingly, obediently willing to put their faith to work. From a dank basement boiler room in New York City to a railroad car on a Grand Central Station siding to a steeltown spiritual experiment to a legacy that continues as the twenty-first century fast approaches—Sam Shoemaker has left us a model for church revival and revitalization that challenges and inspires us with its incalculable possibilities.

Just imagine what could happen if every Christ-centered church in America were to take up that challenge! Just imagine what could happen if every Christian in America would pray Sam Shoemaker's prayer, "Lord, revive Your church—beginning with me!"

CHAPTER 8

THE FELLOWSHIP OF RECOVERY

Recovery Groups

Mike M. was raised Catholic, but didn't believe in much of anything. His father was an alcoholic, and Mike started using drugs and alcohol when he was thirteen years old. He was still using and drinking heavily by the time he was married and after his daughter was born. "I was a terrible person back then," he told us, "a real egomaniac with an inferiority complex."

In 1980, at age twenty-three, Mike hit bottom. "I was completely screwed up. I was out of work and couldn't get a job. I was drinking a lot. My wife had had it up to here with me. I couldn't take all the arguing, so I finally walked out on my wife and little girl and spent the next week just living wherever." After a few days of living "wherever," Mike telephoned his father.

"My dad only had a little one-room apartment, but he said I could sleep on the couch," Mike recalled. "He was in AA, and he told me I needed to go to the meetings with him. That was the beginning of my new life."

As Mike began working the Steps, he discovered things about himself he had never realized before, things that hurt. "I went to meetings almost every night for three or four weeks," he said. "When you start the program, one meeting a week doesn't cut it. I was reading The Big Book and the Twelve by Twelve, and I was seeing myself on every page."

One passage that particularly hit home was this commentary on Step Three in *Twelve Steps and Twelve Traditions*:

> To every worldly and practical-minded beginner, this Step looks hard, even impossible. No matter how much one wishes to try, exactly how can he turn his own will and his own life over to the care of whatever God he thinks there is? . . . [Our instinct cries out], "Nothing is going to turn me into a nonentity. If I keep on turning my life and my will over to the care of Something or Somebody else, what will become of me? I'll look like the hole in the doughnut."[1]

"That was me," Mike concluded. "My ego was so big and I was so stuck on controlling my own life that I just couldn't picture turning my life and my will over to Somebody else. I didn't want to feel like the hole in the doughnut."

Near the end of his first month in AA, a lot of things began to make sense to him. He recognized his own powerlessness. His old inflated ego began to drain out of him like air from a punctured tire. He saw how much his drinking had been hurting those around him. He knew he needed to make amends to his wife.

At one AA meeting, he shared his story and the new insights he was discovering as he had been working the Steps for the past month. There was only one piece of the puzzle that had not yet fallen into place in his mind: his Higher Power. "I'm willing to believe," he told the group. "I want to believe. I just don't know if God is really out there or not."

"If you're really seeking," said one of the AA old-timers sitting across the room, "you'll find Him."

A Spiritual Awakening

That night, Mike went home and sacked out on the couch in the front room of his dad's apartment. There was a large window facing the couch and the drapes were pulled open. As Mike lay on the couch and looked out the window, he saw the moon, full and silvery-white, its face faintly mottled with dry lunar "seas." He pondered the fact that he could look out through that window and see another world, dead and airless. And beyond that world were other worlds with names like Mars and Saturn and Jupiter. And beyond those worlds were oceans of stars, beyond his ability to imagine.

Of course, there's a God, he thought. *There has to be a God.* As he lay contemplating the moon, a light shone in his soul. In the face of such overwhelming conviction, it seemed to Mike that turning his life and will over to this immense Creator-God was only the natural, reasonable thing to do.

"That was my spiritual awakening," Mike told us. "That was the time when I became aware of God and his influence on my life. But it was not a conversion. I didn't become a Christian until about two years later."

After his spiritual awakening, Mike stayed sober for a year and a half. During that time, he borrowed some money and bought a fast-food restaurant. He prayed that his marriage would be restored. His wife, however, could not believe he had changed. Her memories of the old, drunken, self-centered Mike remained fresh in her mind. She wanted nothing to do with Mike.

After a while, Mike began drinking and using drugs again. His discouragement over his broken marriage and the pressures of running his business began to overwhelm him. One of Mike's employees noticed the strain he was under and asked him if he was using drugs and drinking—an unusual question for an employee to pose to the boss. But at twenty-four, Mike was only a few years older than this "kid" who was working for him, and they had a rather laid back relationship. Mike admitted that, though he had kept himself clean for a year and a half, he had recently started using again—and he hated it.

"I think I know someone who can help you," said the

young man. "He's letting me stay at his house for a while. I think you ought to talk to him."

"Who is this guy?" asked Mike.

"He's my pastor."

That evening, Mike had a long talk with his friend's pastor, Reverend Watson. The minister opened his Bible and led Mike step by step, verse by verse, to an understanding of what it means to be a follower of Jesus Christ. That night, Mike prayed and committed his life to the Lord.

"I'm Starting My Life Over"

Several more years passed. Mike continued in his walk with Jesus Christ and he got back into his recovery program with AA. Every day, he prayed that his marriage could be restored, but his wife still refused to talk to him. "I stayed sober almost all of that time," he recalled, "but now and then I'd slip and start drinking or using drugs again. I was in a lot of pain because of the divorce and the fact that I hardly ever got to see my little girl."

After one binge, Mike went to a rehab center in the mountains. He checked in for a week to dry out—and to think. He checked out just before Christmas and went to visit his mother. "The most important thing for me is to stay sober," he told her. "Otherwise I'll end up dead or insane. It's hurting me too much to just see my daughter for a couple hours a week. Right after Christmas, I'm moving to another state and starting my life over."

Two days later, his wife called him up right out of the blue. "Mike, I was wondering," she said hesitantly, "if we could, well, maybe go out on a date." To this day, neither she nor Mike has any idea what prompted her to call—unless it was God Himself.

A few months later, Mike and his ex-wife became man and wife again. Today they have four children, a daughter from their first marriage and a girl and two boys from their remarriage. They have a beautiful life together. God has answered Mike's prayers and restored a marriage that lay in ruins for more than five full years.

"One night after an AA meeting," Mike told us, "I was looking at the moon and something happened. I just came to believe in a Power greater than myself, and I decided to turn my will and my life over to that Power. At that point in my life, I called that God. I didn't keep that commitment perfectly every day. But I was never content to stay in my addiction. Eventually, God brought me into a relationship with Jesus Christ and restored my relationship with my wife.

"I have a philosophy about the spiritual journey I've been on. The Bible says that the only way to God is through Jesus Christ. Jesus said that Himself, and I know it's true. But I believe God uses different things to bring people to Jesus. Some Bible scholars might tell me I'm out to lunch, but I believe that God through the Holy Spirit used a couple of men named Bill W. and Dr. Bob to originate a program called Alcoholics Anonymous. And I believe God is using Twelve-Step recovery groups to bring people to Jesus."

Mike's life proves that point more eloquently than any words we could add.

What Is a Recovery Group?

A Twelve-Step recovery group is a fellowship of people who have come together for one purpose: to find healing from their addictions. Recovery groups come in all shapes and sizes, and they exist for a wide variety of purposes. Some recovery groups average two or three people per meeting. Some average over a hundred. Some are for men only or women only. Some are focused on a single issue, such as alcoholism, codependency, or compulsive overeating. Some gather people with various problems into a single fellowship, all focused on healing their individual addictions by working the same Twelve Steps together.

Whatever its shape, size, or focus, a recovery group should provide eight things:

1. Mutual support

2. The opportunity to listen to the stories of others and learn from their experience

3. The opportunity to confront those who are in denial or otherwise hurting their own recovery

4. The opportunity to learn about addiction and its causes

5. The opportunity to gain insight into one's own issues and motivations

6. The opportunity to work through one's own resistances and penetrate one's own denial

7. The opportunity to express and ventilate emotion

8. The opportunity to become involved in helping others (This is a crucial dimension of the recovery process in that so much of that process is inner-directed and self-focused. If a recovering person does not at some point develop an outward, others-centered focus, he or she will probably become stuck, unable to move all the way through recovery.)

A recovery group is not a treatment center. An alcoholic, typically, does not go to a recovery group to get sober. He first goes to a treatment center for medically supervised detoxification. (Alcoholics who attempt to "detox" themselves without medical supervision risk convulsions and death.) After "detox," the alcoholic joins a recovery program such as AA in order to maintain sobriety.

A recovery group is a *fellowship of healing*. All the components of a recovery group that we have just described should be a part of any recovery fellowship, whether it is secular or Christian. But a *Christian* recovery group has one major dynamic that other recovery groups lack: It is a fellowship with Jesus Christ at the center.

The basis of a recovery group is the support we gain in *relationships*. This concept is as old as the book of Genesis, where God said, "It is not good that man should be alone."[2] God is a relational being. As human beings, made in His image, we too are relational beings. Jesus continually worked and taught in a group process, a process of relationships.

Every major doctrine of the Christian faith has relationship at its core. The doctrine of the Trinity describes God as being in relationship with Himself for eternity—Father, Son, and Holy Spirit. The doctrine of creation teaches that God created man to have a relationship with Himself and with others. The doctrine of the Fall teaches that the relationship between human beings and God was broken by sin. The doctrine of salvation is about restoring that relationship and reconciling human beings to God. The doctrine of sanctification is about being set apart for a relationship with God. The doctrine of the church describes how God is carrying out His plan in history through the family-like "body of Christ," in which each member lives in close relationship to God and other members.

It is not surprising, then, that the process of healing from addiction should occur within a network of relationships. Recovery is a group experience. It cannot take place in isolation.

Getting Started: How One Church Did It

How do you begin a Christian recovery group? Dan Reed, founder and director of Overlake Overcomers[3] told us how the Twelve-Step groups in his church began. Overlake Overcomers is an umbrella designation for seven different recovery groups that meet at the five-thousand-member Overlake Christian Church in Kirkland, Washington. Overlake Overcomers got its start in 1981 when Pastor Robert Morehead asked Reed, who was then six months out of treatment for alcoholism, if he would lead a Bible study for recovering alcoholics.

"I had my doubts about it," Reed recalls, "but I gave it a try. We started with a traditional Bible study format instead of a Twelve-Step Group. There was Scripture study, memorization, and discussion—and it fell flat on its face. The guys in the group were fresh out of treatment, and they were just too toxic for a Bible study. It wasn't meeting their needs. So I went back to the pastor and said, 'Bob, I've been active in AA, and I really think we should use the Twelve-Step approach.' He wanted to know more, so I gave him a copy of *Twelve Steps and Twelve Traditions*. He read it and said, 'Fine. Go with it.' And we did."

The first meeting of Dan Reed's alcohol recovery group was structured like an AA meeting except that those in the group talked openly about Christ as their Higher Power. Members brought their Bibles to the meeting, which was opened with a brief Bible study in which the Twelve Steps were discussed and supported with Scripture—another departure from AA traditions. Most meetings that followed were general discussion meetings, but there were also "topic meetings" devoted to exploring issues such as anger, resentment, or rejection, drawing on both Scripture and AA literature for insight.

Dan Reed's alcohol recovery group met for close to two years before it became an officially recognized arm of the church ministry. There was resistance by some parishioners who worried about having an AA-like environment in their church, replete with smoking and swearing.

It also took some time for church members with chemical dependency issues to feel comfortable in the group. "People were afraid of being identified," said Reed. "They thought, 'I go to this church, and if I attend these meetings people will know I have a problem in this area.'" So in its early days, Overlake Overcomers drew more members from the surrounding community than the church itself.

Over time, the group earned the confidence and support of the congregation. It has grown in numbers and has expanded to cover other forms of addiction besides alcohol. Approximately 150 people meet in seven different groups: Chemical Addiction, Codependents, Codependent Parents, Food Addiction (including compulsive overeating, anorexia, and bulimia), Adult Children Anonymous, Sex and Love Addiction, and Codependents of Sexual Addicts. The entire program is supported by donations from people in the program.

A Typical Meeting

Every Tuesday and Friday night at seven o'clock, all the various Overlake Overcomers groups gather in the Fellowship Hall for what they call "the Front Meeting" (other programs call this "the Big Meeting" or "the Opening"). There are tables with recovery books and literature—some for sale, some free—and refreshments such as coffee, tea, and soft drinks. Baby-sitting is provided free of charge.

The meeting is opened with prayer, a word of encouragement from the Scriptures, and a few minutes for "Praise the Lords"—brief testimonies of the different ways God has been working in people's lives during the week. "When first-timers come into the group," said Reed, "it encourages them to hear that God is really working through the program."

Newcomers are welcomed and "birthdays" in the program are celebrated. A member with a "birthday" stands and says,

"I've been clean and sober for one year this week," or "Three years ago this week I decided to do something about my food addiction." People with "birthdays" are given a round of applause and a small gift such as a bookmark with the Serenity Prayer or a Scripture verse. "You'd think, 'Gee, that's a hokey gift,'" says Reed, "but people look forward to getting that bookmark. The important thing is what the gift represents."

Finally, there is time for announcements, plus the reading of some Scripture promises or a passage from the "How It Works" chapter of The Big Book. The leader of the Front Meeting then asks the individual group leaders to stand and state where they are meeting. That enables newcomers to put a face together with a group, so they know where to go and whom to follow. Then the Front Meeting breaks up and people go to their individual groups. The Front Meeting generally lasts about twenty-five minutes.

Sometimes the format of the Front Meeting varies. On the second Tuesday of the month, a twenty-five-minute video is shown to help orient newcomers to the program. "The video is an educational tool that helps people understand the nature of addiction," says Reed. "It's a lot easier to beat the enemy if you know how it works."

After the Front Meeting, people go to their respective groups—Chemical Dependence, Codependents, the Food Group, and so forth. These groups are then subdivided by prearrangement into smaller groups of about six to twelve people. The leaders of each subgroup have all been trained in a counseling course given by Overlake Christian Church. One leader might conduct a traditional AA-style "Step Meeting," another might conduct a "Topic Meeting" on an issue such as anger or healing memories.

There is no rigid requirement that the groups be subdivided. If a group of fifty or sixty people chooses to meet together, that is allowed. But groups of a dozen or fewer create more opportunity to talk.

The unifying dynamic of all the Overlake Overcomers groups is the Twelve Steps. "We use the Steps exactly as written," Dan Reed told us. "We don't try to 'Christianize' them.

We only change things like 'alcohol' to whatever the addiction is —codependency, food, sexual addiction, or whatever."

Group meetings begin at about 7:30 and end promptly at 8:45. The leader of the group may begin with a brief prayer or a reading of Reinhold Niebuhr's Serenity Prayer:

> God, grant me the serenity to accept the things I
> cannot change, the courage to change the things I
> can, and the wisdom to know the difference.

The rest of the meeting time is devoted to sharing. Meetings are ended on time in order to keep faith with parents of small children and others who need to budget their time. After the meeting, there is an opportunity for fellowship and for perusing the literature tables. Anyone who still needs to talk about issues can do so in a one-to-one setting during the fellowship time.

"The fellowship time after the meeting is very important," says Reed. "Without some unstructured time to just talk and get to know people, the whole experience would be too cold. Our experience shows that fellowship after the meeting is an important dimension of the recovery process."

So that is how one church did it. From tentative beginnings, Overlake Overcomers has become a thriving ministry of both recovery and evangelism. Today, Overlake Christian Church not only exemplifies the principles of Christian recovery in its own community, but also trains people in other churches to do the same.

Other Churches, Other Models

Around the United States and Canada, and to some degree in other countries, churches are using variations on this same theme. Lives are being changed, and thousands of people are discovering hope—not only for recovery in this life but for total spiritual regeneration, now and forever.

In Southern California, the First Evangelical Free Church of Fullerton (where Dave Carder, one of the co-authors of this book, is assistant pastor for counseling ministries) offers one of the most complete Christian recovery programs in the nation.

This network of caring offers support groups (both Twelve-Step and non-Step groups) for chemical dependency, incest, eating disorders, disabilities, infertility, divorce, blended families, and grief. The program begins with an extensive six-week orientation program,[4] and many of the groups are structured for a specific time frame rather than being open-ended as AA groups are.

One of the distinctives of the Fullerton program is that it maintains an aggressive training program for group facilitators. The idea of training facilitators is taboo among many traditional AA people—and even among some in the Christian recovery movement—because AA was built on democratic, rotational leadership. Dave Carder recognizes this tension, but believes that training facilitators is important. "Our experience has been that the facilitators want some sort of guidance and assistance," he said, "so we've done the minimum amount necessary to enable facilitators to feel confident in their roles."

Group facilitators of New Hope meet every Tuesday night. Three out of four Tuesdays are devoted to a facilitator's process group. Facilitators gather for dinner from 6:00 to 6:15; then from 6:15 to 7:00 they work on their own issues together. "It's a recovery group for facilitators," says Carder. "The facilitators process their own issues there. They say things there that they could not say in the groups they lead like newcomers. There's a special camaraderie to that group. It's my group too. I never miss it."

Every fourth Tuesday is devoted to a business meeting. Problems in the groups are sometimes dealt with there, although most problems are handled during the week through contact between the facilitators and the program directors.

(Part 3 of this book contains materials used by the New Hope program at First Evangelical Free Church of Fullerton—a sample brochure, inquirer letter, study guides, and facilitator training material. If you are planning to start a group or program in your church, these materials are available for you to read and adapt so that you won't have to "reinvent the wheel." We've also included in that section a list of books and resources you can use in your groups, which includes two workbooks written by Ron Keller: 12 Steps to a New Day and 12 Steps to a New Day for Teens. Keller has used the material in these workbooks in working with recovery groups in public organizations and schools throughout the country.)

The programs at the First Evangelical Free Church of Fullerton, California, and Overlake Christian Church in Kirkland, Washington, are among the largest and most comprehensive Christian Twelve-Step programs in the country. But Christian Twelve-Step programs are not just for megachurches with memberships in the thousands. No church is too small to become involved in Christian Twelve-Step groups.

The group which currently meets in the Bethany Baptist Church in Presque Isle, Maine, started in a little sixty-member church a few miles away. It was moved to Bethany Baptist because it was handicapped-accessible. The group at Bethany Baptist is largely for chemical dependency and averages around five to seven people per meeting. Lenny W., the contact person for the group, told us, "We encourage people to be involved in traditional AA groups. In one-to-one relationships with the people I sponsor in AA, I share with them who my Higher Power is. I encourage them to try our Christian group and to be open to investigating Jesus Christ."

Sharon G. is the contact person for a Christian Twelve-Step group in Oklahoma. The group has averaged fifteen people per week, all dealing with different issues ranging from drug and alcohol problems to compulsive overeating to gambling addictions to codependency. "What I've really enjoyed about our group," she said, "is knowing that it really doesn't matter what the addiction is, the answer is still the same. The answer is Jesus Christ."

Jane M. of New Jersey calls the Overcomers group at her church a "bridge" for people in need of recovery—and in need of Christ. This 150-member church (average Sunday morning attendance: 350 to 400) sponsors one group with an average attendance of fifteen to twenty people. The group is comprised mainly of people with compulsive overeating problems, but also includes people with issues such as chemical addiction, sex addiction, depression, incest survival, and codependency. "I think many individual people in the group use it evangelistically," she said. "I know I do."

We asked Don T. of Agape Christian Church in Kalamazoo,

Michigan, if he sees Christian support groups as a means of introducing people to Jesus Christ. His reply: "Absolutely! Without a doubt! That's one of the reasons I'm so excited about it." Agape Christian Church is a 450-member church with two Christian support groups, each averaging eight to ten people a week. And there are more support groups on the way. "We're having a 'Small Group Promotional Month' where people sign up for different home groups," Don told us. "I walked into church the other night and the bulletin board was covered with notices: 'We're organizing this support group, that small group. Is there anything else you'd like to see?' It's exploding in our church!"

Suzanne S. of the 1,200-member (average attendance-2,000) Evangelical Free Church of Hershey, Pennsylvania, told us, "Our focus is recovery, but sharing Christ is always in our thinking. As people listen to the sharing and are encouraged to pray, to study the Bible, and to work the Steps, people are coming to a personal knowledge of Jesus Christ." The church sponsors one support group for men and one for women.

How to Start a Recovery Group in Your Own Church

By now the question that is probably uppermost in your mind is "*How*? Where do I begin? What's the first thing I need to do to start a recovery group in my church?"

The process begins when you, as a pastor or layperson in your church, feel a heartfelt burden for people in recovery. Perhaps you are in recovery yourself. Or you may have close friends or family members in recovery. Perhaps you have simply become aware of the enormous potential for evangelism embodied in the Twelve Steps.

So you pray. And you read books and literature about recovery. You read AA classics such as The Big Book and *Twelve Steps and Twelve Traditions*. You study the biblical basis of the Twelve Steps. You learn the traditions that have kept AA and other recovery groups functioning for more than half a century. You discover how AA views recovery group issues such as anonymity, affiliations, controversies, and so forth.

But there is one more crucial ingredient for an effective

Christian recovery program that is all too often overlooked. The people who are designing and structuring the recovery program for your church must understand recovery *from the inside*. This doesn't mean that you have to be a recovering alcoholic or an ACA. You don't have to come from an overwhelmingly dysfunctional background. But if you are not intimately familiar with recovery issues, seek out several people who are. Involve them in the process of designing the program.

At the same time, consider this question as honestly as you are able: If you are not in recovery, why not?

In the Minirth-Meier Clinic book *We Are Driven*, authors Robert Hemfelt, Frank Minirth, and Paul Meier make the case that we are *all* driven, we are all addicted to something in some degree. The reason many of us do not recognize our addictions is that many addictions are actively applauded by our culture: workaholism and success addiction; food addiction (compulsive overeating); preoccupation with fitness, exercise, and diet; preoccupation with sports; compulsive academic overachievement; preoccupation with self-improvement; physical perfectionism (including sun-tanning and cosmetic surgery); preoccupation with homemaking, cooking, and cleaning; preoccupation with computers, music, TV, videos, and movies; money addictions; control addictions (the compulsive need to control people and circumstances); approval dependency; addiction to religious legalism; being a rescuer in relationships; being in rescue-oriented professions; and on and on.

Clearly, the recovery issue is a huge net that draws us *all* in, despite our protests and denials. Can you honestly say you don't see yourself somewhere in that list?

So again, if you are not in recovery, why aren't you? It's a question only you can answer.

Henri Nouwen once wrote, "You cannot lead someone out of the desert if you have never been through the desert yourself." So if you are a nonrecovering person trying to design a program for recovering people, you are at a severe disadvantage. Authorities in the recovery field concur.

"Those of us who are active in recovery," says Bob Bartosch of Overcomers Outreach, "do not think nonrecovering people are able to understand the needs of recovering people.

People in recovery are a different breed of cat. If you don't understand recovery from the inside, you don't understand recovery."

The good news is that a nonrecovery person can go into recovery. All it takes is a recognition of one's own condition and the willingness to take the steps to start working on your own issues. And all we ask is that you prayerfully consider it.

Once you have done your homework and your prayerwork, you are ready to approach the leadership of your church and see if the pastors and the church board are willing to lend their support to a recovery group in your church. Once that support has been given, there are many organizations that can guide you and supply you with video, audio, and printed resources to help you plan the structure for your church's Christian recovery program (for a list of these organizations, see Appendix B).

Nuts and Bolts

Now let's get down to basics—the nuts and bolts and the do's and don'ts of recovery groups:

Focus

Is the group concerned with sobriety from an obsessive-compulsive behavior (such as overeating, alcohol, drug addiction, or workaholism) or recovery from an adult child issue (an adult seeking to resolve childhood issues, such as abuse, neglect, incest)? If so, the group is a recovery group.

Is the group intended to serve as a mutual support system for a current stress factor (divorce, terminal or chronic illness, parenting)? Then the group is a support group, much like Sam Shoemaker's Faith at Work groups.

Facilitating/Leadership

Is the group going to be led by a layman or a professional therapist? Usually the lay-led groups are free and are in keeping with Step Twelve of the Twelve-Step tradition. (Chapter 9, "The Servant of the Group" offers detailed guidelines for this type of leader, the recovery group facilitator.)

Professionally led groups, on the other hand, are often therapeutic, and fees are usually charged. The professionally led groups are often more intense and make use of psychodrama and other therapeutic techniques. Some lay-led groups—usually those for incest victims or life-threatening eating disorders—require that an individual be in therapy or have access to a therapist.

Group Size and Membership

Effective Twelve-Step groups can range in size from three or four people to over a hundred. If each person in the group shares only one issue he or she is facing during that particular week, everyone will have a chance to share even in a group of twenty or thirty people. When it comes to recovery groups, there is no such thing as "one size fits all." The optimum size of your groups will probably emerge after a brief experiment of trial and error.

Some groups are structured and include lectures, workbooks, or scheduled themes for discussion. Others are unstructured and spontaneous. AA is one such unstructured group.

Seating should be arranged in a circle—never in rows. Everyone should be able to see everyone else in the room. The goal should always be "a room without corners" where everyone feels included, where no one can hide in the shadows.

An average recovery group lasts from an hour to an hour and a half. Starting and ending on time is very important. Evening meetings are the norm, but morning and noon meetings can often meet an important need.

Some groups have an open membership, in which people are free to come and go. Such groups may go on for many years with a membership that fluctuates in size and composition. In other groups, people commit to attending for a given period— eight weeks, ten weeks, thirteen weeks—and no new members are admitted after the first meeting. In a closed group, there is no influx of new people, so the group can proceed without continually having to start over and bring new people up to speed. The decision whether to structure a group as open or closed depends on the membership of the group and the issues the group is dealing with. Groups on issues that require an especially high degree of trust and confidentiality (such as incest or rape) are best structured as closed groups.

Ground Rules

In order to have a safe place in which members may share their issues vulnerably and honestly, the boundaries of the group need to be settled in advance. The ground rules governing participation in the group should be spelled out in literature and referenced regularly by group leaders. (A more complete discussion of ground rules may be found in Chapter 9.)

Statement of Purpose

Every Christian recovery group should have a clear statement of purpose. Such a statement helps to focus the program on its goals and enables participants to have a clear sense of why they are there and why the program exists. Both the recovery and evangelistic goals of the program should be boldly stated.

Dan Reed shared with us the Preamble of Overlake Overcomers, which we have reprinted below with his permission. It is based on both biblical principles and the time-tested traditions of AA. It appears in Overlake Overcomers printed material and is read in the orientation for newcomers. It reads:

> Overlake Overcomers is a Christian support group for men and women who have been affected, either directly or indirectly, by the abuse of food, sex, alcohol, or mood- or mind-altering chemicals. We believe that as we look to a loving God for help and put into practice those principles for living which He has given in His Word, we shall find both the strength and the freedom for living happy and productive lives.
>
> We strongly believe that our Higher Power is Jesus Christ, our Savior and Lord. It is our fervent prayer that He will become yours as well. May you find Him now.
>
> We hold no corporate opinions concerning politics, economics, race, philosophies, science or any other matter not immediately bearing upon our

recovery. While we do believe that Jesus is the Christ, the resurrected and living Son of God, we hold no corporate view concerning denominational preference.

Our five-fold purpose, based directly upon the Word of God, is set forth as follows:

1. To provide fellowship in recovery.

2. To be and to live reconciled to God and His family.

3. To gain a better understanding of the disease of addiction.[5]

4. To be built up and strengthened in our faith in Christ.

5. To render dedicated service to others who are suffering as we once suffered.

We practice the suggested Twelve-Step recovery programs of Alcoholics Anonymous and Al-Anon because we believe these steps are the practical application of the life-changing principles which are so clearly set forth in the Scriptures. We welcome anyone who has a desire to stay straight, clean, and sober; anyone who has a desire to rise above the pain and turmoil engendered by the addiction of a loved one; anyone who is not opposed to our general method of recovery. We are here to share our experience, strength, and hope with one another. The loving support and genuine caring of fellow members, coupled with daily prayer and the reading of Scriptures, prepare us to experience total serenity in Christ, no matter what our outward circumstances might be.

Attendance at additional Twelve-Step groups is recommended and encouraged.

We are dedicated to the principles of anonymity and confidentiality. It is understood by all participants that nothing said in these discussions will leave these rooms in any form. Gossip has no place among us, nor will we share these discussions with outside prayer lists.

Our common welfare must come first. Our leaders are chosen not to govern but to serve. There is only one Authority in our group: Jesus Christ, as he expresses His love among us.

Atmosphere of Acceptance

The key to an effective recovery ministry is an atmosphere of unconditional acceptance. People are never judged or criticized for what they share in the group or for what they believe. Atheists and agnostics are received just as warmly as the most orthodox Christian. There should be no condemnation, no finger of accusation, no Bible pounding in a Christian recovery group.

A recovery group is a place where people seek answers. If we want people to continue coming to find healing, we cannot buttonhole them and tell them what they have to believe. We allow them to come as they are, believing as much as they are able to believe, committing as much of themselves as they are able to commit. We accept them. We unconditionally love them. We befriend them.

As Stephen W. told us, "I had a lot of doubts and problems with the beliefs I was raised in. All my life, people told me what I had to believe. They always corrected me when I got it wrong. No one did that in AA. No one tried to change my mind. They just shared their own experience, strength, and hope, and if I wanted to listen, fine. That's how it works."

In every effective recovery group, there is accountability and sometimes even confrontation (especially when a group member is clearly in denial). But the accountability is surrounded by what we call "the warm fuzzies," an atmosphere of total support and caring. The warm fuzzies mean there is a bond of empathy, and that people are listening and identifying with the person who shares. The atmosphere of a healthy recovery group is one of unconditional love.

Unconditional love, said therapist Norm Wright is "a perfect commitment to an imperfect person." This definition implies that we forgive and accept others regardless of their shortcomings—but not that we self-destruct in the process. So, for example, if there is a person in our group who is an abusive and destructive personality, who tries to control the meeting, and who is harming others in their own recovery process, we don't simply say, "Well, we must accept him and love him where he is." Without bitterness or hatred and with as much understanding as we can muster, the facilitator will need to firmly confront his destructive behavior.

Affiliation

A Christian recovery group is not a Bible study, nor is it an AA or Al-Anon meeting. It is modeled on AA, but it is not affiliated with AA. A Christian Twelve-Step group is a fellowship of brothers and sisters in the Lord who come together to learn how to gain control of the areas of their lives that are out of control. It is not intended to take the place of either the church or secular programs such as AA.

A Christian recovery group should never try to pass itself off as an AA, Al-Anon, or other secular support group. Nor should it seek affiliation with those groups. It is, in fact, a violation of AA traditions for an AA group to be affiliated with a church (AA, Al-Anon, Overeaters Anonymous, and similar groups that meet in churches only rent space; they are not sponsored by churches). A Christian recovery group can model itself on the AA framework and traditions, but it cannot call itself Alcoholics Anonymous.

Overlake Overcomers is completely candid about its Christian purpose—and even its evangelistic purpose. "I introduce who we are and what our purpose is," Dan Reed told us. "I say, 'We're Christians in recovery and we're here to recognize that we need help with our addictions. We call upon Jesus as our Higher Power. If Jesus Christ is not your Higher Power, we strongly encourage you to keep an open mind and an open heart. We hope you, too, will come to know this Christ that we talk about and love so much.' "

We should never hide or apologize for the fact that this is a *Christian* Twelve-Step group. It should be boldly stated up front. "Sometimes when we tell people what our purpose is," said Reed, "they get up and say, 'I didn't realize it was all this Bible stuff. I don't want to talk about Jesus, I don't want to talk about God. I'm outta here.' We just say, 'We understand, and you're welcome to come back when you are ready.' People need to know exactly what they're getting into. I don't believe the Lord would honor any effort to hoodwink people in His name."

Richard Peace, professor of evangelism and ministry at Gordon-Conwell Theological Seminary, agrees. "You often find deception employed in certain forms of evangelism. It's almost as if we are trying to trap people in an environment from which they can't escape, dump a message on them, then say, 'We have evangelized.' That never works. The only result is resentment when people find out there's a 'catch.' A church starting a Twelve-Step program has to be up front right from the beginning about the Christian roots of the Twelve Steps and that there is going to be a focus on Christ as the spiritual dimension of recovery."

Involvement with Secular Recovery Groups

We believe that Christian recovery groups should not operate in isolation. They should view themselves as part of a larger network of caring, acting in concert with both the church and with programs such as AA, Al-Anon, Overeaters Anonymous, and the like. There are two reasons for this.

First, we always grow when we learn from others. By exchanging newsletters and ideas with other recovery programs, both Christian and secular, we can adjust our own programs to serve people better—and to serve God better.

Second, by being in touch with the secular recovery community, we can have an evangelistic influence. As Bob Bartosch told us, "Overcomers Outreach is not trying to replace AA. In fact, we encourage people to attend secular recovery groups at the same time they are in their Christian recovery groups. I've been in AA almost eighteen years and I still go to two or three AA meetings a week. And my wife still goes to Al-Anon. It's a fantastic mission field."

Dan Reed agrees. "We encourage people to be involved in AA and other mainstream recovery groups, and not just to attend Christian groups. Christians can have an enormous impact on the secular community, sharing in the meetings, acting as sponsors, and mentoring young people."

But Reed also cautions, "Christians should just be aware

that AA groups frown on any reference to a specific religion. You can talk about spirituality, you can talk about God as you understand Him, you can talk about your Higher Power. But if you talk about Christ or Christianity, you get shot right down."

So don't expect to go into an AA meeting and have an instant platform to preach the gospel. In Twelve-Step groups, evangelism takes place not in pulpits but in relationships. "When I first became a Christian," Mike M. told us, "it was the greatest thing that happened to me. So I went around cornering people and saying, 'You've gotta accept Christ! You've gotta believe such and such!' You start doing that in AA and you ostracize yourself and create a lot of enemies real fast."

Funding

Some recovery groups take offerings. Many do not. Support groups rarely do. Participants in support group programs are usually not wealthy. Some of them are participating in a recovery group because they do not have adequate funds for professional therapy. Still, some support group programs should be supported by those who participate. AA established the practice of taking offerings, and this does provide a sense of dignity since the participants pay their own way.

"Why Didn't We Have These Groups Years Ago?"

Johnny Mendel is the director of the Christian Twelve-Step group meeting at the Mennonite Brethren Church in Reedley, California, as well as the contact person for the AA, Al-Anon, and Alateen groups that rent space from the church. Johnny and his wife Florene began the first AA and Al-Anon groups at the M.B. Church back in 1981, shortly after he came out of rehab. "A couple times in the early days," he recalled, "Florene and I were just sitting there by ourselves, waiting for somebody to show up. But the groups have grown over the years."

Johnny credits AA with saving his life—yet there were times when the AA program could be extremely depressing. "I was raised in a Christian home by a God-fearing mother and father," he told us. "There were times when it was hard for me in those AA meetings. You have people in there who are pimps, gamblers, murderers, ex-cons, prostitutes. The language at the meetings reflects their lifestyle. The really hardened cases curse God and say things about the Lord Jesus you can't even imagine. It gets very, very rank and it really grinds you down. If you are a believer and you love Jesus, you can get old in a hurry in that environment."

For years, secular groups like AA and Al-Anon were the only Twelve-Step groups Johnny knew. One day, he was driving down Freeway 99 through central California, listening to a Christian radio station. A program came on featuring Bob Bartosch of Overcomers Outreach—and Bartosch was talking about Christian Twelve-Step groups! "I was so excited, I almost missed my turnoff!" said Johnny. "I stopped at a pay phone and called my wife and said, 'Did you hear that fella on the radio?' She said, 'I heard! I heard! That's just what we need!' And that's when we started a Christian recovery group in Reedley."

And the message is spreading. "There's another group starting in Visalia," said Johnny, "and one in Hanford and one in Fresno and one in Kingsburg. We had a guy come over from the Baptist church in Kingsburg, and he just bawled, he was so happy to find this program. He said, 'Where has this been? Why didn't we have these groups years ago?' "

"I have another Christian friend who actually stopped going to church because he felt so alone, sitting in that pew, knowing he was an alcoholic. He felt like he didn't belong in church because he couldn't stop drinking. Now he's in a fellowship where there are other Christians struggling with the same problems he has."

Johnny still attends AA, but now he has a Christian recovery group as his spiritual anchor. "I've been sober since March the third of 1981 and my Higher Power is the Lord Jesus. I thank God for AA and I thank God for Christian recovery groups. Christian Twelve-Step groups reach out to nonbelievers and they give believers a place for support and encouragement. They're the greatest group therapy in the world."

CHAPTER

9

THE SERVANT OF THE GROUP

The Principles of Being a Facilitator

"**M**y son was in Operation Desert Storm," Susan Crawford told us, "so the Gulf War was a very stressful time for me. I worried about my son in Saudi Arabia, and about his wife and baby who were left alone in Germany when he was deployed. Those concerns were constantly on my mind, and I was often tempted to turn to food for consolation."

Susan Crawford is the facilitator of a Love Hunger group, one of a growing number of groups sponsored by the First Place program of the First Baptist Church in Houston. Her group is comprised of about ten to twelve members, both men and women. Together, they support each other and share their own struggles as they study the *Love Hunger Weight-Loss Workbook*, a twelve-week interactive program based on the book *Love Hunger* by Dr. Frank Minirth, Dr. Paul Meier, Dr. Robert Hemfelt, and Dr. Sharon Sneed.

"There's a diagram in *Love Hunger* that has been a big help to me for years," she continued. "I've lost about a hundred pounds, and that diagram was one of the tools that made it possible. It's a simple diagram of an empty heart and an empty stomach,[1] and the point is that you don't fill an empty heart by filling your stomach. It helped me realize that there is never a time when *something* doesn't come along to set you up for your addiction, whether you're an alcoholic, a food addict, or a workaholic. There's always something. Whenever I've been tempted to give in to compulsive eating patterns—like during the stress of the Gulf War—that diagram reminds me to turn to the Lord, not to compulsive behavior."

"Despite the Pain, This Is Helping Us"

We asked Crawford how a typical "Love Hunger" meeting flows. "Our group starts with a weigh-in at 7:00 P.M.," she explained. "Everybody has a chance to chat for a few minutes, and the facilitators take time to talk with each person one-on-one about how they're doing. We have prayer, then we go over a fact sheet or log that all the people in the group use to record their triumphs and struggles during the week. We have a little discussion, some time for questions, some time to reward those who are doing well with the program; then we take a five-minute break. After the break—which is usually at 7:45—we get into the *Love Hunger Workbook*. That's where the deepest sharing and the greatest healing takes place. Then we close with prayer requests and prayer.

"People in the Love Hunger group have to deal with the fact that they wear their problems where the whole world can see, in the form of excess pounds. The world looks at an overweight person and thinks, 'What's wrong with this person's life?' Workaholics, sex addicts, and even many alcoholics can hide their addictions, but a weight problem is very visible. Resources like *Love Hunger* and the *Love Hunger Workbook* help us to see that our problems are not unusual, that other people have overcome these problems. That gives us hope we can overcome them too.

"Not long ago, our group was studying Step Three, 'We made a decision to turn our will and our lives over to the care of God as we understood Him.' In the workbook study of Step Three, there is a section on priorities.[2] I asked the group to write down the top five priorities in their lives—not what they *ought* to be, but what their priorities really *are*.

"One woman wrote real quick, while everyone else was still thinking. I said, 'Okay, what did you put down?'

"She said, 'I get up to eat to go to work to come home to eat to go to bed so I can get up to eat again. Those are my priorities.' The *Workbook* really made her face this, that she has to realign her priorities. This began a great discussion in the group about how we consciously need to set authentic priorities in our lives, such as maintaining our relationship with God, having a well-thought-out focus in life, working on our goals for personal growth, and getting exercise."

One of the primary goals of the First Place program is introducing people to Jesus Christ. "Many people in the groups are church members, but many come from outside the church," she explained. "Often, people come to a group just to deal with weight issues. In the process, they find that deeper issues must be dealt with first—emotional and spiritual issues.

"The *Workbook* has you spend a lot of time looking at your childhood, your family of origin, the needs and wounds you feel and how they became a part of your life. I've had to look back at my experiences. Many things that have surfaced for me and others in the group have been painful, yet the consensus of the group is that, despite the pain, this is helping us. The exercises and questions in the workbook force us to go through the pain so we can get past it and be healed."

"It Makes Me a More Confident Facilitator"

Traditional "Twelve Steppers" in the AA mold may object to centering a recovery group around a book study or any other specific curriculum. Today, however, support groups take countless forms. Obviously, book studies and discussion guides are not suitable for every support or recovery group (although every support group should have a literature table with free pamphlets and flyers, plus a few recommended books for sale). Yet many group facilitators find that a book or workbook to study and discuss makes the job easier—and improves the experience for people in the group.

"When I accepted the task of leading this group," Susan Crawford told us, "I was intimidated by the responsibility. I mean, who am I? I'm not a professional counselor! I have no training for handling the deep-seated emotional issues a group like this can open up! I don't think I've had anything scare me as much as this. Every week we deal with issues like physical abuse, emotional abuse, sexual issues. Sometimes, when I open the meeting, I pray, 'Lord, I just don't have the answers for these folks!'

"The *Workbook* makes me more confident as a facilitator. It gives us a focus of authority that I can't bring to the group as a layperson. If there is any professional at all in the group, it is through the book. It is as if Dr. Minirth, Dr. Meier, and the rest of the Clinic team were sitting in with us, interacting with us, sharing their expertise. That helps me feel more assured in dealing with the tough issues in the group.

"The *Workbook* helps to structure the discussion. It points us to the issues that need to be emphasized. In our group, we chose to spend less time on food exchanges, calories, grams, and menus, and more time on personal issues, the support group aspect. The *Workbook* gives people a chance to work on the calories and grams aspect on a day-by-day basis at home, so we can deal with the emotional issues together on a week-by-week basis."

The role of the group facilitator or leader is crucial to the flow and effectiveness of the group experience. There are important advantages in having a facilitator who has been well prepared for facilitating. There are many different ways a facilitator can be prepared and equipped to handle the facilitating role:

- Through the use of supportive curricula such as books and workbooks within the group itself;
- Through the personal reading of recovery and support group literature (from AA classics like The Big Book and *Twelve Steps and Twelve Traditions* to the book you hold in your hands);
- Through training courses (such as the in-depth training which First Evangelical Free Church in Fullerton, California, gives to all its group facilitators in New Hope); and
- Through experience as participants in recovery and support groups (an absolute must for all facilitators).

A Ministry for Laypeople

As you consider the possibility of volunteering to facilitate a group, don't be intimidated by the fact that you are not a professional counselor. Support groups and recovery groups are not seminars put on by experts but places where average laypeople can encourage one another along the path to recovery. No matter what your background, your personality, or your spiritual gifts, God can use you as His agent for recovery and evangelism in a recovery or support group. Virtually any layperson can be an effective facilitator of a Twelve-Step recovery group—*if* that layperson is diligently working the Steps and has been actively involved in Twelve-Step groups.

Don't compare yourself to other group facilitators and say, "I could never lead a group. I'm not like this person or that person." God uses all kinds of people with all kinds of personality traits to achieve His purposes. If you look at the people God used in the Bible, you see a wide range of personality types. The apostle Peter was what psychologists call the "histrionic" personality type: impulsive, unstable, volatile—a strong leader but erratic and undependable.

The apostle Paul, on the other hand, was a classic obsessive-compulsive, a driven personality, perhaps even a workaholic. Paul's protege Timothy appears to have been passive-aggressive, the type that tends to avoid facing issues head-on. Timothy's passive-aggressive nature may have prompted many of Paul's strong exhortations in 1 and 2 Timothy. God used all of these different personalities to achieve His purposes in those early days of the church. The same is true of you today. Whatever your personality type, God can use you as a facilitator as long as you diligently work the Steps yourself and remain open to God's leading.

In the AA tradition, the role of leader or facilitator is shared and rotated democratically. And that practice works well in the AA environment. It may work well in some Christian support groups and recovery groups. But at the Minirth-Meier Clinic, we find that there are advantages in having group facilitators who have been equipped and prepared to understand the group process and to handle any problems that might arise.

The First Evangelical Free Church of Fullerton, California, has a very thorough and intensive facilitator training process. Many churches, however, do not have the resources to provide such a depth of training for their facilitators. To meet this need, we have attempted to make this chapter as complete a resource for facilitators as it can possibly be. In Part 3 of this book, we have also reprinted the facilitator training materials used in the Fullerton program. Feel free to adapt these principles and resources to the needs of your program.

Group facilitating is normally a simple, painless procedure. The preparation is minimal. Support group meetings practically run themselves. The facilitator may need to jump-start the discussion with some personal sharing, but once it has begun, the group dialogue usually develops a life and a direction of its own. For most facilitators, the hardest part of leading a group is knowing how to close the meeting on time.

Yet facilitators should be aware of issues, dynamics, and potential problems in support groups. A facilitator should have good listening skills and a basic understanding of group dynamics. A facilitator should know how to guard against burn-out. There should even be a plan for dealing with such rare but real problems as disruptive individuals and people who are contemplating suicide.

Think of this chapter as a group facilitator's toolbox. In these next few pages we have packed the essential tools you will need to feel confident as a group facilitator.

The Authority Issue

Often, when Christians attempt to structure a "Christianized" recovery group or support group, they fail to understand the dynamics that make traditional recovery programs like AA and Al-Anon work. One of the most fragile of these dynamics is the role of the facilitator. Christians often try to impose a churchlike hierarchical authority onto an AA-style meeting by placing a strong, directive leader "in charge." But in successful groups, no one is truly "in charge." The democratic nature of AA has been one of its selling points ever since the program was founded.

Stephen W. is a recovering alcoholic and director of an urban ministry to homeless people. He continues to be involved in both Christian and secular Twelve-Step groups. He told us, "All of us alcoholics, for some reason, have a real knee-jerk reaction against authority. If we're going to get well, that's something we have to work on. But until we're well, only a genuine Twelve-Step group in the AA tradition can create an environment where we can work on our issues without having Big Brother tell us what to do. AA works so well because no one can order you around. If you try to set up a 'Christianized AA' with one person as the big shot, it'll get unhealthy real quick."

Tradition Two of Alcoholics Anonymous reads, "For our group purpose there is but one ultimate authority—a loving God as He may express Himself in our group conscience. Our leaders are but trusted servants; they do not govern." This is a tradition we ignore at our peril.

Many programs prefer to use the word *facilitator* rather than leader. These words entail subtly different connotations. The word "leader" suggests a person with a measure of authority and control—and the idea of anyone assuming authority and control over a Twelve-Step meeting is completely foreign to over fifty years of practice and tradition in Alcoholics Anonymous.

The role of a facilitator, however, is not one of control or authority. The facilitator's job is simply to get the dialogue started and guide it over any potential rough spots. The qualifications for a Twelve-Step group facilitator are essentially the same as those of a sponsor:

1. A facilitator should have spent a lot of time in a Twelve-Step program—at least three months, and preferably a year or more. Dave Carder suggests that a good rule of thumb is, "You can only facilitate to the level you've participated." For example, a person who hasn't had lots of experience in a rough-and-tumble, confrontational sobriety group shouldn't try to facilitate one.

2. A facilitator must be seriously working the Steps on an ongoing basis.

3. A facilitator must be seriously committed to an ongoing, daily relationship with God through prayer and meditation.

4. A facilitator must have a humble, loving, accepting heart

toward other people, and a desire to see other people find recovery and a relationship with Jesus Christ.

A facilitator of a support group plays a very different role from that of a Bible study leader. A support group facilitator is not an authority but a peer. A support group facilitator does not teach but shares out of personal experience. Bible study groups are important, and we believe that Christians in recovery can benefit from systematic Bible study as well as from a support group. But the role of Bible study leader should not be confused with the role of a support group facilitator.

Step by Step Through a Support Group Meeting

Now let's walk together through a typical Christian Twelve-Step meeting so that you can see how the facilitator functions in that setting.

An average group meets weekly, usually in the evening, although many programs have morning and lunchtime meetings for those who cannot attend evening groups. When starting a new group, it is helpful for the facilitator to take the initiative in sharing personal struggles and powerlessness. For example, the facilitator might say, "The reason I've chosen to facilitate this group is that I am a person in recovery. I need a place where I can come once a week and talk about what it means to live a life that is surrendered to God. I need the encouragement of all of you. I need to be able to share my hurts and failures, as well as my joys and successes." The facilitator sets the tone for the discussion and sharing to follow.

The meeting opens with prayer. Normally, there is also a reading of the Serenity Prayer of Reinhold Niebuhr, the group's Preamble or Statement of Purpose, the ground rules for group discussion, and/or the Twelve Steps.

"Prayer is the most important distinctive of Christian Twelve-Step groups," said Terry Davidson, contact person for the Christian Twelve-Step program at Eastridge Christian Assembly in the Seattle area. "The closest thing to prayer in an AA meeting is when the leader says, 'Let's have a moment to reflect on why we're here.' In AA you certainly won't hear 'Praise the Lords,' prayer requests, or prayer victories. You just don't have that prayer support. It makes such a difference to be in a group that openly acknowledges that Jesus Christ is our Higher Power."

After the opening prayer and the readings (such as the Serenity Prayer, Preamble, ground rules, or Twelve Steps), the facilitator may ask the group if anyone has a specific problem or issue to discuss. Sometimes individuals in the group will ask for help and insight from the entire group on problems they wrestle with, such as anger, loneliness, or temptation. If no one suggests a topic or problem, the facilitator should select a topic or one of the Twelve Steps as a focus for discussion. The facilitator states his or her first name and begins talking about that topic or Step, often accompanied by one or two Scripture verses related to the selected topic or Step. A typical discussion would last about ten to fifteen minutes.

Suzanne S. told us that in the topic or Step discussion at her group in Hershey, Pennsylvania, "We stay away from a Bible study. There are seven of us who take turns leading. My own problem is I like to prepare well for these things, and I have to watch myself that I don't over prepare and leave too little time for people to take over and discuss it. The important thing is to introduce your topic, such as loneliness or anxiety, and get people thinking about it in relationship to biblical truth. We try to have as much time as possible for sharing, because it's in the sharing aspect that the healing takes place."

In the personal sharing time, which follows the topic discussion, each member states his or her first name, then proceeds to share. People talk about their struggles or they praise God for their progress and successes or they request prayer for specific issues. It is all right for some people simply to state, "I'm _____, I have a problem, I'm not ready to share it openly yet. I'd appreciate it if you'd pray for me about it." People are often enormously helped by even that minimal amount of sharing.

About fifteen minutes before time to close, the facilitator may ask if anyone has something to share before the meeting is over. This gives anyone who has been reluctant or inhibited a last chance to speak. The group may then pray brief prayers of thanks, praise, supplication, or intercession. In closing, the group may stand, hold hands, and pray the Lord's Prayer in unison.

The meeting that we have just described typically lasts for an hour, an hour and a half at most.

Suggested Ground Rules for Support Groups

Every group needs to set some boundary lines for the group dialogue. Your primary responsibility as a facilitator is to keep the group functioning within those lines, which we call ground rules. The ground rules of the group should be stated in printed materials, and they should be read or referred to at the beginning of each meeting. If members of the group violate those rules during the sharing time, the facilitator may need to remind the group of the reason for observing certain rules.

The object of ground rules is not to create restrictions, but to create a safe, supportive atmosphere in which sharing can take place as freely as possible. The following are five suggestions for support group ground rules:

1. Above all, everything that is shared in this group must be kept completely confidential. Not even the identity of the members of this group should be disclosed to anyone outside the group.

2. Please try to keep your sharing to no more than five minutes, so that others will have sufficient opportunity to share.

3. Feel free to express your honest emotions—but try to honestly own your own emotions. That means that instead of saying, "My spouse makes me so mad!" we say, "I feel angry when my spouse does so-and-so!" When we own our own emotions, our sentences tend to begin with the word "I" rather than "he," "she," "they," or "you." For the sake of our own recovery, we must take responsibility for our own feelings and responses.

4. Please don't interrupt anyone who is sharing.

5. Please do not engage in "cross-talk." Cross-talk is any conversation directed at another member of the group, whether open or whispered. All sharing should be directed to the group as a whole, not to specific individuals.

6. Please do not give advice to someone who has shared. If another person shares a struggle or a problem, you may respond

by sharing your own experience, strength, and hope—but don't try to "fix" people or their problems.

Other ground rules may be desirable, depending on the specific needs and circumstances of your group. For example, if you have a group with a closed membership and a limited duration, you may want to ask members to make a commitment to attend regularly, to arrive on time, and to stay in the group through the final session.

Any rules governing conduct in a support group should be simple and few in number.

Why Advice-Giving Doesn't Work

There are important reasons for not giving advice in a support group or recovery group. When people give us advice, we suddenly feel defensive. Our denial mechanism turns on. Our rebellious tendencies kick in. We don't want someone telling us what to do. We want to make our own choices. If someone tells us, "You need to do this and this and this," we dig in our heels and grit our teeth and say, "*No way*! I never gave you the right to make my decisions for me!"

Some of us, on the other hand, like to receive advice so we don't have to take responsibility for ourselves. If we follow through with the advice and things don't work out, we can blame the people who advised us for our failures or disappointment. So if people in groups never give or receive advice, how do they gain insight into their problems? The answer: They gain insight by listening to *stories*.

In Twelve-Step groups, people don't tell each other what to do. They just tell their own stories. They share their own struggles, their failures and successes, the solutions they've tried, and which ones worked and which ones failed. In *Christian* Twelve-Step groups there is an added dimension: People have the opportunity to talk openly about what Christ is doing in their lives and how they are able to fit the Twelve-Step program and their Christian faith together.

When one person shares a problem in a meeting, others respond with "crosstalk," or "feedback." They may say, "You know, I really identify with what you're going through. This is where I was and this is what I did and this is how it worked for me." The person with the problem does not feel preached to or coerced. He or she is free to try the other person's solution or discard it.

What works for one person may not work for another. No one can tell another person how to work the Steps.

Learning to Listen

The purpose of a group is to give people the opportunity to share their issues in a safe environment where they will not be judged, advised, preached to, or "fixed." The people in the group—including the facilitator—listen to one another and share their own stories. A support group gives people a place to experience the "warm fuzzies," to be accepted, affirmed, and unconditionally loved. Equally important, it gives them a place to be *heard* and *understood*.

Most people who struggle with addiction issues are adult children of dysfunctional families. Many grew up through childhood, adolescence, and even adulthood with the feeling that they were not listened to or understood by others. Support groups offer adult children the opportunity to be "reparented" in a functional and supportive setting by people who are willing to listen and able to understand.

Most of us consider ourselves good listeners. But the fact is that the ability to listen to others in a truly empathetic and supportive way does not come naturally. It is a skill that must be consciously, diligently learned. The skill of true empathetic listening consists of three components:

1. *The ability to authentically hear what another person is saying and feeling.* This is not as easy as it sounds. We all have a natural tendency to filter what we hear through our own experience, feelings, and biases. We get impatient, we want people to get to the point, we finish their sentences for them, we presume to know what they are saying just as soon as they open their mouths. But to authentically listen to another person means that we try to put ourselves into their outlook, to feel what they are feeling, to elicit the true emotions that seethe beneath the surface of their words.

We listen not just to the content of their sentences, but to the meaning and emotion conveyed in facial expressions, in gestures, in body language, in tone of voice. Often, the nonverbal messages do not agree with the verbal content; when this is the case, the nonverbal message is the more reliable indicator of what the person is truly feeling. Our goal is not just to hear people's words but to truly understand and empathize with their feelings.

2. *The ability to accept that person and his or her feelings without attempting to change, negate, or "fix" those feelings.* This can be the most difficult dimension of listening for people in recovery groups. People in recovery are hurting people. Often when we hear another person share pain, it stirs up our own issues and feelings of pain. We transfer our own feelings onto the other person and are eager to move them out of their own pain so that we ourselves will stop feeling uncomfortable. Often, when we try to "fix" other people, we are really trying to "fix" ourselves and anesthetize our own pain. To be effective listeners, however, we must learn to allow people to feel their own feelings, to grieve their own losses, to apply their own solutions, and to recover at their own pace.

3. *The ability to assure others that they have been heard and understood.* This is the "affirmation" dimension of listening, and it can be the most effective and healing component of all. It involves communicating back to the other person that you hear and that you understand. People who are hurting or ashamed often feel isolated and alone. "I feel so weird—like I'm the only person who ever had this problem," is a comment frequently heard. Empathetic listening and feedback helps the recovering person to feel like a normal part of the human race—and like a fully accepted part of a recovery "family."

Strategies for Listening

Christian writer Ethel Herr expressed in poetic lines the feelings of a person who cries out to be heard. The poem is called "Please Listen to Me":

> If only you would listen
> I'd love to share my heart with you—
> But no, you seldom listen.

Before I've uttered ten words
You interrupt—
You've guessed the rest
And tell it back to me.
Or it reminds you
Of a bigger, better yarn
That you must share immediately.

If only you would listen—
Forgo your chance to show
How rich and full your life has been
You'd understand the way I feel—
What makes me laugh
And cry
And disagree with you.

My hopes and dreams
Might make your life the richer
And draw us closer—
If only you would listen.[3]

There are specific strategies that you can undertake to be a more empathetic listener—and a more effective group facilitator. Some examples:

1. *Practice reflective listening.* This means that you verbally "mirror back" to others what they have shared with you. After a person in the group has shared his or her feelings, you can respond with phrases such as, "I hear you saying . . . Is this what you mean? . . . Am I hearing you correctly?" That person will then be able to respond, "That's exactly how I feel," or, "No, that's not it exactly. Let me explain further." Once that person hears his or her own feelings being expressed by a reflective listener, he or she will feel that those feelings have been heard and understood. This is enormously encouraging to people in recovery. Here are some tips for becoming a better reflective listener:

- When you mirror back to the person who has shared, try to tell that person exactly what you heard them say.
- Try to mirror back the exact meaning of the other person's message, but use different words. This will help the

other person to assess whether you have correctly interpreted the message.

· Do not add or subtract anything from that person's message.

· Focus on feelings rather than facts. The details of that person's story are not as important as his or her emotional response to those events.

· Do not respond with any message of your own. Do not evaluate or analyze. Do not try to persuade the person with logic. Do not argue with what that person feels.

· Express understanding rather than pity. The words, "I know that must have been very hard for you," are much more healing than the words, "I feel so sorry for you."

Here are some examples of short, supportive comments that can help people feel that they were heard and that someone cares and identifies with them.* Note that they are all just one sentence and are not "fixing" types of comments:

1. Uh-uh, hmm, oh
2. That must have hurt an awful lot.
3. Sounds like you have good reason for being angry.
4. Thank you, Harold.
5. I appreciate your courage in sharing that, Mindy.
6. I think I'd be angry also if that happened to me.
7. I feel angry just hearing about it!
8. That *was* a crazy thing for a mother to do to a little girl.
9. That can be very confusing.
10. Thank you for sharing that, Robert.
11. That's got to be hard to live with.
12. What you shared, Frank, really ministered to me. Thank you.
13. Sounds like you're taking some good steps, Carol.
14. It seems so unfair.
15. That's great!
16. All right! Fantastic!
17. As Darlene was sharing it brought up a lot of feelings of when I was treated that way.

* Developed by Dave Osborne for use in New Hope support groups

18. Thanks, Betty.
19. I can really identify with what you were sharing, Pete. I had a similar thing happen to me.
20. I'm glad you're here, Bob.

2. *Be aware of the obstacles to empathetic listening.* These obstacles include:

   • Rehearsing. This is one of the most universal hindrances to good listening. We all tend to frame and rehearse our own replies while another person is speaking—and that prevents us from truly hearing what the other person says. When we catch ourselves rehearsing, we should immediately refocus our attention on listening to the speaker.

   • Identification. This is a self-centered process whereby we select from what the other person shares with us, according to our own interests, feelings, and experience. This is a common block to effective listening. You have probably had the experience of telling someone about an event from your own life only to have that person take over the conversation: "Oh, I know exactly what you mean! The same thing happened to me! Let me tell you . . . ." Inwardly, we respond, "That's not what I meant at all! You're not listening to me!"

   • Filtering. Filtering is a difficult habit to detect in ourselves, because the process itself prevents us from even being aware of it. When our reception of another person's sharing is colored by our own biases, expectations, moods, or issues, we are guilty of filtering, hearing some statements and ignoring others. We alter the meaning of what has been shared. The best antidote to filtering is to listen reflectively. By doing so, we allow the other person to correct any false impressions we might have gained.

   • Mind reading. Many people are quick to make assumptions about the feelings and motives of others based on a scarcity of information. We often try to simplify other people's feelings and motives to a simple "handle" such as, "He's always an avoider," or "She always exaggerates." The fact that a human being is the most complex of all of God's creations should make us stop and think before we assume we know what another person is thinking or feeling.

- Judging. If we judge other people or the statements they make, we shut down our own ability to hear what they are really saying. As much as is humanly possible (and, by the power of the Holy Spirit, *super*humanly possible), we must try to be totally accepting and nonjudgmental as we listen.

- Daydreaming. Distractions are the enemy of effective listening. Sometimes the worst distractions come from within. Even as we make eye contact and nod affirmingly, stray thoughts, fantasies, worries, and memories can cross our minds and block our ability to hear. The person's sharing may itself cause the distraction by setting off a chain reaction of thoughts and associations that shut down further listening. Daydreaming is often a sign of boredom or anxiety, but it is also a sign that we need to become more disciplined and intentional in our listening habits. We must learn to value every word that is said and every feeling that is expressed.

3. *Listen to your own feelings.* Frequently a facilitator can gauge the mood of a group by taking an internal check: Am I feeling angry? Defensive? Depressed? Anxious? Bored? It can often be very helpful for the group to have the facilitator articulate those feelings: "I am really feeling tension right now, and I'm wondering how the rest of you feel." That sort of sensitivity and honesty can sometimes open up issues in the group that need to be acknowledged and addressed.

Problems in Groups

Every group goes through stages and cycles. Every group experiences dissensions and dry spells. This is normal, and the facilitator should not be afraid of these normal passages in the life span of a support group. Here are a few problems to be aware of:

- *People who are angry with God.* It is not only normal but *desirable* to have such people in our support groups. One of the goals of Christian support groups, after all, is to attract non-Christians and to introduce them to an accepting, supportive Christian fellowship—and there to introduce them to Jesus Christ.

Some people in the group may resent the concept of God as a "heavenly Father" because their earthly fathers were distant, abusive, or otherwise dysfunctional. If there are such people in your group, you may want to refer to Jesus in your prayers and sharing rather than your heavenly Father. This helps to point people toward the God of the Bible, as revealed in His Son Jesus, without needlessly conjuring up negative associations. Others may be bitter toward the church and religion. Their negative emotions may have been shaped by judgmental, legalistic, or hypocritical religious people. Still others may be disappointed with God due to unanswered prayer, a terrible tragedy, or simply the anguish of living with their addiction. Many people, when they are new to the recovery process, try to shift the blame for their problems onto God: "Why did God allow me to become addicted?"

People who are angry with God cannot be talked out of their anger. They can only be loved and accepted as they work through their anger with the support of the group. The best way to introduce such people to Christ is to let Christ shine through our own lives, through our caring and our availability as a community of unconditional love.

- *Group denial.* When an individual avoids facing the reality of his or her addiction, that is called "denial." But sometimes an entire group of people can retreat into a denial mindset. As a facilitator, you can actually *feel* this resistance when it occurs. If you or another member share feelings and issues that are too painful for others in the group to face, two or three other members may try to move the group away from confronting those issues. They may attempt various avoidance maneuvers: intellectualizing, making jokes, getting angry, spiritualizing ("Why don't we just pray about this?")—anything to divert the group from the real source of its pain and discomfort.

   If you encounter group denial, use discernment.

Perhaps the group needs your honest confrontation: "I sense that we are not being honest with each other about these issues." Or perhaps the group just needs your patience. Recognize that some people may be too fragile to cope with these issues at this time. Next week's meeting may be a different story.

· *People who leave.* In virtually every support group, there is a core of people who are dedicated to the group, and then there are people who come and go. Some leave because they cannot face the painful truth about themselves and their addiction at this time. Some leave because, for whatever reason, the group is not what they expected. Some leave because the group is either too confrontational or not confrontational enough, and they go to find a group that better suits their needs. Facilitators should not be possessive of the people in their groups. In fact, it is good to point out from time to time, "This group isn't for everyone. Join us, try the group for a while, and if you choose to leave, well, that's okay." The fact that people leave a group is not a sign that either the facilitator or the group has failed. It only reflects that all people—and their needs—are different.

· *Dry spells.* Sometimes even the most open, growing, and alive group will "dry up" for no apparent reason. Intimacy is blocked. Talk becomes superficial, theoretical, intellectual. Feelings are no longer expressed. It could be an "off night." Or it could be a symptom of a deeper problem.

A facilitator who recognizes that a problem exists should confront the matter honestly, personally, and confessionally. "I have to tell you openly," the facilitator might say, "that I have not been honest in sharing my feelings. In fact, I sense that the entire group seems to be operating at a very superficial level lately. I believe the dry spell this group is experiencing is not helping my recovery, yet I don't know how to solve the problem. Do any of you feel the same as I do?"

A more extreme gambit to force people to be more honest with each other is to suggest openly that the group has outlived its usefulness. "If we can't be more open with each other than this," the facilitator might say, "then perhaps this group should disband." This suggestion might be enough to scare the group back to reality and honesty. Faced with the prospect of losing their lifeline, they may struggle to hold onto it.

Or they may not. It may be that the group really has run its course and should disband. The death of a group should not be equated with failure. A successful group can run its course and die, and a failed group can go on and on and on, accomplishing nothing. If a dry spell turns out to be a death knell, the group should be allowed to die with dignity and without regret.

- *People who don't belong.* Some groups are rough-and-tumble, confrontational places where honesty borders on brutality. Other groups are as warm and fuzzy as a comfortable pair of slippers. Putting warm-fuzzy people in rough-and-tumble groups (or vice versa) can be disastrous for all concerned. Some people are too fragile and have too little ego-strength for a confrontational group. And people with intense personalities can overpower a "soft" group.

  Whenever an individual and a group are mismatched, it is the facilitator's responsibility to take the individual aside and explore other options, then possibly recommend a different group to that person.

- *Fearing loss of control of the group.* Dave Carder advises that control of the direction and group experience should be left up to the facilitator. Once facilitators are trained and placed in their groups, however, it is inappropriate for an "inspector"—a pastor or program director—to enter a group to check on its practices. It is also inappropriate for facilitators to discuss with the pastor what goes on inside the support group meeting. These guidelines are spelled out ahead of time to both facilitators and group members so that everybody feels safe within the group.

Drawing Out the Quiet Ones

There is no law that says everyone has to speak in a recovery group. Some will come week after week, never sharing, and sometimes never even making eye contact. They may be shy. They may be going through an emotional upheaval. They may just feel threatened at the prospect of speaking in a group. And that's all right. People can gain a great deal of insight, encouragement, and understanding simply by being with others who share the same issues.

Sometimes people will appear to "check out" of the group. Their eyes will go blank and they will freeze and seem to go inside themselves. *Let them.* Don't distract them. Don't try to attract their attention. They are doing hard work. They have heard someone share a story or an idea that connects with their experience. They are identifying, processing, concentrating. They can only do one thing at a time. Let them finish the job they are working on, and they will "check back in" to the meeting when they are ready.

There will be other times when you will sense that certain people in the group really have something they need to say, but for some reason they just can't or won't. There are things you can do to help the quiet ones feel more comfortable sharing their feelings with the group. You can make a point of talking to them after the meeting. "We're really glad you're here," you might say, "and I want you to know it's okay to just sit and listen as you've been doing. Over time, you'll become more comfortable with the group.When you have something you wish to share, you'll know you're among friends."

A more direct way of involving quiet people is for the facilitator to pose a question ("What solutions have you found for this problem?"), then nod to the person on the right or left and go around the circle. Often, the quiet people in the group really want to share, but won't unless it is "their turn."

Problem People

Occasionally, a group will be disrupted or distracted by what we call "problem people." For the most part, problem people do not deliberately set out to cause problems for the group. People come into a Twelve-Step group from a variety of backgrounds and experiences, with a wide array of issues and hurts. In many cases, disruptive behavior is just a symptom of the hurt that person is feeling—and perhaps even a defense mechanism against the pain of honestly facing his or her issues. In other words, problem behavior is often a form of acted-out denial.

Problem people can be helped to face their issues so that they can work *with* the group instead of *against* it. As we help them see their issues more clearly, they will be able to blend with the group and to move more confidently toward their own recovery. Here are seven basic forms of defensive or disruptive behavior that occasionally crop up in recovery groups:

1. *The angry, emotional outburst.* The expression of honest anger and emotion is okay in recovery groups. The group and the facilitator can be very helpful in furthering the recovery process by accepting and supporting a person who is expressing strong emotion. The pain of honestly confronting their issues causes some people to weep, some to yell, some to swear. A healthy group understands that these people may be releasing feelings that have been repressed or denied for years—and that those feelings are simply coming out explosively, like the *bang!* of an over-inflated balloon.

However, there will be times when people express emotion or anger in a way that is totally inappropriate and disruptive to the group. The facilitator needs to use discernment in such cases. Is this a one-time problem which is unlikely to recur? Are others in the group accepting of the person, or does the person's behavior frighten and intimidate the group? Even if the ground rules of the group have been violated, it may be wise to "bend the rules" a little if the facilitator decides that the outburst does not threaten the safety and supportive atmosphere of the group.

When such a disturbance takes place, it may be best to encourage that person to step out of the room for a moment, then come back and share his or her feelings in a more appropriate way. But if this person has a history of repeatedly venting rage against the group, it might be appropriate to refer him or her to a therapist, an anger management class, or a more confrontational group. In extreme cases, a disruptive person might have to be barred from the group entirely. Though we care for the individual, the good and the safety of the group must always come first.

2. *Joking and clowning.* Clowning also calls for discernment on the part of the facilitator. A recovery group should be a place where both tears and laughter can be freely expressed. However, some people use their sense of humor to keep themselves—and even the rest of the group—from getting too close to the pain of an issue. Others use humor to draw attention to themselves. In either case, the "face of a clown" is probably a cover-up for a great burden of pain. If a "clown" repeatedly creates distractions that prevent the group from getting to serious issues, the facilitator should talk to the disruptive person in private.

3. *Monopolizing the group dialogue.* When a person talks overmuch in the group, it is often a sign that he or she doesn't feel listened to in ordinary relationships. Over-talkative people usually do not realize that they are monopolizing the time. The best way to deal with monopolizers is to set a time limit as part of the group's ground rules—and to enforce it fairly.

Another reason some members may monopolize the time of the group is self-absorption or narcissism. As Dave Carder told us, "People in recovery have a tendency to become very narcissistic at first. They are like infants. The whole world revolves around them. People in pain don't have a lot of energy for anything or anyone else. They are working on their issues and grieving their losses, so they talk a lot about I, I, I. Some church people see people in recovery as too self-absorbed, but that self-absorption is just a stage in the process. Of course, recovering people can't stay at that narcissistic stage. They have to be helped beyond their self-absorption."

How do we help people move beyond the narcissistic stage? "We tell people straight out," says Dave, " 'You can't remain stuck in that self-centered phase. You've got to move outside of yourself and become involved with other people's recovery. You've got to become a good listener to other people's issues. That's the only way to really keep your own recovery moving forward.' "

4. *People who are "stuck."* "In our program," says Carder, "we have a saying: 'Everyone is responsible for his or her own

recovery.' No one is going to do it for you. It's your life. If you don't take responsibility for yourself, no one else will."

John 5 tells the story of a man who for thirty-eight years had lain beside a pool that was reputed to have healing properties. When Jesus saw this man, he asked him the simple question, "Do you really want to get well?"

Good recovery groups ask that question.

The answer the man gave Jesus is not unlike the answer of many people who are "stuck" in their recovery process: "Sir, I have no man to put me into the pool when the water is stirred up; but while I am coming, another steps down before me."[4] He made an excuse for remaining "stuck" in his miserable condition.

Some people in recovery are like him. They like to look as if they're getting help, without taking responsibility to make real changes in their lives. This crippled man had grown comfortable in his role as victim of an affliction. It was predictable, he knew exactly what each day would be like, and he could bask in the pity of others.

People like him need help—sometimes confrontational help —in order to become "unstuck" and start making real progress toward genuine recovery.

5. *"Fixing" others.* People who give advice and try to "fix" other people are the most well-intentioned of problem people. They are trying to help and to stop others from hurting. They often have no idea that they are violating the rules. Christians are often the worst offenders because the Christian culture teaches that there is a Bible verse for every problem we face. Here again, the best way to deal with "fixers" is by having a "no advice" rule stated clearly in the ground rules—and by gently yet impartially enforcing the rule.

6. *Seductiveness.* People who repeatedly wear seductive clothing, sit in a revealing way, or speak and gesture flirtatiously, may be engaging in "seductive behavior." This behavior is seriously distracting and disruptive to the group. Many people are not consciously aware of their seductive behavior; others deliberately use sexuality to gain attention, win friends, or control situations in the meeting.

Seductive behavior should be privately but directly confronted; there's no effective way of "hinting around" about it. We find that it is best to approach the person in a one-to-one setting and state frankly how his or her behavior is affecting the group. Be specific about what the person wears, does, or says that you feel is inappropriate. Be prepared for any reaction. He or she may agree with you, get angry, ridicule you for your "prudishness," or leave the group entirely. Again, the needs of the group supersede the needs of the disruptive individual.

7. *Drunk and disorderly behavior.* People who come to a recovery group meeting intoxicated are extremely rare. Dan Reed of Overlake Overcomers told us, "In the past ten years, I've only had two or three situations when someone was drunk or belligerent and tried to disrupt a meeting. A couple of us just escorted the individual outside and asked him to come back after he had sobered up. In all the years I've been with Overlake Overcomers, no one has ever gotten violent."

"I Want to Die"

Dr. Frank Minirth was very concerned about Judy.

Judy was one of about a dozen people attending a Life Care seminar on depression that Dr. Minirth was conducting. Of all the people participating that week, Judy had shared the least. On the second day of the seminar, Dr. Minirth felt sure that the reason she was so quiet was not that she was shy, but that she had withdrawn into her feelings of depression.

Following the afternoon lecture, the group gathered for a sharing time. Various people around the room talked about insights they had gained into their own struggles with depression. Judy, however, sat silently with her arms folded across her chest and her eyes downcast. At one point, she quietly excused herself and left the room. She returned about twenty minutes later and resumed her melancholy posture.

The better part of an hour passed as several others shared. During a brief lull in the conversation, Judy spoke up. "I need to say something," she murmured softly, her face drawn into a mask of deep emotional pain. "I would just like to ask everybody in this room to forgive me."

"Forgive you for what?" asked Dr. Minirth.

"I would just like to know that you forgive me, that's all," she said, biting her lip as if to keep some terrible truth from spilling from her lips.

Dr. Minirth had a strong suspicion. When someone asks forgiveness when no apparent wrong has been committed, that is frequently the sign of a person who is trying to die. "I think we should all just pause right now and pray for Judy," said Dr. Minirth.

One by one, the members of the group prayed, coming at last to Judy herself. Softly, almost inaudibly, she began to pray. "Lord," she said, "I haven't prayed in years." And she proceeded to pour out her pain and disappointment to God. Then she began to sob. The woman sitting next to her put an arm around Judy.

At that moment, Dr. Minirth made an assumption about Judy—an assumption that turned out to be correct. He said, "Judy, what have you done to harm yourself?"

"I took some pills, Dr. Minirth," she said. A gasp went around the room.

"What kind of pills? And when did you take them?"

"Lithium. A whole bottle. I think it was around thirty-eight pills. I took them about an hour ago, when I left the room."

Dr. Minirth had Judy rushed to the hospital. Her stomach was pumped and she stayed in the hospital overnight. She was able to rejoin the group the next day. Throughout that day, the group supported her and prayed with her. They gave her a card with a personal note from each member. At the end of that day, she smiled and told everyone, "This group has been used to bring me back to God. This is the first time I've ever been in a group that accepted me, where people loved me for who I am. I couldn't believe that you stood by me and loved me even after I tried to kill myself. That made me realize that the body of Christ is important. It made me realize that I want to be a part of the body of Christ too."

Sometimes a person like Judy comes into a group, feeling despondent and desiring a final end to pain. No one truly wants to die, but sometimes a person becomes so depressed that he or she can see no other option. That person then becomes a likely candidate for suicide. As a facilitator, you can take positive steps when a person appears suicidal or discusses suicidal feelings in the meeting. The following is a list of guidelines for dealing with potentially self-destructive people:

- If someone mentions suicidal feelings, don't ignore or deny those feelings. Face them directly and involve the group in discussing them.
- Talk frankly about the subject. Sometimes people are afraid that if they say the word "suicide," they will plant the idea in someone's mind. But the idea is already there. The tragedy is that the suicidal person is alone with those thoughts and has no one with whom to do a "reality check."
- Involve the group. Tell the entire group that the recovery process brings out pain, and that many of us want to find ways to stop the pain. Encourage people to talk about their own experiences of self-destructive thoughts. This will help the suicidal person to feel less alone with the problem. When the entire group is willing to speak openly about the suicidal person's issues—loneliness, hopelessness, depression—that person will feel the friendship and support of the group, and the chances of committing suicide will be reduced.
- Listen carefully and nonjudgmentally. Don't say things like, "Suicide is a sin," "Suicide is bad," or "People who kill themselves go to hell."
- If the person threatens suicide, take it seriously. Don't dare him or her to "go ahead and do it." Don't say, "You wouldn't really do that." Don't offer glib reassurances. Act on the premise that the intention is real.
- Don't express shock or dismay. Express love and understanding.
- Take action. If it is possible to do so, remove the means of suicide from the person's reach.
- Stay with the suicidal person.
- Get immediate help from people or agencies specializing in crisis intervention and suicide prevention.

A final word: If the person succeeds in committing suicide, don't absorb that tragedy as your own personal failure. When people are determined, no other person has the power to stop them.

When to Refer to a Professional Counselor

Sometimes a person in the group exhibits problems that are beyond the group's abilities. He or she may need medical evaluation and psychological assessment. When a person in the group demonstrates one or more of the following symptoms, the facilitator should encourage that person to seek professional evaluation or counseling from a psychiatrist, psychologist, counselor/therapist, or medical physician:

- Suicidal feelings, characterized by a strong sense of hopelessness, a lack of desire to live, a feeling that he or she cannot control self-destructive urges, a history of previous attempts, and/or a specific suicide plan.
- Homicidal feelings, characterized by anger, rage, or hatred that he or she feels cannot be controlled, and/or a definite plan to hurt or injure another person.
- Psychosis, characterized by an inability to think, to remember, to communicate, to respond emotionally, to interpret reality and behave appropriately; or characterized by delusions, hallucinations, and grossly disorganized behavior.
- Neurosis, characterized by extreme anxiety, hysteria, obsessive-compulsive behavior, phobias, or debilitating depression.
- A medical condition, such as extreme headaches, migraines, or other physical problems that prevent him or her from functioning normally.
- Ongoing substance abuse.
- Any situation that is too intense for the facilitator and the group to adequately cope with.

Legal Issues

Virtually every jurisdiction in the country has laws that require reporting certain acts to the authorities, even if those acts are disclosed in the confidential setting of a support group. If a man in a group said, for example, that he was engaged in child abuse, trafficking in child pornography, or exposing himself at schoolyards, the facilitator of that group could actually be liable to criminal prosecution if he did not report this man to the authorities.

The reporting requirements and the official agencies involved will vary from state to state and county to county. It is important to understand the reporting requirements in your particular jurisdiction.

For the sake of safety and trust in the group, you may want to consider making an announcement before each meeting (particularly in groups dealing with sexual addiction) to this effect: "We have to abide by certain restrictions according to the law. So we would caution you to be careful about sharing about any activities which we would be required to report to the appropriate authorities."

Preventing Burn-Out

Burn-out is that "I've had it!" feeling that often follows many stressful weeks in a repetitive situation. Fortunately, burn-out is preventable. There are a number of steps you can take to keep from becoming "weary in well-doing" as a support group facilitator.

One of the best ways to avoid burn-out is to approach the facilitating task with the right attitude. Tell yourself, "I am facilitating this group for the sake of my own recovery. I am not here to save the group. I am not responsible for the success of this group. I am not responsible for anyone's recovery but my own."

All too often, facilitators carry the burden of the group on their shoulders. They worry, "What if I do or say something stupid? What if nobody comes? What if nobody shares? What if people drop out of the program? What if the group flops? What if nobody gets better?" Such thoughts generate stress—and stress leads inevitably to burn-out.

If you are considering becoming a group facilitator, you should carefully weigh this question: "Why do I want to be a facilitator?" For some people, taking on the role of facilitator may actually be an extension of their addiction. This is especially true of those who are addicted to volunteerism, to rescuing others, or to controlling others. This is not to say that those who wrestle with such issues are unfit to lead groups. We are only recommending that this question be considered with care and with a recognition that the power of denial is strong.

Another suggestion for preventing burn-out is to rotate leadership of the group with one or more people. This enables group facilitators to enjoy time off from the chores and burdens and allows them to spend more time simply receiving the nurture of the group. And there is an added benefit: as you rotate leadership and give increasing numbers of people experience in facilitating groups, you create a nucleus of people who are equipped to lead new groups as the recovery program expands.

The Servant Role

The role of a facilitator is not the role of a master but of a servant. The servant of the group has a high calling. He or she is engaged in a task of lasting value, of eternal worth. It is a ministry of helping others find healing from addiction, from emotional pain, and from the power of sin.

The group facilitator is a servant not only of the group, but of Jesus Christ and His kingdom. It is such an vitally important task that Jesus will not entrust it to experts and professionals. He will only entrust it to the most ordinary and humble of people—

To people like *you*.

CHAPTER

10

BUT WHAT IF . . . ?

Questions and Answers

For several years, Dr. Richard Fowler and Dr. Robert Hemfelt have crisscrossed the country conducting "Love is a Choice" seminars on codependency. Everywhere they go, they find people who are hungry for a biblical understanding of addiction and recovery. "Whenever we tell people in the seminars," said Fowler, "that the Minirth-Meier Clinic is producing a book on how to start Christian recovery groups in churches, the response is always, 'Wow! That's what we need! When is it coming out?' Growing numbers of Christians are aware of their need for a Christian atmosphere in a recovery group and for insight into using the Twelve Steps as a vehicle for evangelism."

The "Love Is a Choice" seminars offer an opportunity for participants to write down questions for Drs. Fowler and Hemfelt to answer. In this chapter, we have combed through those questions to select the ones most frequently asked in relation to recovery groups and the Twelve-Step process. Here are those questions and our answers:

We keep hearing about the "disease" of alcoholism or the "disease" of chemical dependency. Is addiction a sickness? Or is it sin?

At the Minirth-Meier Clinic, we do not call addiction a disease. We call it a *disorder*.

It is the vogue these days to refer to addiction as a disease. The problem with that word is that it sounds like something you catch, like a virus, rather than something you choose to do. Recovery does not take place until the addict takes *responsibility* for his or her choices. By calling addictions such as alcoholism diseases, we risk conveying that the addict is not responsible for the addiction.

Many factors make up any addiction, whether it is an addiction to chemical substances or pornography or work or rage. These factors may be genetic, generational, early environment-related, physiological and metabolic, or stress-related. All of these factors contribute to the disorder of addiction. But the overriding factor in every addiction is *choice*. What gives the addict hope is the fact that he or she can make choices.

On the other hand, many Christians view the issue of addiction as simply a matter of sin. Their prescription is, "Pour your booze down the drain, read your Bible, pray—and that will be the end of it." Now, we recognize that, in a small percentage of cases, God does provide an instantaneous miracle of healing. But in most cases, He chooses to let the natural consequences of sin take their course. Just as a broken arm takes six weeks to heal, victory over the addiction disorder usually takes time as well—time and intensive treatment.

Those who prescribe "just read your Bible and pray" for people with compulsive-obsessive behavior do not fully understand the nature of sin from either a biblical or psychological point of view. The Bible clearly teaches that sin is a complex issue, rooted in the disordered nature of the human condition. That is why the apostle Paul writes, "For what I am doing, I do not understand. . . . For the good that I will to do, I do not do; but the evil I will not to do, that I practice."[1]

The term *disorder* recognizes that the addicted person has a physical, psychological, or emotional factor that inclines him or her toward addictive behavior. But the existence of a disorder does not diminish the importance of choice and responsibility. No matter how tenacious our addictive agent may be, we always have the power of the Holy Spirit—and the power to choose.

Only Christianity addresses the issues of sin and responsibility. Because Christians in recovery understand both the disorder dimension and the sin dimension of addiction, we are uniquely qualified to minister to the needs of addicted and recovering people.

Why do people talk about "codependency" as if it was something wrong or harmful? Doesn't the Bible teach us that we should be dependent on one another?

The Bible teaches that as Christians we are to be *interdependent*—that we are to support one another, pray for one another, love one another, and bear one another's burdens. In fact, that is exactly what Twelve-Step support groups are all about: people finding recovery through a process of support and interdependence. But there is a big difference between interdependence and codependency.

Codependency may be defined as "an unhealthy involvement in another person's addiction." This involvement is itself a form of addiction—an addiction to a relationship with an addicted person. A codependent person enables another person's addiction by supplying money or opportunities to indulge in that addiction, by making excuses for the addicted person, by accommodating oneself to the addicted person, and so forth. Whereas interdependency is conscious, healthy dependency, codependency is an unhealthy, out-of-control dependency, rooted in addiction and obsessive-compulsive urges.

People in recovery are seeking to break free of the bondage of codependency by means of an interdependent relationship with other recovering people. They rely on and encourage each other, but they are not codependent with each other. They are not co-involved in addiction, but in the process of becoming well and whole.

Many recovery issues are centered around "poor self-esteem." My codependency recovery group is always saying that I should be assertive, that I should be more positive about myself and try to build strong self-esteem. But my Christian friends tell me the Bible says to "turn the other cheek" and to be "meek and lowly." Who is right?

Many Christians confuse "self-esteem" with the sin of pride. In fact, there is nothing unbiblical about having a healthy sense of self-worth. Quite the contrary. The Bible teaches that we have great worth as human beings. We were made in the image of God, and God loved us so much that He sent His Son to die for us. As Christians we are children of God, heirs of His kingdom, a royal priesthood.

Unfortunately, some very poor Bible teaching in many quarters today is contributing to a tragic misunderstanding of what having good self-esteem means. This teaching has come to be called "Worm Theology," a name derived from the lines of the Isaac Watts hymn:

> Alas, and did my Savior bleed?
> And did my Sovereign die?
> Would He devote that sacred Head
> For such a worm as I?

We do not believe that Jesus died for worms. We believe He died for men and women of worth. We were made in God's image, and even though that image in us has been defiled and broken by sin, God through Christ has made a decision to love us, to reconcile us, and to reshape His image in us. Our sense of self-worth rests not in anything we have done, but in the fact that God has invested His love and worth in us through Jesus Christ.

For many Christians, faulty theology actually hinders the recovery process. Jane M. observed that, because of their beliefs, codependency is a hard issue for many Christians to resolve. "Bad theology keeps many Christians in denial," she told us. "A lot of the verses we were nourished on in Sunday school can be twisted around to a codependent's delight. Like 'turn the other cheek,' which to many Christians means 'become a doormat.'"

We agree. When interpreting Scripture, we must study each passage within the framework of the entire Word of God. "Turn the other cheek" is not the full counsel of God on the subject of responding to abuse. In many instances, the Scriptures also call to loving confrontation with those who sin against us, not just for our good but for theirs as well, and for the sake of the relationship (see Matthew 18:15 and Galatians 6:1). And "meekness," as the word is used in the New Testament, does not mean weakness, but *strength under control.*

Healthy self-esteem is not pride or arrogance. Quite the opposite. Invariably, it is the self-important, arrogant snob who actually has the *lowest* self-esteem. If that person had a healthy sense of self-worth, he or she wouldn't have to go around *acting* important.

The issue of self-esteem is actually a paradox, and that is why it is so widely misunderstood. Low self-esteem causes us to be more preoccupied with self. Healthy, God-directed self-esteem —far from making us more egocentric, narcissistic, or prideful— actually *diminishes* those tendencies and allows us to become less self-centered.

Having healthy self-esteem means that we do not beat ourselves down, nor do we puff ourselves up. We simply accept ourselves, secure in the knowledge that God by His grace has accepted us, cleansed us, and forgiven us by His grace through Jesus Christ.

Why do people need Twelve-Step groups? Why can't they just get better by praying, reading the Bible, and relying on the Holy Spirit?

When we put this question to evangelism professor Richard Peace, he replied, "Going to Twelve-Step groups is getting better by prayer, reading the Bible, and relying on the Holy Spirit! That's what the Twelve Steps are all about!"

Some Christians are under the mistaken impression that Twelve-Step groups are being promoted as a substitute for Christian disciplines such as prayer and Bible study. Nothing could be further from the truth. At the Minirth-Meier Clinic, we endorse Twelve-Step groups (particularly Christian groups) as places where people can learn and practice these Christian disciplines.

Not only do the Steps encourage recovering people to make daily contact with God, but they also encourage other vitally important Christian disciplines and values. The Steps begin with repentance, and they lead the recovering person toward deeper humility, honesty, confession, restitution, prayer, service, and witnessing—all essential components of the Christian faith.

To say that Christian Twelve-Step groups are a substitute for the church would be like saying that Youth for Christ, the Navigators, or the Minirth-Meier Clinic is a substitute for the church. No one ever asks, "Why do people need the Billy Graham Evangelistic Association? Why can't they just be evangelized by praying, reading the Bible, and relying on the Holy Spirit?" People understand that the Graham Association is not a substitute for Christianity; it is a tool that God uses for the benefit of His kingdom. The same is true of the Twelve Steps.

I have heard that AA and the Twelve Steps are part of the New Age movement—and even satanic. Aren't the Twelve Steps really a spiritual heresy?

AA is a nonsectarian spiritual program with roots in the evangelical Oxford Group. The Twelve Steps are a proven, common-sense approach to spiritual and emotional wholeness that the evangelical church of the 1990s is only slowly beginning to embrace. The Steps embody both an intensely realistic application of biblical truth and a profound understanding of human psychology.

Are Satan and the New Age movement also at work in secular Twelve-Step programs? Unquestionably so. That, in fact, is why we at the Minirth-Meier Clinic feel so strongly that the church must begin to make greater inroads into the recovery movement and to start Christian Twelve-Step programs. The fact that Satan is active in the world should not force us to retreat, but spur us to advance!

Richard Peace warns that much of the anti-New Age backlash that we see today in evangelical circles actually has the effect of encouraging rather than deterring the New Age. "The New

Age issue is a smoke screen," he told us. "It has never been a coherent movement—just a loose alliance of various ideas, practices, and perspectives. The nearest thing to a structure in the New Age movement is the New Age bookstore in town. The danger I see is that evangelicals, having just discovered the New Age a few years ago, may give it new power by making it the enemy.

"I'm concerned about those who are quick to condemn certain programs and ideas as 'New Age.' For example, a lot of New Agers meditate. But to say that Christians should therefore avoid meditation is to deny the Psalms!

"Are there New Agers in Twelve-Step groups? Of course there are! But what are they using? A Christian program! The Twelve Steps are a profoundly *Christian* concept. New Agers in Twelve-Step programs ought to be worried about being 'corrupted' by Christianity, not the other way around!"

On close examination, we find significant differences between the Twelve Steps and New Age philosophy. For example, the gurus of the New Age movement proclaim every individual to be his or her own god, with the ability to tap into the unlimited potential of the self. Step One, however, says, "We admitted we were powerless. . . ." There are similar discrepancies between New Age philosophies and the other eleven Steps. The reason there is such a strong dissonance between New Age philosophies and the Twelve Steps is obvious: Unlike the New Age movement, the Twelve Steps are rooted in biblical Christianity.

Aren't Twelve-Step groups really an addiction in and of themselves? Aren't people in recovery just trading one addiction for another?

Some Christians in the codependency field encourage recovering people to work through their recovery within a limited time frame. Dave Carder told us, "Our goal is to provide a safe place to start the recovery process. We run a two-year program here at First Evangelical Free Church of Fullerton—though that doesn't mean you can't stay longer. Everyone has different needs. Some people will always be vulnerable and may always need a group in order to keep moving toward recovery. But our hope for the average person is that he or she will eventually 'graduate' from the need of a weekly recovery meeting.

"This is where we differ from sobriety groups such as Alcoholics Anonymous. AA says, 'You need to stay in AA to stay sober.' And I've known people in AA who tended to substitute meetings for recovery. They never got beyond sobriety to actually working on the fundamental issues that made them drink in the first place. Our goal is to help people get to a place in life where they don't need to stay in a meeting to stay well.

"We tell our people that once they've had six months of sobriety under their belts, they are probably strong enough to start working on the adult child or inner child issues that prompted them to start drinking in the first place. Sobriety is not our only goal. Recovery is our goal, and sobriety is the initial step in the process toward recovery."

Jane M., contact person for a Christian recovery group in New Jersey, offers another perspective. Several years ago, a woman in her church started a recovery group and asked Sue to attend. Sue was surprised when the woman told her that the group was only scheduled to last twelve weeks.

"What do you do at the end of twelve weeks?" Sue asked.

"Well, then you have it," the woman replied.

"I had been in Overeaters Anonymous for six years," Sue told us, "and I knew I didn't 'have it.' But we did the group for twelve weeks. A few weeks after it ended, the woman started coming to OA. It turned out she didn't 'have it' either."

Whether an injury is physical, emotional, or spiritual, people heal at different rates. Some people may experience sobriety in six months or two years or ten years. And all of us—whether we are recovering from an addiction or just seeking to live the committed Christian life—should be "working the Steps" all of our lives. If that is exchanging one addiction for another, then all we can say is that a lifetime spent living the principles of the Twelve Steps is about the healthiest addiction anyone has ever discovered!

And there is another important consideration: Let's suppose that you have been completely cured of your addictions, and Twelve-Step meetings are no longer necessary. There is *still* a vital reason for you to be involved in a Twelve-Step program: *the opportunity to share Christ through the Twelve-Step process.* As a person who has been through the recovery process with the help of God, you now have a story to tell. You can share your experience, strength, and hope so that others can discover the truth that you've already found: Jesus Christ is the Lord of Recovery.

You've just called the Twelve Steps "the healthiest addiction anyone has ever discovered." Is it ever possible for Twelve-Step groups to become an unhealthy addiction?

Twelve-Step groups are a powerful tool for recovery. However, like any other useful tool (such as a pack of matches or a chainsaw), the tool of the Twelve Steps can be—and has been—misused. The fact that a tool can be misused is no reason to do away with matches, chainsaws, or Twelve-Step groups.

For some people, a recovery group is just another crutch in a collection of crutches. We have seen marriages destroyed by Twelve-Step groups. For example, Helen, a pastor's wife, went into secular psychological counseling and was referred to a secular codependency group. In the process of dealing with her issues, she uncovered a long repressed memory of having been sexually abused as a child. At that point, Helen pushed her husband away. "I don't want to be touched," she told him. "Stay away from me. I don't want to be around you." They were later divorced.

Before going into counseling and the support group, intimacy had not been a major problem for Helen. But after she identified her issues, she reacted in an extreme way. She used her past issues as a defense against having to deal with her present issues. Instead of moving forward, she retreated from true recovery. Occasionally, people use their codependency issues as an excuse to move away from relationships and wholeness.

As Christians in recovery, our focus should not be on taking scabs off old memories and reopening old wounds. Our focus should always be on healed relationships with God and others. Our goal is to live a fully functional life in the here and now.

When we set up Twelve-Step groups in the church, aren't we really bringing worldly psychological principles into the church? Isn't it enough to simply teach the Word of God in our churches?

In secular programs such as AA, the Twelve Steps are a spiritual tool for recovery from addiction. In the hands of Christians, the Twelve Steps also become a vehicle for evangelism and for teaching the Word of God. Though the Steps do not mention Jesus Christ by name, it should be clear that a program that calls for repentance, humility, honesty, confession, restitution, prayer, service, and witnessing could hardly be called "worldly."

In American Christianity, there are many people who mistakenly believe that psychology and the Bible do not mix. At the Clinic, we have a saying: "People are down on what they are not up on." Much of the hostility many Christians feel toward psychology comes from a misunderstanding of both psychology and the Word of God. The truth is that there is a lot of psychology in the Bible. The Psalms, Proverbs, the teachings of Christ, and the New Testament epistles are filled with insight into the workings of the human mind, human emotions, and human relationships.

An understanding of the Bible is our primary basis for understanding what makes people tick. But the Bible does not give us all knowledge on all subjects. Much of the information that we rely upon to live our daily lives comes not from the Bible but from so-called "secular" sources. The physical sciences have revealed fascinating secrets of the universe, from the intricate structure of the atom and of the DNA molecule to the vast scale of the galaxies. Medical science has revealed healing wonders ranging from aspirin and penicillin to artificial hearts and promising new treatments for cancer. The fact that none of this information is found in the Bible does not in any way diminish the value or the authority of God's Word.

Similarly, the sciences of psychology and psychiatry have given us many profound insights into the workings of the human mind and emotions. Christian psychologists and psychiatrists are able to address both the spiritual and emotional needs of people because they start from the firm foundation of biblical knowledge, then add the insights gained through scientific research and clinical experience.

In recent years, a spate of Christian books has condemned the Twelve Steps, the recovery movement, and the entire field of psychology, whether secular or Christian. In a recent best-seller, one well-known pastor complains, "I have no tolerance for those who exalt psychology above Scripture, intercession, and the perfect sufficiency of our God. And I have no encouragement for people who wish to mix psychology with the divine resources and sell the mixture as a spiritual elixir." This pastor expresses little empathy for the very real problems many Christians face. His prescription for every emotional or psychological issue, from abuse to addiction to schizophrenia, is "sharing Scripture and praying with someone."

At the Minirth-Meier Clinic, our theology is biblical and Christ-centered. We emphatically do not place *anything* in authority over the Word of God. But it is clear both from experience *and from Scripture* that "sharing Scripture and praying with someone" does not solve all emotional and spiritual problems. Many people need help from other Christians in order to recover from trauma, emotional disorders, and sin. Those other Christians may be trained practitioners of medicine, psychiatry, and psychology, or they may be fellow strugglers in a support group. But there is a wealth of biblical counsel and practical example to show the validity not only of the Bible and prayer but of mutual support and counseling.

It was the all-sufficient power of God, working through Jesus Christ, that called forth Lazarus from the tomb. But when Lazarus came out of the tomb bound hand and foot by graveclothes, Jesus commanded those around Lazarus to unbind him. This is a powerful analogy of our role in partnership with God as we seek to set free people held captive to addictions and sin. The Lord is the source of all life and power, but he commands us to unbind those who are bound by toxic addictions and toxic emotions.

In 2 Corinthians 1:3–4, Paul tells us that God comforts us in our troubles so that we can be experienced, empathetic comforters to others who are in trouble. This is the foundation of the support-group concept. The ministry of encouraging, counseling, supporting, and confronting one another—which embraces both psychological counseling and the support group concept—is found in such passages as Proverbs 27:17, 1 Corinthians 12:20–26, Galatians 6:1–2, and Hebrews 10:23–25.

In Romans 12:3–8, Paul says that there are many members in the body of Christ, but not all members have the same function. Among the different functions (or spiritual gifts) Paul lists is the gift of "exhortation"—in the original Greek, *paraklesis,* which means to be alongside someone as a comforter and counselor. We believe in the perfect sufficiency of God—but the Scriptures clearly teach that God is at work in the world and in human lives through us, His people—pastors, laypeople, and yes, even Christian psychologists and psychiatrists.

Some years ago, a seminary student was referred to the Minirth-Meier Clinic in Dallas. He was severely depressed and out of touch with reality. He experienced wild delusions and heard nonexistent voices. He was clearly psychotic, and the source of his psychosis was unquestionably a chemical imbalance in the brain. Our doctors knew that if this dopamine imbalance went untreated for more than six months, his psychosis would probably become permanent. If he was treated with the proper dosages of medication, the young man's emotional health would be restored.

Our doctors treated him with the correct medications, and postponed biblical counseling—and for very good reason. Psychotic people are so out of touch with reality that they cannot apply the Bible correctly. After hearing or reading a Scripture passage, they might literally pluck out their eyes or claim to be Moses.

Only a few days after we began treating this seminary student, he regained his grip on reality. Once his medical problem was under control, we began a program of biblically based counseling. The man's own pastor joined with us in the counseling, and together we were able to help this young man relieve his level of stress and repressed anger, which—together with a genetic malfunction—had caused his dopamine levels to become imbalanced. Today this young man is fully recovered. He is a successful, loving, and empathetic pastor.

Just a few months later, we had a very similar case. This

second patient was also a seminary student and like the first, he was psychotic, depressed, delusional, and he was hearing nonexistent voices. Again, the cause of his psychosis was a dopamine imbalance. There was one major difference between his case and the previous case: This second young man's pastor was vehemently opposed to psychiatry. He was convinced the only way to help this young man was to get him out of the clinic and into biblical counseling—which this pastor succeeded in doing.

This second seminary student is still psychotic. He never received the medication that would have saved his sanity. He is in an institution, and he thinks he is a United States senator. All his potential for Christian ministry has been lost because a well-meaning but misguided pastor failed to understand that there are some very important truths that are not found in the Bible—one of which is the truth about medical treatment for people with a chemically-based psychosis.

There is a saying, "All truth is God's truth," and we agree. Every idea which *claims* to be true must be examined through the filter of God's Word. If the claim to truth stands up to the scrutiny of God's Word, then we can use that truth. If the claim contradicts God's Word, then that claim must be rejected. God's Word is the final authority.

This principle is certainly valid with regard to an idea known as the Twelve Steps. In Minirth-Meier books such as *The Path to Serenity, Love Is a Choice, Kids Who Carry Our Pain*, and *We Are Driven*, we have repeatedly examined the Twelve Steps and the claims of the recovery movement according to God's Word. At the Clinic, we have seen God use the Twelve Steps as a powerful instrument to heal broken lives and introduce great numbers of recovering people to Jesus Christ.

There is no question that God is at work through the Twelve-Step recovery movement. The only question is whether we as Christians will obediently respond to what God is doing through Twelve-Step groups, joining in partnership with Him to bring the good news of recovery and eternal life to hurting people—or whether we will turn our backs on this unprecedented opportunity for ministry and evangelism.

What is the role of the pastor in starting and encouraging Twelve-Step groups in the church?

The pastor's role is crucial. The success of Christian support groups depends in large part on the attitudes of the people in the church, and the pastor plays a major role in shaping those attitudes. The task of raising consciousness regarding recovery issues begins with the pastor. If the pastor has an open, empathetic heart for people with addiction issues, his attitude will permeate the congregation. Even in the most supportive congregations, there will always be a few who are critical and negative. A supportive pastor can do a lot to curb such criticism.

One of the hardest things a pastor has to come to terms with regarding Twelve-Step groups is that he has no control over the group. Dave Carder told us, "When you do a program like this, pastors sometimes panic. They feel apprehensive because they're not sure where it's going and how it works and who's in control. The group does not report to the pastor. The pastor isn't welcome to stroll in and observe, as he can in other church programs. The only control the pastor has is in facilitator selection and training and in the selection of recovery literature, curriculum, and in the general rules governing the group.

"Once the group is started, the pastor's control is gone. I know how hard that can be because I'm a pastor myself. But the pastor has to let go of the group. He can't run it. In most cases, he shouldn't even be in the group. If he needs a group where he can deal with his own issues, he probably should go to a group outside the church. He'll feel safer if he does."

While writing this book, we interviewed dozens of people around the country who are involved in Christian Twelve-Step groups. If there was one piece of advice we heard consistently in interview after interview, it was this: "Get the support of the pastor."

So the role of the pastor in encouraging Christian Twelve-Step groups is vital but delicate. His support is necessary, even though his personal presence in the meetings is not recommended. One of the people we interviewed, Don T. of the Agape Christian Overcomers in Kalamazoo, Michigan, summed up the importance of the pastor this way: "I don't know where we'd be without the support and encouragement of the pastoral staff at our church. If the recovery program is going to succeed, the church has to stand behind it and support it.''

Should Christians only attend Christian recovery groups, or should they also attend secular groups such as AA, Al-Anon, and Overeaters Anonymous?

That is a personal choice for each individual to make. In some secular support groups (particularly those which involve issues such as chemical addiction or sexual addiction), the language used is frequently offensive to Christian sensibilities. Many secular meetings are also shrouded in a haze of tobacco smoke, although there are increasing numbers of nonsmoking meetings available. Of course, there are also many secular support groups where there is no more blue air and blue language than at the neighborhood bridge club.

Some Christians are willing to brave the swearing and smoking of some rough-and-tumble support groups in order to make an evangelistic difference. Other Christians may not feel strong enough to go into such an environment. As Johnny Mendell told us, "The language gets very, very rank and it really grinds you down." But if you feel God calling you to that very needy mission field, you should go.

Why is there such a wide gulf between churches and the secular recovery movement?

The rift between churches and the recovery movement goes back beyond the early days of Alcoholics Anonymous. In those days, the disorder of alcoholism was not widely understood. Most churches looked down upon alcoholics as "moral degenerates," and alcoholics in turn wanted nothing to do with the people and institutions that had so harshly judged them and written them off.

This standoff continues today. Most long-time members of AA take the position, "We'll rent the space and use your church building, but we don't want your church people at our meetings. Church people have no more right in our meetings than the landlord has a right to go snooping through his tenant's closets." Many AAs fear that Christians will come into their recovery groups, point fingers, and say, "You rotten people! You lousy bunch of drunks!" They fear that Christians will judge, preach, and fix people, all of which would work against the recovery process and take away the alcoholics' freedom to tell their stories.

"There's a coolness on both sides of the equation," evangelism professor Richard Peace told us. "The secular recovery movement doesn't trust the church and vice versa. But with the pervasiveness of Twelve-Step recovery groups in our culture, it's incumbent upon pastors, churches, and Christians in general to take another look at Twelve-Step groups. We in the church don't need to have outside groups doing Twelve-Step programs. We ought to be doing these programs ourselves. The Twelve Steps are so profoundly Christian that they belong in the church."

We do not want Twelve-Step groups to become churches or to replace the church. Rather, we are trying to bring the biblical principles of the Twelve Steps back into the church where they originated and where they belong.

I'm not involved in Twelve-Step groups, yet I sometimes come in contact with people who are in recovery. What can I do to be a witness to people in recovery, even though I'm not in recovery myself?

People who are working the Twelve Steps are seldom very far from their recovery books and their daily journal. It's their lifeline—like a dialysis machine for someone with kidney disease. They cling to their books and their journal for dear life.

Be on the lookout for people carrying or reading these materials. If you see someone reading The Big Book or other Twelve-Step literature in a hotel lobby, a coffee shop, the student union, or wherever, that's the time to initiate the conversation. God brought you and that person together. If you make the connection, God will provide the spark. People in recovery are very open.

*What is our gospel? What is the message we are supposed to
carry to others? Should we share the gospel in a different way
in the Twelve-Step process than we would in any other setting?*

Whether we share Jesus Christ in a Twelve-Step sponsoring
relationship or with a needy stranger in an airport or at the
kitchen table over a cup of coffee, our gospel is the same—and it
is very simple. When you sense an opportunity to share the gospel with someone, the message you share can be as basic as this:

"To receive God's forgiveness in your life, you first admit
that you are a sinner and that you have done wrong." For scriptural support, you may share Romans 3:23 with that person.
"Second, recognize that Jesus Christ, the Son of God, died on
the cross in payment for your sins." Refer to Romans 6:23. "Finally, trust Jesus Christ as your Savior and Lord of your life."
Share John 1:12. "Would you like to express your commitment
to Jesus Christ in a prayer? If so, you can say these words with
me:

> Lord Jesus,
> I invite you into my life.
> I confess that I am a sinner.
> I thank you for dying for me.
> I ask you to take control of my life.
> I trust you as my Savior."

As we've noted in earlier chapters, not everyone who is a
Christian actually has a single moment to point to as the exact
instant of conversion. For some, becoming a Christian was a
gradual process of faith and spiritual growth. But whenever there
is an opportunity to help a spiritually seeking person make a
conscious, deliberate decision for Christ, as outlined above, we
help to give solidity and definition to that person's faith.

Sharron G. of Oklahoma shared with us how she has been
able to creatively marry two different evangelistic approaches
together—the Twelve-Step process and Evangelism Explosion.
"I went through the Evangelism Explosion training at our
church," she said, "and then we went out in teams to call on
people in their homes and share the gospel. These were people

who had visited our church and filled out visitor cards. There were many occasions in our EE calls—I'd say about a third of the time—that the people we called on had experienced problems with alcohol or drugs, either at that time or in the past. So I was able to share that part of my life, and how God had helped me through the Twelve Steps. Then I shared the EE presentation and led many of them to Jesus."

After these people made a commitment to Christ, the Christian Twelve-Step group became a vehicle for follow-up and a setting where discipleship could take place. "A lot of these new converts were a little reluctant to go into a Sunday school class," Sharron told us, "because they didn't feel they fit in yet. But they feel perfectly at home in a Christian Twelve-Step group in the church. It's exciting to see the spiritual growth that is taking place in many of these lives." This is a beautiful example of how we as Christians can adapt ourselves and our gospel to any given situation, and in the process bring needy people into a life-changing encounter with Jesus Christ.

At the Minirth-Meier Clinic, we stand on John 14:6, which says that Jesus is *the* Way, *the* Truth, and *the* Life. There is no other way. Alcoholics Anonymous is not the way. The Twelve Steps are not the way.

Jesus Christ is the *only* Way.

CHAPTER 11

I HAD RATHER BE A DOORKEEPER

A Challenge to Each of Us

"You asked about my medal. I haven't told the story of it to anyone, and you will see why, when you hear about it. I am not very proud of it, for I didn't deserve it; and yet there isn't a thing I can do about it, without revealing a story that cannot be told just now, for it would get my new friends into trouble. . . . You may tell the story as long as my name is never attached to it."

This is the beginning of a letter that an American GI, who was stationed in the Pacific during World War II, wrote to his pastor in New Jersey. The letter was reprinted in Sam Shoemaker's book, *Faith at Work*.

Tomorrow I go off to the battlefield: I may never get home again, and I want someone to know that I don't deserve that medal. I didn't earn it, and I shouldn't have it. It happened this way:

I was captured by the Japanese with five of my pals. We were marched along through the jungles, with bayonets in our backs. As we marched along toward the Japanese camp, I had to see my comrades one by one killed, mutilated, and torn limb from limb. They were men with whom I had spent three years—not three years of casual friendship either. When you live with men, night and day, winter and summer, when you work with them, suffer with them, fight with them, you become attached to them more closely then you'll ever become with any other man the rest of your life. As I watched them fall, I knew that within a few minutes I, too, would be killed as they had been. But, somehow, at that moment, my only thought was, the sooner the better. Life for me was over.

I said the Twenty-third Psalm. (Do you remember the time you made me come back to church for a whole afternoon to learn it because you insisted that I learn my Bible?) I said the Lord's Prayer, and then I started to think things over. A good bit of the Yankee spirit stayed with me. Die I must, but I determined not to let my captor see my fear. Trembling from head to foot, marching in mud up to my ankles, with a bayonet sticking in my back, I began to whistle the way I used to when I was a small boy and had to go through a dark street. So I whistled as loud as my trembling lips would let me.

After a while, to my surprise, I realized that I was whistling a hymn that we used to sing, "We gather together to ask the Lord's blessing . . ."

Well, as I whistled it over and over, I did think of our church and the various individuals in it. I realized for the first time how much the church had. It had molded my character and given me the stuff to be able to take what the Army gave me, and take it knowing I was not alone—that God was with me. I thought how the church stood for eternal life. At any moment now, I, too, would be dying. That sharp point at my back would start me on the journey to eternity. But, now, I was no longer afraid. Were my five friends whom I had seen killed in heaven now? Would they welcome me soon?

Suddenly, from my reverie, I became aware that someone had joined me in whistling. No, it couldn't be, but it was—my Japanese captor! He, too, was whistling the hymn. Soon we both broke into words, he in Japanese and I in English: "The wicked oppressing, now cease from distressing. . . . He forgets not His own."

One after the other were the hymns we whistled and sang, as we marched through the jungle mud, with me in the front and my captor in the rear, with his gun at my back. Gradually, the power of the hymn made me relax, and it must have had the same effect on him, for soon I felt his gun fall into place. And, still later, he caught up with me, and we sang, he in Japanese and I in English.

I wondered if his thoughts were as mingled as mine. Here we were, marching along, lifting our hearts in unison in Christian praise to a Christian God of Peace, and yet I was being led to the slaughter by him.

I was interrupted in my thinking by his words in perfect English: "I never cease to wonder at the magnificence of Christian hymns." Startled by his English, I jumped and we both laughed. Soon we were talking. I asked where he learned to speak English, and he replied that he had gone to Christian mission schools.

"Not Glory Kindergarten?" I asked.

"Why, I started in Glory Kindergarten. How do you know it?"

Then I told him how, in Sunday school, we had studied about Congregational schools and churches. We had raised money for Glory Kindergarten and had sent over gifts for it. I spoke of the gift of the picture we sent and the letters we had back from the teachers. He remembered the picture and added that, when the picture was presented, he had helped fix the flowers for the Japanese beauty-corner where the picture was placed. Then followed a conversation that it is impossible to relate—one that few men have ever had with one another—when surface things are swept away and the soul stands out on top.

We talked of war and how the Japanese Christians hate it, of Christianity and its power in the world, of what it would mean if people should ever dare really to live it, of the incomparable value of the missionaries, of Kagawa, of our own ideals for our own homes, our jobs, and our future families. And, finally, at his suggestion, we knelt in the mud and prayed for suffering humanity around the world, for His peace "that passeth all understanding," and for peace again on earth and goodwill toward men.

When we arose, *he asked if I would take him back as a prisoner to the American headquarters!* He said this was the only way he could live up to his Christianity and thus help Japan to become a Christian nation. And, on our way back, he found in various foxholes other Japanese Christians and they too joined me as we walked toward the American headquarters.

I shall never forget the hope and joy that came into their eyes, as my Japanese friend unfolded to them, one by one, as he met them, how we found each other, and where and why they were being taken. All the way back we talked of the Christian religion.

You know, after being born into Christianity, I had taken its teachings for granted. I never shall again. I know now from these Japanese friends what Christ can mean to an individual or a nation that has lived under a hideous system of heathen gods. I know that it means the difference between Japanese atrocities and my own Japanese friends with their high Christian ideals.

When we neared camp, by mutual agreement, they put on poker faces and somber looks, and I, gun in hand, marched them into their prison camp. After the war is over, they will spend their lives keeping alive and spreading an ever-growing Christian community.

So you see I don't deserve a medal for the most wonderful experience of my life.[1]

Heathen Gods

Why should we share Christ through the Twelve-Step process? Why do we need the Twelve Steps?

Sam Shoemaker said in *Christ and This Crisis*, which was written in the midst of World War II, "We are fighting for the re-Christianization of a de-Christianized nation. If America is to accept the place of leadership in the world of the future which events seem to be asking her to take, something must happen to the soul of America that has not happened."[2]

And eleven years later Shoemaker challenged the church again: "It looks as though our world, in the next twenty-five years, would go either way up, or way down. Which way depends, frankly and almost totally, upon whether we can so put ourselves at God's disposal that He can bring to the world, through people like ourselves, the thing which it needs most. We cannot doubt either His power, or His willingness: any blockage must be on our side. If all of us will try to get the ways open to Him, and become His agents and His instruments, we may make possible that flooding down of God's free and plentiful Grace which is, among all our human needs, the sorest need of our time and our world."[3]

Many Christians believe that our world has missed the mark. It has gone down, rather than up, since Sam Shoemaker gave us that challenge in 1948. And since Shoemaker felt that the rise or fall of our world depended upon Christians, we must acknowledge that the church—and more particularly each one of us—has missed the mark.

In this book, we have shared with you just a handful of the stories we have heard of people whose lives have been turned toward Jesus Christ as a result of the Twelve-Step process. We

began with stories from the 1930s and '40s and '50s—the movement of the Holy Spirit among alcoholics and church members
and the country club. We told the stories of people in recovery
and support groups in our own era. In secular Twelve-Step
programs such as AA and Al-Anon, many people (like Scott and
Darcy Jennings in Chapter 5) have been set on a spiritual journey
which has led to Jesus Christ. Others have been brought back to
a previously abandoned faith by working the Twelve Steps in
secular programs. The secular programs are not *designed* to bring
people to faith in Jesus Christ, but because of God's grace and
the biblical origins of the Twelve Steps, many people happily do.
Unfortunately some secular programs interpret "God as we understand Him" from an increasingly meaningless (and even New
Age) perspective. The words of that anonymous GI should
haunt us: "I had taken [Christian] teachings for granted. I never
shall again. I know now . . . what Christ can mean to an individual or a nation that has lived under a hideous system of heathen gods." As we look around us at the cults and New Age
deceptions that are sweeping so many souls into their nets, we
have to admit that our own society is rapidly becoming "a hideous system of heathen gods." People in recovery are hungry
for real spiritual power to plug into. They long for a Higher
Power with a name and a face. Some, like Scott and Darcy Jennings, will find the God they are searching for. Others may come
under the control of "heathen gods."

Evangelical Christians, concerned about those who are lost
without Jesus Christ, cannot be content with the fact that a for-
tunate few will beat the odds and discover Jesus Christ in their
secular support groups. There is so much more we can do to
reach those who wander in confusion and darkness, searching for
the "Unknown God." There is so much more that we can do in
an intentional, purposeful way to enable recovering people to
move from a "Higher Power" to the Highest Power of All.

"I Had Rather Be a Doorkeeper . . ."

Sam Shoemaker summed up the Twelve-Step process in the
ending stanzas of his poem, *I Stand by the Door*, the apologia for
his life:

Go in, great saints, go all the way in—
Go way down into the cavernous cellars,
And way up into the spacious attics—
It is a vast, roomy house, this house where God is.
Go into the deepest of hidden casements,
Of withdrawal, of silence, of sainthood.
Some must inhabit those inner rooms,
And know the depths and heights of God,
And call outside to the rest of us how wonderful it is.
Sometimes I take a deeper look in,
Sometimes venture in a little farther;
But my place seems closer to the opening. . . .
So I stand by the door.

I admire the people who go way in.
But I wish they would not forget how it was
Before they got in. Then they would be able to help
The people who have not yet even found the door,
Or the people who want to run away again from God.
You can go in too deeply, and stay in too long,
And forget the people outside the door.
As for me, I shall take my old accustomed place,
Near enough to God to hear Him, and know He is there,
But not so far from men as not to hear them,
And remember they are there, too.
Where? Outside the door—
Thousands of them, millions of them.
But—more important for me—
One of them, two of them, ten of them,
Whose hands I am intended to put on the latch.
So I shall stand by the door and wait
For those who seek it.
"I had rather be a doorkeeper . . ."
So I stand by the door.

PART 3

ESTABLISHING A SUPPORT GROUP OR RECOVERY GROUP IN YOUR CHURCH

CHAPTER

RECOVERY GROUP PROGRAM RESOURCES

From First Evangelical Free Church, Fullerton, California

A generation ago, Christians weren't allowed to bring their real problems and hurts into the church. Depression, marital stress, chemical dependency, and other issues of dysfunctionalism could not be openly named in church. The problems were there, all right, as evidenced by all the "undesignated" or "unspoken" prayer requests hesitantly voiced at Wednesday-night prayer meetings.

Today, however, these issues can be confronted honestly, in an atmosphere of caring, within the context of Christian recovery groups and support groups. It's not that the church has invented something new. Rather, the church is rediscovering the support group dynamic that has been a feature of healthy church life ever since the days of the New Testament.

In 1981, a program of support groups and recovery groups was started at First Evangelical Free Church of Fullerton, California. It began with one group and has grown into an array of ministries involving more than 1,500 people.

Some of these people are new parents, seeking recovery from the parenting they received, along with help in building stable, functional homes for their own children. Some have alcohol and drug addictions. Some come for support as they grieve the loss of a marriage or a loved one. Some are struggling with teens in crisis. All are reaching out to find a surrogate family system that shares their hurt and their life experiences—a place where they can be nurtured and reparented by a loving God.

Some of these groups are "open"—that is, individuals are free to come, participate in the group, and leave as they please. In this sense, the groups are much like the original recovery groups of Alcoholics Anonymous. Open groups are good for people who are at an early stage in the recovery process, who feel apprehensive or uncertain about the process, or who need additional, immediate support for a time of crisis.

Other groups are "closed." They require registration and have a fixed membership and fixed number of weeks they meet (usually twelve to twenty-eight weeks). The advantage of closed groups is that a fixed membership creates a bond of trust and enables members to feel safe. Closed groups encourage a level of intimacy and vulnerability that can be very healing for people in recovery.

The following pages will give you a behind-the-scenes look at how the program operates at First Evangelical Free Church of Fullerton—the kinds of groups we have, how they are structured, how they function, and how we prepare our facilitators. You will see the letter we send to all inquirers and newcomers; the study guides we use in our open groups; and the materials we use to train our facilitators.

We have a saying in our program: "Every man is responsible for his own recovery. Every woman is responsible for her own recovery. No one is going to do it for you." As people take responsibility for their own lives, their own choices, and their own recovery, healing takes place. We have seen this principle in action in the lives of hundreds of people.

My prayer, and the prayer of my coauthors, is that you will

use and adapt these materials and ideas to your own group, and that by God's grace you will see this same healing take place in your own life and your own church.

DAVE CARDER

New Hope Introductory Brochure

THIS BROCHURE is given to individuals who enter the New Hope program, one of a number of recovery programs at First Evangelical Free Church of Fullerton. The New Hope program is comprised of a number of individual groups meeting on different days of the week and focuses on the issues of adult children of alcoholics. Other programs at First Evangelical Free Church of Fullerton include Liontamers Anonymous for people with a chemical dependency, Psalm 139 for people with physical handicaps, Vista for victims of incest, Temple Builders for people with eating disorders.

Welcome to New Hope

You are not alone. One estimate says there are approximately 40 million adult children of alcoholics in the USA today, and even more people are recognizing that they grew up in a dysfunctional home, even though alcohol was not a problem.

Robert Subby in *Lost in the Shuffle* said there are roughly four types of troubled family systems that seem to stand out as prime breeding grounds for codependency:

1. Alcoholism, chemical dependency, and other compulsive behaviors
2. The emotionally or psychologically disturbed family systems
3. The physically abusive and sexually abusive family systems
4. The fundamentalistic or rigid dogmatic family systems

In our family of origin we did not feel safe to share our feelings. We learned that there were certain things we were not to talk about and found it difficult believing that anyone could accept us just the way we were or be there for us when we needed them. We found ourselves living by three unwritten rules: "Don't talk; don't trust; don't feel."[1]

We trust you'll find New Hope to be a safe place where: 1) you can talk about what you need to talk about; 2) let yourself feel your emotions; and in the process, 3) discover that there really are people whom you can trust.

God has provided us with many options to avail ourselves of in our recovery process. New Hope is only *one* of the options. There are Bible studies, therapy groups, books, tapes, Christian counselors, and seminars that you may also find helpful.

We encourage you to come for at least six weeks before you make a decision whether or not this group is for you. The journey is not an easy one and there may be times when you'll be tempted to give up. During those times you may find it helpful to talk with someone about your thoughts and feelings.

Stay with it. *There is hope for you!*

"Now may the God of hope fill you with all joy and peace in believing, that you may abound in hope by the power of the Holy Spirit." Romans 15:13

Based on the acrostic HOPE, the objectives of the group are:

H—Healing of painful childhood memories.

He heals the brokenhearted
And binds up their wounds.
Psalm 147:3

"For I will restore health to you
and heal you of your wounds," says the LORD,
"Because they called you an outcast."
Jeremiah 30:17

O—Open sharing of feelings and emotions.

> Rejoice with those who rejoice, and weep with those
> who weep.
> Romans 12:15

P—Prayer.

> Confess your trespasses to one another, and pray for
> one another, that you may be healed. The effective,
> fervent prayer of a righteous man avails much.
> James 5:16

> The LORD is near to all who call upon Him,
> To all who call upon Him in truth.
> Psalm 145:18

**E—Encouragement toward growth and responsible living
and a feeling of self worth based upon God's love.**

> Therefore comfort each other and edify one another,
> just as you also are doing.
> 1 Thessalonians 5:11

> But, speaking the truth in love, [we are to] grow up
> in all things into Him who is the head—Christ.
> Ephesians 4:15

NEWCOMERS	**VIDEO**	3 Weeks
	ROLES, RULES, BIRTH ORDER	3 Weeks
OPEN GROUPS	**CHARACTERISTICS**	Open
	CHARACTERISTICS	13 or 15 Weeks
CLOSED GROUPS	**CHARACTERISTICS**	13 or 15 Weeks
	WORKBOOKS	13, 24, or 28 Weeks
	ANY GROUP and/or **FACILITATOR**	Repeat

Video

The New Hope video is divided into three segments and serves as an introduction to what our program is about. New Hope members share from their own experience and Pastor Dave Carder explains how God is in the process all the way.

Roles, Rules, Birth Order

These three weeks provide the newcomer an opportunity to discuss some of the roles and unwritten rules of alcoholic/dysfunctional families and to identify different characteristics that are often associated with a person's birth order.

Open Group Characteristics Study

Open groups are for anybody and do not require a commitment of consistent attendance. The fifteen characteristics of adult children of alcoholic/dysfunctional families from *The Twelve Steps: A Spiritual Journey* (San Diego: Recovery Publications) are discussed. We have developed study guides for each characteristic that include questions for group discussion and relevant Scripture passages for personal reflection at home.

Closed Group Characteristic Study

Closed groups are limited to an agreed-upon number of people who decide to commit themselves to working together for a specified period of time. Groups have a choice of using either the same list used in open groups or a list of thirteen characteristics from *Adult Children of Alcoholics*, by Janet G. Woititz.

Closed Group Workbook

We are currently using two workbooks in our groups. Many people find *When I Grow Up I Want to Be an Adult* (thirteen weeks) a good study to work through as preparation for *The Twelve Steps: A Spiritual Journey* (twenty-eight weeks). Both are published by Recovery Publications.

Discussion Groups

Occasionally, we will offer a closed Twelve-Step discussion group for those between the two workbooks (thirteen weeks).

Couples Group

We have a group for married couples, which goes through the workbook *God, Where Is Love,* by Clair W. Participants need to have been through at least twenty weeks of New Hope and have an interview with the facilitators in order to join (thirteen weeks).

Volunteers

The New Hope program functions because of the support of volunteers. It is their help that enables New Hope to continue being a safe place to recover. Everyone counts!

Facilitator Training

A facilitator is not a therapist, nor is he/she a teacher. A facilitator is not one who has "arrived" and pretends to have it all together. A facilitator is a fellow traveler who continues to work his/her own recovery and helps keep the group a safe place. We encourage people as part of their Twelfth Step to consider becoming facilitators and giving back to the group something of what they have received.

Criteria to be a Facilitator:

1. You must have participated in New Hope for at least twenty weeks.
2. You need to be participating in a group presently.
3. Training either takes place before the regular New Hope meeting or on a Saturday morning.
4. You may facilitate up to the level at which you have been a participant.

New Hope Support Group
"A Miracle in Process"

The Problem

We took on the behavior patterns of the alcoholic disease and/or dysfunctional family early in childhood and carried them into adulthood. Even though we may never take a drink ourselves, we have acquired unhealthy ways of relating with others that have given us difficulty, especially in intimate relationships.

We have stuffed many of our feelings from our traumatic childhood and have difficulty feeling or expressing our emotions because it hurts so much. Our comfortable feelings, such as joy or happiness, can also be difficult to express. Our being out of touch with our feelings is the larger part of our denial. We have learned in our dysfunctional families the three unwritten rules: "Don't talk; don't trust; don't feel," and are still unknowingly living by those rules today.

We often feel isolated and afraid of people and authority figures. Angry people and personal criticism frighten us. Some of us take on compulsive behaviors ourselves or marry a compulsive person and try to fix them, or both.

Many of us live life as victims and are attracted by weakness in our love, friendships, and career relationships.

We are terrified of abandonment and will do almost anything to hold on to a relationship rather than experience the painful feelings of being abandoned. We received this from living within an alcoholic/dysfunctional environment where no one was emotionally "there" for us.

This is a description, not an accusation. We have learned to survive by becoming reactors rather than actors. What we have learned, we can unlearn in the Solution.

The Solution

In the Solution we learn that even though our parents gave us our physical existence, we can now look to God, our Heavenly Father, as the initiator of our new life. We look to Him to lead us to a new level of experience and to give us direction toward a life of wholeness and healing of the past. We learn we do not have to remain prisoners of our past.

Recovery starts when we begin to learn about the disease. We learn that it is three-fold: we didn't cause it; we can't control it; we can't cure it. By becoming educated about the disease, we begin a process that eventually leads us to forgive our parents and to release them to God. We learn to focus on ourselves in the here and now and to detach from our obsession with the alcoholic/dysfunctional person. We learn to love ourselves and others, even though this may sometimes take the form of "tough love."

We experience new freedom as we find there are people we can begin to trust. We learn to allow ourselves to feel our feelings, and then to express them. We learn that in Christ, we are accepted. With God's help and the Twelve Steps based on Scriptures, we can begin to recover from our dysfunctional past, turn our lives in a new direction, and be freed from the shame that has bound us.

Rules for Small Discussion Groups

1. While others are talking, please let them finish without interruption.
2. No fixing—we are to listen, to support, and be supported by each other in the group, not to give advice. Please save any questions you might have until after the group is dismissed.
3. Speak in the "I" form instead of "we," "they," or "you." This helps us take responsibility for our feelings and accept them as being valid. For example:
   "I believe . . ." rather than "They say . . ."
   "I felt angry that . . ." rather than "She made me so angry . . ."
   "I think . . ." rather than "Don't you think . . ."
   "I felt hurt when . . ." rather than "He hurt my feelings . . ."
4. Keep sharing to no more than 5 minutes in order that others in the group will be able to share.
5. Try to share from the heart as honestly as you can. It is OK to

cry, laugh, and be angry in the group; there will be no condemnation from others.

6. What is shared and who you see in the group is to stay in the
   group and not to be shared with anyone else.

New Hope
Inquirer Letter

THIS LETTER is sent to all individuals who inquire into the New Hope program for adult children of alcoholics. It explains each phase of the recovery group program—how long each phase lasts, what takes place in the groups, what sorts of resources are used. Similar letters are sent to those who inquire into Liontamers Anonymous, Vista, Temple Builders, and other recovery programs at First Evangelical Free Church of Fullerton, California.

Dear Inquirer:

The following is a description of our New Hope program. New Hope is our group for adult children of alcoholics and other dysfunctional families.

You may find it helpful to open the New Hope pamphlet to page 6 as you read about how we operate.

New Hope meets for an hour and a half once a week. We have both a Friday morning and a Tuesday evening group. The first twenty-five minutes are spent reading the Problem, the Solution, announcements, and a testimonial.

Opening Session:

The meeting starts with a person reading the *New Hope Guidelines for Large Group Leader*. We have a copy of the Serenity Prayer written in large print on a board for everyone to read together. After the *Problem* and the *Solution* (pages 8 and 9, NH pamphlet) have been read, someone gives his/her testimony. All of this takes place with everyone together.

After the big meeting, the group is divided into newcomers, characteristic groups, and workbook groups.

Newcomers

A person is considered a newcomer the first six weeks. The first three weeks we show a segment of the New Hope video. We then divide the people into groups of about ten each and have them discuss a question or two about what they have just seen. At the end of these sessions, some time is allowed to answer questions about the program.

Weeks 4, 5, and 6 are used to discuss *Roles, Rules,* and *Birth Order*. We cover one topic each week.

Open Characteristic Groups

After completion of weeks 4, 5, and 6 people may join an open characteristic group. We have these groups because of the number of people that come, our limited space, and the limited number of available facilitators. We use a different list of characteristics in these open groups than we do in the closed groups. This allows for less repetition. We have developed a study guide which provides some structure for those groups desiring it.

Closed Characteristic Groups

As space and facilitators become available, we form closed groups out of these open ones. An announcement is made in the big meeting and a sign-up sheet is made available for those that are interested. Some people make the mistake of thinking they cannot seriously start working on their recovery until they get into a closed group. We have found that this is *not* the case.

Closed Workbook Groups

The next step after going through the characteristics is a workbook study. People may choose between two different workbooks, but many find *When I Grow Up I Want to Be an Adult* a good preparation for the Twelve-Step workbook. The Twelve-Step book is set up for twenty-eight weeks, but some groups shorten it to sixteen weeks.

Facilitator Training

It is our hope that, at some time in their recovery, people will want to give back some of what they have received by becoming a facilitator. This is a fulfillment of 1 Corinthians 1:3–4 and Step 12. We have a self-help training manual and a video series we use in our training program. The bulk of our training centers around teaching listening and responding skills and ways of keeping the group a safe place to share. We offer the training and then allow people to decide if they will facilitate after they have been trained and have seen what is involved. We have a separate group for current facilitators, so they can share a meal, fellowship, and process some of their issues together. We want facilitators to continue working on their own recovery in the groups they facilitate, but this gives them an extra opportunity to deal with personal issues or problems they may be having in their groups. The group ends with a time of prayer for the New Hope meeting.

Once a year we also have a retreat for the facilitators. The church covers the cost as a way of saying thank you for their help.

Materials

You will notice a bibliography listed in the back of the New Hope pamphlet. There are a number of materials in the secular market we have found helpful, but as with anything (Christian or secular), they need to be read with discernment.

Miscellaneous

Outside speakers: Approximately once a quarter we will have a special speaker come in and speak for part or all of the opening session on some relevant topic.

Refreshments: We have hot coffee, tea, and cookies available at every meeting. An offering basket is placed on the table to help defray costs.

Book table: We sell related books and tapes before and after the meeting. We get a discount at a local Christian bookstore and pass the savings on to our people.

Council

The New Hope council consists of five volunteers who divide up the responsibilities of ordering materials, set up and clean up, refreshments, testimonies and greeters, handling the money, and the book table. The council members serve for thirteen weeks.

Hopefully, this will answer most of the questions you may have. Feel free to change the format to meet your needs. The enclosed New Hope pamphlet is complimentary. For further copies please send $1.00 to help us cover postage and printing. You may reproduce any of our materials for your group. We only ask that you give appropriate credits on the materials.

God bless you in your new endeavor. If you start a group, please let us know so we can include it in the next update of the national list of Christian ACA groups!

In Christ,
The New Hope Leadership Team

Guidelines for Large Group Facilitator

This sheet serves as the guide for the individual who volunteers or is asked to lead the Big Meeting for the first 20-30 minutes of New Hope. The sheet is laminated in plastic so the same copy can be used over and over with the different large group leaders. The leader is also responsible for finding two other individuals to read the problem and the solution. Finally, the group leader either shares his/her testimony or calls on the individual who has agreed to do so beforehand. The necessary announcements are given at the end of the Big Meeting while the offering is being taken.

Facilitator reads the following:

1. Hi, my name is _____. This is the regular meeting of New Hope, our support group for adult children of alcoholics and those who were raised in dysfunctional homes. We hope you will find this is a safe place where, together, we can finally shed our denial and our defenses and learn to admit to ourselves and others how hurt, angry, and wounded we have felt as a result of growing up in a dysfunctional and/or alcoholic household. Admit it . . . experience it . . . and release it to God through prayer, meditation on His Word, and open and honest sharing with one another.

2. Please stand and repeat the Serenity Prayer with me.

> God, grant me the serenity to accept
> the things I cannot change, the courage
> to change the things I can, and the
> wisdom to know the difference.

3. Read the Problem and the Solution.

4. We hope you have identified with the Problem and have an open mind about working, one day at a time, toward the Solu-

tion. It takes time. Please be very patient with yourself and with us. If you are a member of another Twelve-Step program, you will find this another way to focus on the same suggested Steps.

We have found that it takes a minimum of six meetings in a row to start coming out of denial. We encourage you to try this, let God lift you up, and let us support you. This program is not easy, but it works if you stay with it and are willing to work toward inner growth.

Facilitator may now share his/her testimony for ten minutes. Please try to present your story about growing up in an alcoholic and/or dysfunctional family, giving group members an idea of the strength/growth you've achieved so far, as a result of this program. Leave them with a sense of hope and encouragement. Be sure to let them know why New Hope is important to you and how you think it will benefit others through their participation.

Open Group Study Guides*

Dear Friend:

This New Hope Study Guide has been created to help facilitate personal reflection and group discussion in our open groups. Not all of our groups use the discussion questions. Some just read the common characteristics and have open discussion. Those desiring more structure use the questions. Every week we hand out one characteristic to each person and just repeat the process every fifteen weeks.

The Scripture passages are for personal reflection at home. The fifteen common characteristics are taken from *The Twelve Steps: A Spiritual Journey* (San Diego: Recovery Publications). Thank you,

The New Hope Leadership Team

NEW HOPE Common Characteristic #1:

"We have feelings of low self-esteem that cause us to judge ourselves and others without mercy. We try to cover up or compensate by being perfectionistic, caretaking, controlling, contemptuous and gossipy."

Related Scripture (For personal use)

Psalm 103:8–14
Isaiah 46:4
1 John 3:1

1. Do you find that you tend to be hard on yourself?
2. Do you struggle with feelings of low self esteem? If so, how?
3. Share a time in your childhood when you felt worthless.
4. How about a recent time?

* This study guide was originally developed by Dave Osborne for use in New Hope.

5. Do you ever find yourself being perfectionistic, caretaking, controlling, contemptuous, or gossipy? If so, how does it affect your relationships?

NEW HOPE Common Characteristic #2:

"We tend to isolate ourselves and to feel uneasy around other people, especially authority figures."

Related Scripture (For personal use)
Psalm 25:16
Psalm 56:9b
Psalm 68:5, 6
Hebrews 4:15–16

1. Did you tend to isolate yourself as a child? Do you still have that tendency?
2. How did you feel in relationship to authority figures as a child?
3. How do you respond to authority figures today?
4. What kind of connection can you see between your perception of authority figures and your perception of God?

NEW HOPE Common Characteristic #3:

"We are approval seekers and will do anything to make people like us. We are extremely loyal even in the face of evidence that indicates loyalty is undeserved."

Related Scripture (For personal use)
2 Corinthians 3:5
1 Thessalonians 2:4
Ephesians 2:8, 9

1. How did you seek approval as a child?
2. What do you find yourself doing now to try to make people like you?
3. Have you ever or do you currently find yourself still compromising your values in order to keep someone's approval? If so, how?

4. Do you find yourself remaining overly loyal today when perhaps the loyalty is undeserved?

NEW HOPE Common Characteristic #4:

"We are intimidated by angry people and personal criticism. This causes us to feel anxious and overly sensitive."

Related Scripture (For personal use)
    Psalms 69, 70 and 71
    Psalm 145:8
    Psalm 147:3

1. Who was the angriest person in your home growing up? What did you fear when they got angry?
2. How do you respond when you are criticized? Do you tend to launch a defensive attack, withdraw, ignore, or minimize the situation?
3. How do your responses to angry or critical people affect your relationship with them?
4. Who are the angry and critical people you struggle with now?
5. How do you respond to yourself when you are angry or critical?

NEW HOPE Common Characteristic #5:

"We habitually choose to have relationships with emotionally unavailable people with addictive personalities. We are usually less attracted to healthy, caring people."

Related Scripture (For personal use)
    Psalm 146:5–10
    Matthew 11:28–30
    Hebrews 2:18

1. When you were a child, how did people in your family respond when you cried or got angry?
2. How do you feel about yourself when you cry or get angry?
3. Do you find yourself choosing relationships with people who are emotionally unavailable?

4. What do you think you need from a person in order to feel that they are "emotionally there" for you?

NEW HOPE Common Characteristic #6:

"We live life as victims and are attracted to other victims in our love and friendship relationships. We confuse love with pity and tend to 'love' people we can pity and rescue."

Related Scripture (For personal use)
Psalms 9 and 13
Psalm 25:16–22
Psalm 35:10

1. Do you find yourself attracted to people you can help?
2. Can you share a time when you had a difficult time determining love from pity and rescue?
3. Was there anybody you tried so hard to help when you were a child?
4. Share a time you felt like a victim.

NEW HOPE Common Characteristic #7:

"We are either super-responsible or super-irresponsible. We try to solve others' problems or expect others to be responsible for us. This enables us to avoid looking closely at our own behavior."

Related Scripture (For personal use)
Psalm 51
Psalm 139:23, 24

1. As a child did you see yourself as being super-responsible, super-irresponsible, or perhaps a combination of both?
2. How do you see yourself today?
3. Has being super-responsible or super-irresponsible kept you from looking closely at your own behavior?
4. Do you have difficulty determining what you are responsible for and what you are not responsible for?

NEW HOPE Common Characteristic #8:

"We feel guilty when we stand up for ourselves or act assertively. We give in to others instead of taking care of ourselves."

Related Scripture (For personal use)
    Proverbs 4:23
    1 Corinthians 6:19, 20
    3 John 9, 10

1. Were you ever put down for acting assertively when you were growing up? If so, how did you feel when it happened?
2. How do you feel now when you say no to someone?
3. Do you ever find yourself taking care of others and neglecting yourself?
4. How have you been neglecting yourself?

NEW HOPE Common Characteristic #9:

"We deny, minimize or repress our feelings from our traumatic childhoods. We lose the ability to express our feelings and are unaware of the impact this has on our lives."

Related Scripture (For personal use)
    Matthew 26:36–44
    Mark 3:5
    John 11:35
    Hebrews 5:7–9

1. What feeling do you have the most difficulty expressing?
2. What is it you fear would happen if you let yourself freely express that feeling?
3. Who do you feel safe with in expressing your deepest hurts?
4. Some people deny their pain by using a substance or some compulsive behavior pattern. Others make everything funny, get depressed, get angry, try to help others, spiritualize, stay very busy. How do you keep yourself from feeling your pain?

NEW HOPE Common Characteristic #10:

"We are dependent personalities who are terrified of rejection or abandonment. We tend to stay in jobs or relationships that are harmful to us. Our fears can either stop us from ending hurtful relationships or prevent us from entering into healthy, rewarding ones."

Related Scripture (For personal use)
    Deuteronomy 31:6
    Psalm 27:10
    Psalm 56:3

1. Is there a job, relationship, or any situation you realize is harmful to you now but you continue to subject yourself to?
2. Share a time when you felt rejected or abandoned and what that was like for you.
3. What was your greatest fear as a child?
4. What is your greatest fear today?

NEW HOPE Common Characteristic #11:

"Denial, isolation, control, and misplaced guilt are symptoms of family dysfunction. As a result of these behaviors, we feel hopeless and helpless."

Related Scripture (For personal use)
    Proverbs 14:8
    Romans 5:8
    Romans 8:1
    2 Corinthians 7:6
    Galatians 6:2
    1 John 1:9

1. Some people distinguish between guilt (I've done something wrong) and shame (I am what is wrong). In your family was there a distinction or were you equated with your behavior?
2. What were you shamed for when you were a child?
3. What do you still feel guilty about today?

4. How would your life change if you were no longer bound by guilt and shame?

NEW HOPE Common Characteristic #12:

"We have difficulty with intimate relationships. We feel insecure and lack trust in others. We don't have clearly defined boundaries and become enmeshed with our partner's needs and emotions."

Related Scripture (For personal use)
Psalm 41:9
Psalm 139:1–18

1. Share an experience as a child when you trusted someone and felt that they let you down.
2. What about yourself makes you feel insecure?
3. If we don't bond with people we may find something else to try and bond with. This could be a job, sport, hobby, pet, computer. What do you substitute for intimate relationships?
4. What boundaries are easy for you to maintain and which are more difficult?

NEW HOPE Common Characteristic #13:

"We have difficulty following projects through from beginning to end."

Related Scripture (For personal use)
Lamentations 3:21–25
Psalm 119:89–90
Philippians 1:6

1. Do you find yourself having difficulty following projects through? Share a project you are currently having trouble completing.
2. How does this difficulty in following through impact your relationships?
3. Share a time from your childhood when a parent expressed disbelief that you were capable of performing a certain task.

4. How would your parents react if you were to become more successful than they have been? (Or, how have they reacted if you have become more successful?)

NEW HOPE Common Characteristic #14:

"We have a strong need to be in control. We overreact to change over which we have no control."

Related Scripture (For personal use)
  1 Chronicles 29:11–14
  Psalm 37:23, 24
  Psalm 104
  Colossians 1:13–17

1. What areas in your life do you feel a strong need to be in control of?
2. Who exercised the most control in your family as you grew up and how did they do that?
3. When you feel like you are not in control of what do you do?
4. What kind of change is hardest for you to accept?
5. When you are not in control, how do you feel?

NEW HOPE Common Characteristic #15:

"We tend to be impulsive. We take action before considering alternative behaviors or possible consequences."

Related Scripture (For personal use)
  Psalm 103:8–14
  Isaiah 30:18
  Isaiah 48:17
  1 Timothy 1:16

1. Who in your family was the most impulsive while you were growing up?
2. How have your impulsive actions resulted in physical or emotional pain for yourself?
3. How has someone else's impulsive behavior left you physically or emotionally hurt?

New Hope Facilitator Focus Series

TRAINING MANUAL

Dear New Facilitator:*

Hopefully when you are done with this five-part focus series, you will have a better sense of how to facilitate a small group. You know, facilitating a small group is in a sense a paradox. On the one hand, it is very easy to do. Go to a meeting; read the rules; watch the clock; share your own adult children issues; and there you go! Easy, right? Well, not always. The majority of the time things go pretty smoothly. But there are a few times when things don't go as planned. Someone may act up in the group (i.e., try to fix someone), for example. What do you do? This training manual will answer some of the questions you may have, as well as discuss what a facilitator does and what he/ she needs to be aware of in working with groups.

The purpose of the training is *not* to teach you to be a therapist or an expert group leader. None of us would lead groups if that were the case—there would be too much pressure! You can never facilitate a group perfectly. You learn about facilitating by, first, maintaining your own recovery and, second, by experiencing a *week at a time* the different situations in your group. We call this on-the-job training. You have already been on the job (that is, in support groups) for a while now. You will find that you rely on your past experiences in groups to help you facilitate your current groups. You have witnessed, in the past, what makes these groups flow and what makes them awkward. We are merely trying to expose you to some tools we find helpful in facilitating groups. I hope you will find them beneficial!
God bless you,
The New Hope Leadership Team

* Originally developed by Curt Grayson for use in New Hope, this series has been revised to be included in this section.

FOCUS GROUP #1
Your Recovery
The Key to Being a Facilitator

This may surprise many of you who expected this first session to be a long explanation of what a small group leader does—the psychological themes or a checklist of do's and don'ts for how a facilitator should behave. But before we proceed to talk about the specific how to's of facilitating small groups, we need to focus on something far more profound—what actually makes a leader effective. Understanding why you want to facilitate a small group and what effect being a leader has on your recovery from your personal adult child issues is critical. Here are some questions to ask yourself and discuss in the group:

1) Why do I want to be a facilitator in a small group?

2) How do I think or feel that becoming a facilitator will affect my own recovery process?

Many adult children who have led small groups describe the problem of burn-out in being a small group facilitator. They find that they lose interest in the group or feel that being a facilitator causes them to be forced into the role of "leader" so they no longer feel they can share their own experiences (good or bad) in the group. If you feel you are responsible for the success of each of your group members' recovery, then you will definitely burn out. Remember: You are responsible for your own recovery—not anyone else's. What a relief! This hopefully takes the pressure off you so you can simply maintain your own recovery, even as you facilitate.

3) Discuss in the group what you are doing to help maintain your recovery while you are facilitating a group. When you feel the pressure to be a "looking-good" leader, what resources do you have to help you get back to basics—i.e., talk, trust, and feel?

The Not-So-Secret Ingredient

Most small group facilitators who appear to be successful in their groups are those that recognize an important fact about their own recovery: They have to regularly attend the group and work on their own issues in order to maintain their recovery. Regular attenders at Twelve-Step meetings "absorb" how support groups work. God, through the group, works in you His miracle of healing. And as your eyes, ears, heart, mind, and soul are being changed and restored, you become "the human sponge." When you are growing every week in your own recovery, many of the issues you face on how to facilitate groups are answered almost instinctively!

Key Points to Remember:
- Understand why I want to be a facilitator.
- Maintaining my own recovery is the only foundation that gives me the proper perspective to be a healthy facilitator.
- Build practical steps to protect against facilitator burn out.
- If I maintain my own recovery as an adult child, I am on my way to gaining the needed insights into how to facilitate a group.

FOCUS GROUP #2
New Hope
Support Group Goals and Objectives

Today, we want to give the small group leader a better sense of what New Hope is all about. Many people come to the group expecting a variety of things to happen. Some come without any clue of what will occur. Each of you has memories of your New Hope experiences, from your first day until now. We have found, however, in talking with people who come through New Hope, and especially with new small group facilitators, that they are still not sure what the overall goals and objectives are at New Hope.

1) Share in your group what your feelings and perceptions were on your first visit to New Hope. (Go ahead—be honest.) Many people come to New Hope for different reasons. Some have been to other support groups. Most have not. Feelings such as fear, anticipation, and relief are part of what newcomers feel.

2) Now that you have been coming, how have your perceptions of New Hope changed?

New Hope Goals

Here is a list of some of the goals we hope are achieved through the New Hope support group:

1. Increased self-awareness
2. Reduced feelings of isolation
3. Validation of feelings
4. Reinforcement of reality
5. Support and encouragement
6. Identification of dysfunctional patterns
7. Goals
8. Establish positive decision-making habits
9. Increased self-confidence
10. Healing of relationships with God, others, and ourselves

1) In your group talk about each of these points. How do you see your growth in (or struggles with) each of these areas?

It is hard when you are facilitating a group to identify whether a group is obtaining these goals or not. It is good to recognize that these are areas of growth that *support groups*—not Bible studies or therapy sessions—*can* achieve. Remember, people are coming to New Hope with preconceived ideas about what goes on here. Many people have a variety of expectations and needs when they walk through the door. Until they experience a support group, they may confuse it with other kinds of group settings. Two of the most common misconceptions about support groups are that they operate as psychotherapy groups or Bible studies. Let us look at the differences:

Psychotherapy—This type of group focuses on how people feel about each other in the group. This may bring up a lot of feelings (especially negative ones), which is why this group should be led by a trained therapist. Cross Talking is frequent and is analyzed by the group and the therapist. Individual or group therapy is a valuable experience and many people in the group have been in therapy where it has been a vital part of their recovery process. At New Hope, we are not trained to do therapy, and it is not the focus of what happens in support groups. You may experience situations as a group facilitator where someone is hurting enough (e.g., extreme anger, withdrawal, tears.) to need professional counseling. We encourage them to seek this and provide them with a list of Christian professional therapists. This is not to say, however, that support groups do not have therapeutic qualities. They do! Support groups help people understand and cope better with their lives. But they function differently than therapy groups.

Bible Study Group—New Hope is not a Bible study group. For Christians this can be a hard one to understand because Bible study groups have been such an important part of our Christian experience. Bible studies focus on teaching a particular truth from the Bible in some structured way. We do not use the Bible during our meetings, although individuals in the group may mention a passage that was helpful in their recovery that week. Be careful that a person doesn't guide the support group towards Scripture reading. This can offend some people who are struggling in their relationship with God (at least at the moment). Also, a person who uses a lot of Bible verses may not be honestly telling you their feelings about their life or problems.

We do recommend regular attendance at Bible studies outside of New Hope and feel that they are appropriate and helpful. 2) In the group, talk about times where you have seen support groups turn into therapy groups. How about Bible study groups? How did you feel about it? What did you do?

Remember, none of us will be able to prevent the group from ever taking a detour into a Bible study or therapy group. Leaders who have identified what New Hope is trying to be and what it is not trying to be will hopefully have a better chance of steering the ship in the right direction. This is the important point.

Key Points to Remember:

- The focus of a support group is to allow each person an opportunity to share his/her experiences without being fixed or preached to.
- We grow in support groups by listening to what others have done on their journey of recovery and freely sharing our own lives. This helps break through the barrier of isolation.
- Support groups are not the same as Bible studies or therapy groups. People in your group may need both and we encourage it.

FOCUS GROUP #3

What Does a Facilitator Do, Anyway?

If you are participating in the focus series you may be asking yourself "What does a facilitator do?" What is his/her role? Good question! People define the role of the facilitator in a variety of ways depending upon what the purpose of the group is. Here is a definition that might be helpful: *A facilitator is a servant leader who helps others grow by helping them learn how to develop their own skills and resources.*

This is probably a good time to talk about the difference between a leader and a facilitator. A leader is someone who usually has a set agenda for teaching and exercises a fair amount of control over how the group participates in the process. A facilitator, on the other hand, believes more in equal-member-participation emphasis in the group. The facilitator is *first*, a *member* of the group, and then helps to structure or arrange the time and flow of the meeting. This is a great relief when you think about it because a very important part of being a good facilitator is being able to share your own needs in the group. Once you quit sharing your own recovery issues, you create a distance between you and the other members in the group. This is not good! The next thing that usually happens is you become "looking good kid" all over again—only going to meetings because others *need* you or because you are *supposed to*. Remember, the key to being an effective facilitator is to continue to maintain your own active recovery!

Most of us came to this facilitator training program having already participated in some small groups. (This means we have some established leadership concepts based on experiences modeled for us by those who have facilitated those small groups.)

1) Discuss in the group what your experiences have been in the small groups. What were some positive experiences? How about the negative? What could the facilitator have done differently to make it a better experience for the group? (Remember, the goal here is not to pick apart any particular small group leader, but to focus on what happened and how you felt about it.)

Once we understand our past group experiences, we can see

how they influence what we expect of other facilitators or of ourselves, as new facilitators.

Here are two basic responsibilities of facilitators:

Provide structure—Use the Rules for Small Groups to keep track of what we call boundary issues—that is, time, place and guidelines for what constitutes appropriate sharing in the group. Reading the rules at the beginning of every meeting reminds new and old-timers alike about the support group structure and what they can expect as group members.

Expectations—After you help group members understand what the structure of the meeting is like, they can better grasp what to expect from the facilitator, themselves, and others. Remember our discussion in the last focus group where we talked about people having different needs, fears, and expectations when they come to a support group? For many, this is a very new experience, and they need a lot of structuring of their expectations, especially early on. Fortunately, in most groups, there are a few seasoned support group attenders that can help the facilitator deal with situations that develop!

2) Look at the Rules for Small Groups. Discuss in your group what each rule means for you and why it is important.

RULES FOR SMALL GROUP DISCUSSIONS

1. While others are talking, please let them finish without interruption.

2. No fixing. We are to listen, to support, and be supported by each other in the group, not to give advice.

3. It's OK to feel angry here and to express your anger in the group. We will hear you, but try to remember there are others in the room as well.

4. Speak in the "I." Talk about how something or someone made you feel. Example: I felt sad when . . . , etc.

5. Keep sharing to no more than 5 minutes in order that others in the group will be able to share.

6. Try to share from the heart as honestly as you can. It's OK to cry, laugh, be angry in the group. There will be no condemnation from others.

3) Were you surprised by some of your or other peoples' responses to what the rules are all about? Did you learn something new?

4) Discuss in your group how it feels to use the rules.

Key Points to Remember

- A facilitator is someone who helps others grow by helping them learn how to develop their own skills and resources.
- A facilitator provides structure (i.e., time keeping and rules for acceptable discussion). This helps to put members and the facilitator at ease because people clearly know what is expected of them and of other people.
- Facilitators are not responsible for whether or not other people do their recovery. They are only responsible to do their own recovery; and they provide boundaries for the group so it is safe to talk, trust, and feel.

FOCUS GROUP #4
Listening To Lead
Effective Listening Exercises

Did you know that one of the main reasons people come to support groups is that they currently are not, or in their childhood were not, listened to? There may be a lot of talking going on but they don't feel understood at a deeper level. Let's look at the definition of empathetic listening and then consider how it applies to us as small group facilitators.

Empathetic listening is the ability to stand in another person's shoes without avoiding, denying or fixing that person. The empathetic listener feels what the other person is feeling and communicates understanding. Notice, there are three parts to empathetic listening: 1) an ability to perceive with sensitivity what others are feeling or saying; 2) the capacity to let others know that they are understood; and 3) the ability to allow the person's feelings to exist without invalidating, fixing, or controlling those feelings.

Sometimes this is easier said than done, especially when you see someone hurting and you want to stop that hurt with some tidbit of recovery wisdom. Most people who "fix others" do not do so because they are consciously trying to control them. They do so more likely because they (as is the case with most of us) don't like others to suffer through something, especially when they feel something could be said to stop that suffering. Other people's pain often reminds us of what we've been through, so we relive that experience emotionally when we watch them hurt. Part of effective leadership is to be able to listen empathetically and to allow other people to grieve in their recovery.

1) Discuss in your small groups the question, How do I feel when others in the group are going through something I have experienced?

Because people come to support groups to be heard and to listen, the facilitator in a group must set an example of how safe it is to do just that. My experience has taught me that trying to give someone specific suggestions or tell them what they can do to solve a problem *usually* backfires! If your suggestion was right, you lose because they didn't learn to figure it out on their own. So then they become dependent *on you*. If your suggestion was wrong, they will blame whatever action they took *on you*! You can't win either way! This is why it is important, even if people attempt to coax a directive from you, that you resist. In the long run, those people will learn that they need to arrive at their own decisions. The goal in support groups is to learn by sharing your own experience and to listen to what other people have done in similar situations. Notice the difference. When people share their own experiences, it helps others in the group to see what *has* or *has not* worked for them. It allows each person in the group to choose what *they* will do.

LISTENING TO YOU!

The reason we emphasize listening to others is to keep the facilitator alert to potential problems in the group situation. One of the tools you have to identify problems is to use "yourself as the instrument." What does this mean? Listen to what your own gut is telling you regarding what is happening in the group. If you are feeling anxious, bored, angry, passive, you may be feeling the mood of the group. Sometimes you can say, "You know, right now I am feeling something and I wonder how other people feel." Sometimes sorting out your own issues from what is floating around the group is tough. As a facilitator, tuning in to your own feelings can be helpful in opening any problems occurring in the group.

2) Discuss in your group what it means to listen to "your own gut". How can this help your personal recovery and guide the group in a positive way?

SPEAKING IN THE "I"

We talk a lot about speaking in the "I". What does that mean, anyway? It means that when you share a feeling, instead of saying, "He made me angry when he said something," you say, "I felt angry, sad, depressed, fearful, when he did that." This is an important distinction, because in support groups we are learning to own our feelings and responses to events that happen to us, *not to blame others.* We had no control over the events of our childhood; but as adults, we do have some choice of how we respond. We are no longer automatically victims of others' actions! When we own our feelings about something that someone did or said to us, we begin the process of setting better boundaries so we can choose how we will respond to that action. (Feel the difference?) As adult children, we struggle with this concept a lot because we were victims as children.

3) Discuss in your group what speaking in the "I" means to you and examine the affect it has on recovery in support groups.

4) Think of some examples of statements that are not in the "I" form and rewrite them so that they are like the one that follows: "My husband made me so mad when he didn't come home like he said he would!" Now here it is in the "I" form: "I felt angry when my husband didn't come home for dinner."

ACTIVE LISTENING

Active listening means that you are more than just casually sitting there, listening to the content of what a person says. You also notice nonverbal messages. Body language and facial expressions are important indications of what people are feeling about what they are saying. If they are incongruent (i.e., a person says he is happy when his face is frowning or tense), then you might suppose that the person speaking is not being honest about or even aware that maybe he is not as happy as he would have you believe.

5) Think of other kinds of nonverbal messages that are sent out in a group. What are they? What do you do when they don't match what a person is saying?

REFLECTIVE LISTENING

Many times when we talk to each other we think we understand what the other person is saying. But communication studies show that we listen very little to what people actually say! In fact, we listen only to part of a message, then begin to plan what we are going to say in response! This means that we may be missing most of the message but are responding as if we've heard the whole thing. This can cause problems! This is why it is so important to check out or feed back to people what you thought you heard them say. This may sound almost insulting to those who consider themselves good communicators, but it is amazing how much we can miss in others' messages.

6) Break into groups of three and take turns in the role of the sender, receiver, and observer. Practice your listening skills. Take ten minutes each as the sender (the one who talks). Talk about an experience you had last week while the listener hears what you are saying. After about two minutes or so of listening, feed back to the sender what you heard him say. Listen for the five "w's"— who, what, when, where, and why. The observer may take notes to get the facts down in helping the feed-back process. Do this several times until the ten minutes are up.

7) Well, how did it go? What were some of the more difficult parts of the exercise?

8) How do you think reflective listening can help you as small group facilitators?

Key Points to Remember

- Empathetic listening is the ability to stand in the other person's shoes without avoiding, denying, or fixing that person. Allow them to feel what they are feeling and communicate to that person that you understand.
- Sometimes people in the group need to hurt or struggle with their recovery without being offered solutions. *Support, yes! Fix, no!*

- Listen with your gut to what your feelings are about the group process.
- When we and others speak in the "I," we are accurately recognizing that we are not victims anymore and that we can choose how we respond to what others do to us.
- People send messages verbally and nonverbally. We can listen and watch for both to see if they are congruent (i.e., saying the same thing).
- Checking out a sender's message helps to clarify if we accurately heard what they said. (It's hard work!)
- Remember, good communication takes a lifetime to learn and even then we don't listen perfectly! The goal in this exercise was simply to make us aware of our own personal communication patterns.

FOCUS GROUP #5
Problem People and Situations

Probably one of the most frustrating aspects of being a facilitator is dealing with those people who come in and out of support groups. Remember from our last session, we pointed out that people come into New Hope with a variety of expectations and experiences from previous support groups. Some that come in have been in other Twelve-Step meetings and are comfortable with the kind of sharing that goes on. Others have had little or no experience in support groups and may attempt to disrupt the meeting in a number of ways. It is important to understand that those who do this rarely do so because they are consciously mean or wish to disrupt the group. Each person is at a different stage of recovery and may or may not understand why he or she is unable to obey the rules or is creating a problem.

Before we take a look at some of the problems that develop in groups, please discuss in your group your past experience of being in a meeting. When there were problems, what were they? How was it handled? How did you feel about it?

We use several types of defenses in groups (you notice I said "we," not "they," because we all do them) when we feel threatened or unsafe emotionally. As you read the following list of defenses, or roles, be careful not to stereotype anybody in your group into a certain role for your own convenience. People can play several roles and can change at different times according to where they are in their recovery. All these roles are in some way a form of denial, where people are pushing away the pain of getting in touch with painful memories or experiences.

FIVE ROLES

1. SILENCE/WITHDRAWALS—A person using silence simply does not talk in the group. He may not even establish eye contact with any group member or with you, as a facilitator. In New Hope we do not have a rule that people have to talk in a group. As a matter of fact, we realize that some people may be intimidated by the group setting or may be shy or may be going through something difficult at that moment.

What you can do: It is okay to let people in the group say absolutely nothing! You would be surprised how much people soak up by simply listening to what others are saying. As a facilitator, you can go over to the silent member after group, (when it is convenient), and tell the person you appreciate his coming to the meeting. Reaffirm that he need not speak during the meeting until he is ready to do so.

Discuss what it has been like to have people in your group who have been silent and how you felt about it.

2. MONOPOLIZING—There are always people in the group who have a lot to say but don't recognize they are talking too much. It is important to recognize that these people rarely perceive their amount of talking as *too much*! They may always talk that much or that fast, which may also be a reason people tune them out when they want to be heard.

What you can do: As a group facilitator, it is not your job to fix this person, but you can use the rules to reinforce that each person has a limited time to share if all are to get an opportunity to do so. The monopolizer in your group may need therapy or to attend another AC meeting, on another night of the week, to get more time to share his or her particular issues.

Discuss in your groups when you have seen someone monopolizing the group time. How did you respond? How about others? How did they respond?

3. HUMORIZING—Being funny in a group can be occasion-

ally helpful when the mood is somber and people are feeling down. Our solution statement in the New Hope packet states, "You will probably see laughter and tears in our meetings." Those of you who have been coming for a while know what we mean! When we describe humorizing as a problem, we mean excessively filling up the space with jokes or other distractions that make people laugh. The family clowns will tend to do this, especially when something in the group is touching a nerve close to where they are hurting.

What you can do: Talk to that person afterward and let them know that, although laughter is good, the goal of the meeting is for people to deal with serious painful issues in their lives. Let them know that laughter and cutting up keeps everything at a surface level, which is not good for the group or for you either. The humorists may be scared to talk about how much they are hurting. It is often said that laughter and tears are similar expressions of emotion, and we've found this to be repetitive.

If the person keeps joking, others in the group may need to talk to him or her about how the humorizing makes them feel. This is okay for the group to do. These people may have never heard how their antics affect others. Don't worry if someone says, "I feel like I can't talk about anything serious when joking is going on in the group." Believe me, they will eventually get the message.

Discuss in your groups when you have been in a group where someone else was cutting up or laughing to the point of distraction. How did you feel? How did it affect the group process?

4. ADVICE GIVING—We also call this fixing. Often, as an individual shares in the group, others give answers or opinions about what that person should do to solve the problem. They may do so out of good motives (i.e., stop that person's pain). But people come to support groups, as we've talked about earlier, not to be told how to solve problems, but to have the freedom to express themselves. Dysfunctional families often tell children what to do or give them very little choice in what happens to them. One of the most healing aspects of a support group is having the freedom to express your ideas or experiences and being accepted without having to change! This can be especially

hard for Christians because we are used to having a Bible verse for every dilemma or situation in our lives.

What you can do: Remind the person who is giving advice about the rule stating advice is not allowed in the group.

Discuss a time you have seen advice giving or fixing happening in a group you have been in. How did it make you feel? How did it affect the group?

5. SEDUCTIVE BEHAVIOR—This need not be sexual seduction necessarily. People can use their natural charisma in meetings to focus on their problem. It is important to observe when this happens, especially in the case of sexual seduction. This may manifest itself in what a person wears, how they sit, or in what they say during the meeting. A person who wears seductive clothing week after week or sits in some revealing way or tends to say seductive things can distract the group. Seductive people are not always aware of what they are doing or how their behavior comes across to other people. Some seductive people *are* aware of how they come across, and they use their behavior to win friends or control meetings.

Seduction is often learned as a defense against growing up in a dysfunctional family. Sex can become a drug like any other drug and can even become an addiction. There are excellent support groups now for people that struggle with sexual addiction. Our goal as facilitators is not to tell someone he or she is a sexual addict, but to be aware of seduction and how it affects the group.

What you can do: It is probably best if the seductive person is taken aside after the meeting, or called on the phone, and given feedback about his or her behavior. Be specific about what you observe—noting clothing, position, or language, as well as the affect the behavior has on the group. Some people may get mad and never come back or argue that they are not being seductive. That is okay. Remember, our goal is to keep the group safe and focused on recovery. If they would like, they can bring it up at the next meeting and ask the group what their feelings are.

Discuss in your group when you have been in a group where there has been seductive behavior. How did this make you feel? How did it affect the group?

6. EXTREME ANGER, EMOTIONAL OUTBURST, OR IN-

APPROPRIATE BEHAVIOR—Occasionally in New Hope meetings, people are going through so much pain in recovery that they are not about to obey the rules of the group. They may become angry, yell at the group, insist on talking about what they want, or in some other way, behave inappropriately. This could be caused by a number of things. Some people have been holding feelings in for a long time, and they are finally letting off steam that is proportional to the pain!

What you can do: If they have been fairly appropriate in the group before, they probably won't lose control again. You can only ask them to step outside for a few minutes so they can blow off some steam, then come back to the group and talk about their feelings when they are more calm. After the meeting you might suggest privately that they get additional support in the form of a second weekly meeting or from a therapist.

7. HISTORY OF EMOTIONAL PROBLEMS—Some people come into New Hope with a history of emotional illness. They may or may not be currently in treatment (outpatient or inpatient) and may possibly be on medication which helps them cope.

What you can do: Our goal is not to push these people away but to remind them with extra sensitivity that we are glad they are here but it seems they are having a tough time remembering the rules for discussion and that if they are going to stay they need to follow the rules. Another option is to tell them that sometimes not everybody is ready for a support group and that is okay. Tell them that they are not bad people because they can't stick with the format. You may recommend that they talk to a therapist. Our goal is not to be a collecting house for people with severe emotional problems. There are many other resources that would be much more helpful for people with disruptive problems. Let their therapist decide which would be best for them. We don't have the expertise to handle these problems.

Discuss in you group meetings where someone was inappropriate. How did you feel? How did it affect the group?

8. SUICIDAL THREATS—Very rarely in New Hope meetings, someone comes in who may appear depressed or may actually mention wanting to die or end it all because he is hurting so much. All of us probably at one time or another have felt dis-

couraged about our recovery and have thought or talked about wishing we weren't alive. For the majority this can be a normal complaint about the process; but we still have hope, and through therapy and support groups, we find a reason to keep on going.

Discuss in your group if you have ever felt this way and what you did to get help during those low moments.

SUICIDE PLAN—A more serious situation arises when people have a plan for how they will kill themselves and have access to the tool, or weapons, to perform the act. This is a very dangerous combination! If you are facilitating a group and someone hints that he or she has the tools and the plan, you should, during or after the group, ask what his or her plans are. It is good to mention to the group, when someone acts this way that sometimes recovery makes us all feel helpless and we want to stop the pain of the hurts we feel. This will help the suicidal person not feel so embarrassed or isolated. You might also get others in the group talking about their own experiences with feeling suicidal. This hopefully will put the person at ease.

At the conclusion of the meeting, you can either get one of the leaders of New Hope to help you with the situation or follow the procedure below:

1. Assess again if they have a plan and access to weapons. (Get their name, address, and phone number.)
2. Determine if they have attempted suicide before.
3. Ask if they are currently seeing a therapist. Get them to tell you their therapist's name, address, and phone number. Ask them if you can call their therapist or 911 to get some help for them.
4. Stay with them (you or someone else) until help arrives. If they leave or run away, use the information you obtained from them so the police can find them.
5. Remember, you can only do what you can do. You have no power to stop someone from killing himself. You are only a support group facilitator, not a psychiatrist!

Key Points to Remember

- People who disrupt meetings often do so unconsciously or are afraid to deal with deeper issues in their lives.
- 5 roles to watch for: Silence/withdrawal, monopolizing, humorizing, advice giving, and seductive behavior.
- Some people, because of their past experiences, may not be ready for New Hope small groups. If this happens, you have permission to not let them disrupt your group. (We will back you on this!)
- If someone is suicidal, follow the plan enclosed or seek help from a New Hope leader.
- Remember, we are small group facilitators, not therapists, police, pastors, or other professionals! If we have realistic expectations of ourselves, we will not do recovery work for others; we will only do our own recovery work!

Resources For Christian Recovery Groups And Support Groups

Books, Workbooks, and Video for Study and Group Discussion, Arranged Alphabetically by Subject

Adult Children of Alcoholics; Adult Children of Dysfunctional Families—see also Codependency

The Adult Child of Divorce by Bob Burns and Michael J. Brissett, Jr. (Nashville: Thomas Nelson).
A book for those in one of the largest "adult child" groups. The authors map out a complete recovery program that shows how a child's development is affected by divorce. This book points the way to emotional healing, forgiveness, and breaking the transgenerational cycle.

Adult Children of Alcoholics by Janet Woititz (Deerfield Beach, FL: Health Communications, Inc.).
What children of alcoholics need is basic information to sort out the effects of alcoholism in their lives. Dr. Woititz's groundbreaking book is the first to provide this crucial material.

Forgiving Our Parents, Forgiving Ourselves by David Stoop (Ann Arbor, MI: Servant).
Step-by-step, readers learn to construct a psychological family tree that will help them uncover family secrets and habits that have profoundly shaped their adult identity. As they begin to understand their family of origin, readers will be able to take an essential step of forgiveness and gain spiritual healing.

Free to Forgive: Daily Devotions for Adult Children of Abuse by Dr. Frank Minirth and Dr. Paul Meier (Nashville: Thomas Nelson).

"We all have holes in our souls," say the authors. "We all experience painful moments of loneliness, abandonment, or simply feeling like a nobody." The founders of the Minirth-Meier Clinic offer insight and wisdom—one "nugget" of truth for each day of the year—from God's love letter to us, the Bible.

Healing for Damaged Emotions by David Seamands (Wheaton: Victor).

In the beginning, God created us with minds, spirits, wills, and emotions. But soon thereafter, sin entered the world and our emotions have been among its victims. This book helps readers deal honestly and successfully with their inner hurts—the results of emotions damaged by sin.

New Hope Video (available from New Hope, First Evangelical Free Church, 2801 North Brea Boulevard, Fullerton, California 92635; cost $16.00).

Introduced by Chuck Swindoll and hosted by Dave Carder, Curt Grayson and others, this three-part video (each part in 20 minute segments) features sections on rules and roles of dysfunctional families; the structure and process of the New Hope Group; and the place of the church and use of Scriptures in recovery. An excellent tool to help individuals understand what New Hope is all about and how it works.

New Hope Facilitator Training Video (available from New Hope, First Evangelical Free Church, 2801 North Brea Boulevard, Fullerton, California 92635; cost $50.00).

Five 50-minute segments in a self-training format prepare participants to facilitate both open and closed groups. Segment topics include listening skills, group process, group safety and rule enforcement, affirmation responses, and a model for working through difficult emotional turmoil based on a review of Jesus' experience in Gethsemene.

Putting Away Childish Things by David Seamands (Wheaton: Victor).

Many of us have childish behavior patterns that hinder our growing up in Christ. This book shows how to move toward the maturity God desires for every believer.

Secrets of Your Family Tree by Dave Carder, Earl Henslin, John Townsend, Henry Cloud, and Alice Brawand (Chicago: Moody).
This book deals with specific aspects of dysfunctionality as they are passed down from generation to generation, using two biblical families as an example. The authors explain the role of the church in healing dysfunctional symptoms and provide steps for recovery.

Unfinished Business by Charles Sell (Portland: Multnomah).
Sell reveals the influence of childhood families on the adult life, and the relationship between personal struggles and past experiences. Based on extensive research of family traits common in dysfunctional homes, Sell provides a way to resolve the inner conflict.

The Way Out of the Wilderness by Earl Henslin (Nashville: Thomas Nelson).
The first recovery book to show dysfunctional families portrayed in the Bible, illustrating God's ability to heal and restore. A ground-breaking book that helps the spiritually-minded face the reality of their codependencies and addictions.

Alcohol—see the Twelve Steps

Chemical Dependency (Alcohol and Other Drugs)—see the Twelve Steps

Codependency

Beyond Codependency by Melody Beattie (New York: Harper & Row).
This follow-up to *Codependent No More* offers recovering codependents a practical plan for rebuilding their lives and mastering the art of self-care and self-love.

Codependent No More by Melody Beattie (New York: Harper & Row).

This book explains what codependency is, what it isn't, who's got it, and how to move beyond it.

Day by Day Love Is a Choice: Devotions for Codependents by Dr. Richard Fowler, Jerilyn Fowler, Dr. Brian Newman, and Dr. Deborah Newman (Nashville: Thomas Nelson).

This recovery devotional is a compact daily companion to *Love Is a Choice*. Its 365 meditations are designed to help the reader discover a biblically based, truth-centered view of relationships to God and to hurting or addicted loved ones.

Kids Who Carry Our Pain by Dr. Robert Hemfelt and Dr. Paul Warren (Nashville: Thomas Nelson).

How do we break the cycle of codependency? How do we keep from passing our childhood wounds down to our own children? The relationship we had with our own parents influences our relationship with our own children—but we can stop the pain and build strong, healthy, happy family ties. This book points the way with compelling stories and profound insights. An excellent resource for groups on codependency, parenting, divorce and single parent issues, and family intimacy.

Love Is a Choice by Dr. Robert Hemfelt, Dr. Frank Minirth, and Dr. Paul Meier (Nashville: Thomas Nelson).

Probably the definitive book on codependency from a Christian perspective. If you have been trying to "fix" an addicted loved one; if you are exhausted from trying to please other people; if you are plagued by guilt, or if you are trapped in a destructive relationship—this book is for you.

Love Is a Choice Workbook by Dr. Robert Hemfelt, Dr. Frank Minirth, Dr. Paul Meier, Dr. Deborah Newman, and Dr. Brian Newman (Nashville: Thomas Nelson).

This interactive workbook takes the life-changing principles of *Love Is a Choice* a step further. More than just questions and answers, this workbook is lively reading, packed with stories and graphics that bring the truths and insights of *Love Is a Choice* alive.

Pain and Pretending by Rich Buhler (Nashville: Thomas Nelson).

The popular radio talk show host helps those scarred by the pain of divorce, chemical dependency, and abuse reach into their pasts and uncover the roots of their problems.

Setting New Boundaries: Daily Devotions for Those in Recovery by Mark MacDonald, Kevin Brown, and Ray Mitsch (Nashville: Thomas Nelson).

In recovery, the key to a balanced life lies in learning to set new boundaries in relationships. This daily devotional from the counselors at the Minirth-Meier Clinic is for anyone in recovery.

When Victims Marry: Building a Stronger Marriage by Breaking Destructive Cycles by Don and Jan Frank (San Bernardino: Here's Life).

The authors reveal how dysfunctional childhood affects marriage. Blending personal insight with years of counseling experience, they offer a team approach and a proven ten-step process for emotional recovery.

Control Addiction

Imperative People by Dr. Les Carter (Nashville: Thomas Nelson). For "those who must be in control," this book confronts the reader with such questions as: 1) Do your emotions control your actions? 2) Are you driven by duty? 3) Do you act superior, yet feel inferior? 4) Do you have a craving for control? An excellent resource for groups dealing with control addictions, codependency, and church leadership.

Divorce/Infidelity—see also Adult Children of Dysfunctional Families

Torn Asunder: Recovering from Extramarital Affairs by David Carder (Chicago: Moody).

A practical how-to book to help couples get back on track after infidelity. Includes discussion of how to process anger, the history of infidelity within the family system, the required recovery process, exercises for rebuilding intimacy, and material for a couple's Twelve-Step infidelity recovery group. Also offers help for the children in this marital setting, the spouse who is attempting to recover alone from this experience, and friends supporting marriages recovering from infidelity.

Eating Disorders (Compulsive Overeating; Anorexia; Bulimia)

Beyond the Looking Glass by Remuda Ranch (Nashville: Thomas Nelson).
Recovering from anorexia and bulimia is not simple or instantaneous. This daily devotional helps women take the time and effort to face their pain and shame and restore wholeness.

Food for the Hungry Heart: Daily Devotions for Overeaters by Cynthia Rowland McClure (Nashville: Thomas Nelson).
The perfect daily companion to *Love Hunger*. Each day's meditation shows the reader how to turn to God rather than food for true satisfaction.

Love Hunger by Dr. Frank Minirth, Dr. Paul Meier, Dr. Robert Hemfelt, and Dr. Sharon Sneed (Nashville: Thomas Nelson).
Overeaters crave food to satisfy their hunger for love. People with a food addiction have a codependent relationship with food. Part 1 of this book explores the emotional causes of compulsive overeating and the addiction cycle, and explains how to feed the hungry heart. Part 2 is a ten-stage life plan for body, mind, and soul—a plan not only for controlling weight but for achieving spiritual and emotional healing. Part 3 is the Love Hunger Cookbook, filled with indexed recipes and workable menu plans to fit any lifestyle, plus a guide to nutrition and calories.

Love Hunger Weight-Loss Workbook by Dr. Frank Minirth, Dr. Paul Meier, Dr. Robert Hemfelt, and Dr. Sharon Sneed (Nashville: Thomas Nelson).
This recovery program, which is proven effective by hundreds of support groups at the Minirth-Meier Clinic, is now available in a powerful twelve-week interactive workbook. Powerful, practical, and filled with encouraging stories and memorable graphics. Also contains menus, snack choices, and a list of recommended frozen dinners and main dishes.

The Thin Disguise: Understanding and Overcoming Anorexia and Bulimia by Pam Vredevelt, Dr. Deborah Newman, Harry Beverly, and Dr. Frank Minirth (Nashville: Thomas Nelson).

The most complete, authoritative book on how to understand and overcome anorexia and bulimia in women, combining sound medical knowledge, psychological principles, and the spiritual principles necessary for recovery. Authors include the nutritional information necessary to reprogram the anorexic's and bulimic's eating habits and advise them how to change their eating habits to regain healthy nutrition.

Emotional Pain (Shame)

The Child in Each of Us by Richard Dickinson (Wheaton: Victor).
In each of us lives a child who desires to live freely and be loved, but often that part of us has been stifled. This book helps heal the wounds of childhood and break cycles of negative thoughts and actions.

Hiding from Love by Dr. John Townsend (Colorado Springs: NavPress).
Victims of shame, betrayal, and abuse often find themselves imprisoned in patterns of emotional withdrawal. These patterns affect relationships with self (self-esteem), with others, and with God. Dr. Townsend, co-director of the Minirth-Meier Clinic West in Southern California, helps the reader identify, understand, and move beyond the emotional pain that cripples relationships.

Released from Shame by Sandra D. Wilson (Downers Grove: InterVarsity).
Counselor Sandra D. Wilson examines destructive patterns of thinking and feeling and acting that affect the children of dysfunctional families, describes her own healing process from having grown up in such a family, and offers help and encouragement to others who are beginning their journey of recovery.

Grief

A Very Present Help: God's Promises for Those Who Are Grieving (Nashville: Thomas Nelson) Arranged topically, this collection of Bible passages walks readers through the various stages of grief as it provides comfort and reassurance that the readers are not alone in their experience.

Incest Survivors

A Door of Hope: Recognizing and Resolving the Pains of Your Past by Jan Frank (San Bernardino: Here's Life).

The author describes nine symptoms experienced by women with a traumatic past. While integrating numerous vignettes from her own life and from women she has counseled, Frank walks readers through ten steps to healing.

Legalism/Religious Addiction

Toxic Faith by Stephen Arterburn and Jack Felton (Nashville: Thomas Nelson).

This book explores the issues of religious addiction with insight and compassion that comes from both personal and clinical experience. It points the way toward a pure, realistic relationship with God.

Marriage

Passages of Marriage by Dr. Frank and Mary Alice Minirth, Dr. Brian and Dr. Deborah Newman, and Dr. Robert and Susan Hemfelt (Nashville: Thomas Nelson).

Marriages go through certain well-defined stages (or "passages") of emotional and spiritual development. This book examines the passages from "Young Love" to "Realistic Love" to "Comfortable Love" to "Renewing Love" to "Transcendent Love," and shows couples how to negotiate successfully the twists and turns of each stage. A beneficial resource for groups on couples support and family intimacy.

Men in Recovery

Father and Son by Gordon Dalbey (Nashville: Thomas Nelson).
Dalbey offers a powerful and compassionate exploration of the devastating wound inflicted on most men by their own fathers. He shows that the only pathway to authentic manhood is through the Father God, who comes to men and heals them exactly where their earthly fathers have wounded and forsaken them.

Healing the Masculine Soul by Gordon Dalbey (Dallas: Word).
This book offers men new hope for walking in true manliness by

yielding to God. It is an answer to men struggling with the extreme definitions of masculinity, showing that there can be a natural, balanced portrayal of manhood by following goals set by God, and not society.

The Man Within: Daily Devotions for Men in Recovery by Ted Scheuermann, Larry Stephens, Dr. Brian Newman, and Bob Dyer (Nashville: Thomas Nelson).
Packed with stories, Scripture, and the principles of the Twelve Steps, this daily devotional is for men who have made a commitment to spiritual growth and emotional health.

Uneasy Manhood by Robert Hicks (Nashville: Thomas Nelson).
Why do I have so few real friends? Why is my relationship with my father so disappointing? Why am I driven to work so hard? A book about the fears and frustrations of manhood.

You Take Over, God. I Can't Handle It. by Kevin Brown and Ray Mitsch (Nashville: Thomas Nelson).
A daily devotional to help young men recovering from drug and alcohol addiction.

Mothers

Mothering: The Complete Guide for Mothers of All Ages by Dr. Grace Ketterman (Nashville: Thomas Nelson).
The Medical Director of the Crittenton Center in Kansas City, Missouri—and an accomplished mother and grandmother—offers practical, godly insight for mothers of every age group on such issues as self-care, adolescent peer pressure, child development, self-esteem, absent fathers, disabled children, grandparenting, and more.

Shame—see Emotional Pain

Stress

Together on a Tightrope by Dr. Richard Fowler and Rita Schweitz (Nashville: Thomas Nelson).
A practical manual for couples who are balancing on the tightrope of stress. This is a book for people facing: job loss; financial setbacks; family upheaval; problems with in-laws; critical illness;

grief; moving; any other kind of "emotional overload." *Together on a Tightrope* is designed to help couples handle the storms of life.

Support Group Issues

The Lies We Believe by Dr. Chris Thurman (Nashville: Thomas Nelson).
Dr. Thurman uncovers the common lies that make us unhappy and ineffectual in our lives, our careers, our families, and our relationship with God, including:
Self-lies—"I must have everyone's love and approval."
Worldly lies—"You can have it all."
Marital lies—"You should meet all my needs."
Religious lies—"God's love must be earned."
An excellent resource for groups on codependency, religious addiction, workaholism, depression, or marriage and family intimacy issues.

The Truths We Must Believe by Dr. Chris Thurman (Nashville: Thomas Nelson).
The key to emotional health is knowing the truth, facing the truth, and living by the truth. The truths we must believe include:
You don't have to please everyone.
You are going to die.
You are not entitled.
Your childhood isn't over.
A valuable resource for men's and women's groups, emotional health support groups, codependency groups, or any setting where people want to live a full, well-adjusted Christian life.

The Twelve Steps (including Chemical Dependency; Alcohol)

One Step at a Time: Daily Devotions for People in Twelve-Step Recovery by Cynthia Spell Humbert, Betty Lively Blaylock, and Dr. Frank L. Minirth (Nashville: Thomas Nelson).
The cofounder and two counselors of the Minirth-Meier Clinic teamed up to create 365 devotions to help people understand

the biblical principles of the Twelve Steps. The emphasis is on practical application in this book of meditations.

The Path to Serenity by Dr. Robert Hemfelt, Dr. Richard Fowler, Dr. Frank Minirth, and Dr. Paul Meier (Nashville: Thomas Nelson).

Like The Big Book of AA, *The Path to Serenity* is a journey through the Twelve Steps—but from a biblical Christian perspective. "We've found that our patients have had difficulty walking through the Twelve-Step process without the involvement of a God who has a name, a face, and a history of interacting with people just like them," say the authors. Packed with life-changing insights and dramatic stories of people who have overcome addictions to alcohol, drugs, sex, pornography, destructive relationships, controlling, overeating, overwork, and more.

Serenity: A Companion for Twelve-Step Recovery, Complete New Testament, Psalms and Proverbs, with meditations by Dr. Robert Hemfelt and Dr. Richard Fowler (Nashville: Thomas Nelson).

The perfect day-by-day companion for people who are "working the Steps." Contains the beautiful and easy to read New King James Version text, plus the Twelve Steps, the Serenity Prayer, and eighty-four encouraging meditations (seven for each Step) that underscore what the Bible says about the Steps. More than five hundred verses are highlighted and keyed for easy reference, so that the reader can gain an overview of the biblical principles of recovery. An indispensable tool for all recovery groups.

12 Steps to a New Day by Ron Keller (Nashville: Thomas Nelson).

An interactive workbook that will take the reader on a personalized journey through the Twelve Steps. Those recovering from obsessive-compulsive behavior and drug or alcohol addictions will learn to understand and apply the principles behind the Twelve Steps.

12 Steps to a New Day for Teens by Ron Keller (Nashville: Thomas Nelson).

This interactive workbook is designed for teenagers as it takes them through the Twelve Steps as a spiritual journey. They will learn to apply the principles to make sound personal decisions for the dilemmas of daily living.

Twelve Steps: A Spiritual Journey by Ron Halverson (San Diego: Recovery).

This workbook gives a full explanation of the Twelve-Step program as a spiritual journey, with explicit, detailed exercises for individuals and groups to use in working each Step. Adapted from the Twelve Steps of Alcoholics Anonymous, this material is written primarily for adults whose lives have been negatively affected by substance abuse, violence, or other inappropriate behavior on the part of their caretakers. The biblical references aid Christians in confronting their past and surrendering their lives to God as part of their journey in recovery.

A Walk with the Serenity Prayer: Daily Devotions for People in Recovery by Dr. Frank Minirth, Dr. Paul Meier, Dr. David Congo, and Jan Congo (Nashville: Thomas Nelson).

This daily devotional offers people in recovery the chance to live throughout the year in the realistic truths of the Serenity Prayer.

Women in Recovery

Days of Joy: God's Promises for Women in Recovery (Nashville: Thomas Nelson) Scripture verses directed to specific issues women confront as they work through their recovery from addictions, codependency, and obsessive-compulsive behaviors comfort and strengthen.

I Can't. God Can. I Think I'll Let Him. by Jane Cairo, Sheri Curry, Anne Christian Buchanan, and Debra Klingsporn (Nashville: Thomas Nelson).

A daily devotional written for teenage girls struggling to recover from alcohol, drug, and food addictions.

A New Beginning by Al Ells (Nashville: Thomas Nelson).

This is a daily devotional that helps sexually abused women come to terms with their inner pain. Each devotion includes a Scripture reading, message, and concluding prayer that comforts, guides, and assists the abused in their recovery.

The Woman Within: Daily Devotions for Women in Recovery by Janet Congo, Julie Mask, and Jan Meier (Nashville: Thomas Nelson).

This book of recovery meditations is written by women, for women—and specifically for women who have made the choice to face their problems and grow through them.

Workaholism

Pace Yourself: Daily Devotions for Those Who Do Too Much by Ric Engram (Nashville: Thomas Nelson).

This is the 365-day companion to *We Are Driven.* "In our society, drivenness is an accepted way of life," says the author. *Pace Yourself* is a refreshing journey toward serenity and mastery over those factors that fuel our drivenness.

Time Out: Daily Devotions for Workaholics by Gary E. Hurst, Mike Kachura, and Larry D. Sides (Nashville: Thomas Nelson).

Most workaholics work compulsively to avoid pain and anxiety. These 365 meditations are designed to help recovering workaholics put family and personal growth before the demands of their work.

We Are Driven: The Compulsive Behaviors America Applauds by Dr. Robert Hemfelt, Dr. Frank Minirth, and Dr. Paul Meier (Nashville: Thomas Nelson).

We brag about our drivenness. We praise the workaholism and people-pleasing of others. Perfectionism, materialism, addiction to exercise and physical conditioning—these are the compulsions our society admires and encourages. With dramatic narrative and incisive clarity, the authors show us how these compulsions are rooted in issues of shame, negative messages, codependency, and cultural idolatry. An effective resource for men's or women's support groups, parenting groups, and codependency groups.

Notes

Chapter 1: I Stand by the Door

1. Sam Shoemaker, *Faith At Work* (New York: Hawthorn, 1958), 80–82.

2. *Alcoholics Anonymous Comes of Age: A Brief History of A.A.* (Alcoholics Anonymous, 1957, 1985), 253.

3. Helen Smith Shoemaker, *I Stand by the Door: The Life of Sam Shoemaker* (New York: Harper & Row, 1967), 192.

4. *Alcoholics Anonymous Comes of Age*, 270.

5. Helen Smith Shoemaker, *I Stand by the Door*, 177.

6. Ibid.

7. *Alcoholics Anonymous Comes of Age*, 270.

8. See Matthew 9:10–13.

9. Helen Smith Shoemaker, *I Stand by the Door*, ix–x.

Chapter 2: One by One

1. Sam Shoemaker, "The Most Unforgettable Character I've Met: Red Cap No. 42." *Reader's Digest*, February 1946, 51.

2. Sam Shoemaker, *Revive Thy Church, Beginning with Me* (New York: Harper, 1943), 9.

3. Sam Shoemaker, "The Most Unforgettable Character," 53.

4. Sam Shoemaker, *Revive Thy Church*, 15.

5. Sam Shoemaker, "The Most Unforgettable Character," 51, 52.

6. Sam Shoemaker, *Revive Thy Church*, 15.

7. Ibid., 91.

8. Sam Shoemaker, "The Most Unforgettable Character," 52.

9. Sam Shoemaker, *Revive Thy Church*, 18.

10. *Alcoholics Anonymous Comes of Age*, 59, 60.

11. Ibid., 63.

12. Helen Smith Shoemaker, *I Stand by the Door*, 94.

13. Ibid., 94.

14. *Alcoholics Anonymous* ["The Big Book"], 3rd ed. (New York: Alcoholics Anonymous World Services, 1976), 179.

Chapter 3: We Came to Believe

1. J. Keith Miller, *A Hunger for Healing* (San Francisco: Harper San Francisco, 1991), xv.

2. See Acts 2:14–42; 17:2–4, 10–12; 18:27–28; Ephesians 4:14; 1 Timothy 4:6; 2 Timothy 3:16.

3. 2 Corinthians 12:9–10.

4. Psalm 18:2.

5. Quoted by Tim Stafford, "The Hidden Gospel of the Twelve Steps," *Christianity Today*, 22 July 1991, 17.

6. Miller, *A Hunger for Healing*, 32.

7. See 2 Timothy 3:5.

8. Sam Shoemaker, *Faith at Work*, 83.

9. M. Scott Peck, *People of the Lie* (New York: Simon & Schuster, 1983), 76.

10. Helen Smith Shoemaker, *I Stand by the Door*, 24–25.

11. Ibid., 25.

12. Ibid., 26.

13. Sam Shoemaker, *Faith at Work*, 83.

14. Ibid., 142–145.

Chapter 4: Walking the Walk

1. Psalm 139:23–24.

2. Matthew 5:23–24.

3. Ralston C. Young, "On the Right Track," 167–171.

4. Mark 14:38.

5. Sam Shoemaker, *Faith at Work* (New York: Hawthorn, 1958), 83.

6. Psalm 96:2.
7. Sam Shoemaker, *Faith at Work*, 82.
8. Ibid., 82.

Chapter 5: Taking the Twelfth Step
1. Matthew 28:19.
2. Helen Smith Shoemaker, *I Stand by the Door*, 27.
3. *Alcoholics Anonymous* ["The Big Book"], 14–15.
4. *Alcoholics Anonymous Comes of Age*, 65–66.
5. "Dr. Bob's Last Major Talk," *A.A. Grapevine*, November 1991, 5.
6. Sam Shoemaker, *Revive Thy Church*, 32.
7. Ibid., 36.
8. Ibid., 34.
9. Ibid., 35–36.
10. Ibid., 42.
11. Ibid., 36–37.
12. Ibid., 33–34.
13. Ibid., 42–43.
14. Ibid., 37–38.
15. Ibid., 39–40.
16. Ibid., 40–41.
17. Ibid., 41.
18. Helen Smith Shoemaker, *I Stand by the Door*, 26.
19. Sam Shoemaker, *Revive Thy Church*, 42–43.
20. Ibid., 43–44.
21. Sam Shoemaker, *Faith at Work*, 197.

Chapter 6: The One-to-One Connection
1. 1 Corinthians 4:16; cf. 1 Thessalonians 1:6.
2. Shoemaker, *Revive Thy Church*, 106.
3. Ibid., 106–107.
4. Ibid., 108.
5. Ibid., 108–109.
6. Ibid., 109–110.
7. Ibid.
8. Ibid., 110–111.

Chapter 7: Revive Your Church

1. Sam Shoemaker, *Revive Thy Church*, 88–89.
2. Ibid., 85.
3. Ibid., 91–92.
4. Ibid., 85–86.
5. Ibid., 97–98.
6. Ibid., 98.
7. Ibid., 94.
8. Ibid.
9. Sam Shoemaker, *Faith at Work*, 161–163.
10. Ibid., 163–165.
11. Sam Shoemaker, *Revive Thy Church*, 95–98.
12. Sam Shoemaker, *Faith at Work*, 189–192.
13. Duncan Norton-Taylor, "Businessmen on Their Knees," *Fortune*, October 1953, 248.
14. Sam Shoemaker, *Faith at Work*, pp. 302–306.
15. Norton-Taylor, "Businessmen on Their Knees," 253.
16. Ibid., 255–256.
17. Sam Shoemaker, *Faith at Work*, 302–306.
18. Helen Smith Shoemaker, *I Stand by the Door*, 203–205.
19. For more information about The Philadelphia Experiment and Employment Anonymous, contact The Pittsburgh Experiment, 1802 Investment Building, Pittsburgh, Pennsylvania 15222; Telephone (412) 281-9578.

Chapter 8: The Fellowship of Recovery

1. Alcoholics Anonymous, *Twelve Steps and Twelve Traditions* (New York: Alcoholics Anonymous World Services, 1953), 35–36.
2. Genesis 2:18.
3. Overlake Overcomers of Kirkland, Washington, is not affiliated with Overcomers Outreach of La Habra, California.
4. At the beginning of each new orientation session, leaders explain the rationale for this six-week orientation: "We have found that it takes a minimum of six meetings in a row to start coming out of denial." Some authorities in the Christian recovery field have expressed to us that they prefer to have a shorter orientation and get people started in their support groups as quickly as possible. These are decisions that each program must

make for itself, taking into account the needs and issues of its own participants.

5. Note: At the Minirth-Meier Clinic, we prefer to call an addiction a disorder rather than a disease. For a complete explanation, see Chapter 10.

Chapter 9: The Servant of the Group

1. Dr. Frank Minirth, Dr. Paul Meier, Dr. Robert Hemfelt, Dr. Sharon Sneed, *Love Hunger* (Nashville: Thomas Nelson Publishers, 1990), 37.

2. Dr. Frank Minirth, Dr. Paul Meier, Dr. Robert Hemfelt, Dr. Sharon Sneed, *Love Hunger Weight-Loss Workbook* (Nashville: Thomas Nelson Publishers, 1991), 86–87.

3. "Please Listen to Me," by Ethel Herr, copyright © 1974 by Ethel Herr. Used by permission.

4. John 5:7.

Chapter 10: But What If. . . ?

1. Romans 7:15, 19.

Chapter 11:   I Had Rather Be a Doorkeeper

1. Sam Shoemaker, *Faith at Work*, 233–237.

2. Sam Shoemaker, *Christ and This Crisis* (New York: Revell, 1943), 16.

3. Sam Shoemaker, *Revive Thy Church*, xi.

Chapter 12: Recovery Group Program Resources

1. Claudia Black, *It Will Never Happen to Me* (Denver: MAC, 1982).